# EXPLORATIONS IN SOCIOLOGY
British Sociological Association
VOLUME 29

# The Making of Scotland:
## Nation, Culture and Social Change

EDITED BY
**DAVID McCRONE
STEPHEN KENDRICK**
AND
**PAT STRAW**

306.09411
m138m

**WITHDRAWN**

EDINBURGH UNIVERSITY PRESS
*in conjunction with*
THE BRITISH SOCIOLOGICAL
ASSOCIATION

© British Sociological Association 1989

Edinburgh University Press
22 George Square, Edinburgh

Set in Itek Times Roman
by Carto-Graphics, Edinburgh and
printed in Great Britain by
Redwood Burn Limited,
Trowbridge, Wiltshire.

British Library Cataloguing
  in Publication Data
The Making of Scotland:
  nation, culture and social change.
1. Scotland. Social conditions, history
I. McCrone, David
II. Kendrick, Stephen
III. Straw, Patricia
941.1

ISBN 0 85224 631 5
     0 85224 658 7 pbk

# CONTENTS

|  | |
|---|---|
| *List of Contributors* | ix |
| Introduction: Understanding Scotland<br>*David McCrone, Steve Kendrick and Pat Straw* | 1 |
| 1. Conjectural History, Sociology and Social Change in Eighteenth Century Scotland: Adam Ferguson and the Division of Labour<br>*John D. Brewer* | 13 |
| 2. Nationality, Social Change and Class: Transformations of National Identity in Scotland<br>*John Foster* | 31 |
| 3. Scotland is Different, OK?<br>*Tony Dickson* | 53 |
| 4. Scotland, Social Change and Politics<br>*Steve Kendrick* | 71 |
| 5. Shetland in the World Economy: A Sociological Perspective<br>*R.J. Smith* | 91 |
| 6. Welfare, Government and the Working Class: Scotland, 1845–1894<br>*Ian Levitt* | 109 |
| 7. Patronage and Professionalism: The 'Forgotten Middle Class', 1760–1860<br>*A.A. MacLaren* | 123 |
| 8. The Domestication of 'Fallen' Women: The Glasgow Magdalene Institution, 1860–1890<br>*Linda Mahood* | 143 |
| 9. Representing Scotland: Culture and Nationalism<br>*David McCrone* | 161 |
| 10. The Social Construction of Tradition: The Restoration Portraits and the Kings of Scotland<br>*S. Bruce and S. Yearley* | 175 |
| 11. Culture, Social Development and the Scottish Highland Gatherings<br>*Grant Jarvie* | 189 |
| 12. 'We're Off to Wembley': The History of a Scottish Event and the Sociology of Football Hooliganism<br>*H.F. Moorhouse* | 207 |
| *Index* | 229 |

# Introduction: Understanding Scotland

DAVID McCRONE, STEVE KENDRICK AND PAT STRAW

The chapters in this volume are based on some of the papers presented at the British Sociological Association's annual conference held in Edinburgh in March 1988. The topic of the conference–sociology and history–tapped one of the richest seams of social-science research in recent years, including over thirty papers on Scottish themes. There can have been few such occasions which brought together a wealth of sociological and historical research on Scotland, and it would seem to reflect the considerable current health and dynamism of the analysis of Scottish society. The first chair of sociology was founded at a Scottish university just under twenty-five years ago, somewhat later than south of the border, but the output of sociological research as reflected in this and other volumes would seem to point to the sound establishment of sociology in (and of) Scotland.

However, the social analysis of Scotland faces particular problems and challenges stemming from Scotland's peculiar constitutional status: it is a nation but not a state. On the one hand this poses problems in dealing with Scotland to do with its nature as an object of study. On the other hand, Scotland's constitutional subordination has had marked effects on the resources available for the study of Scotland as a professional activity.

*Studying Scotland: Problems of Resources and Problems of Definition*
There are hardly any mechanisms at the Scottish level for funding academic research other than in the form of government sponsorship of research that is closely related to policy. Other than this, funding decisions are overwhelmingly made south of the border. Sociology, indeed the social sciences, are not exceptional in this. Indeed, historians of Scotland have long pointed to the 'extraordinary situation' (Smout n.d., p. 11) of Scottish schoolchildren, who can go through the education system 'without encountering more of Scottish history than a few tales of the heroes at the primary level'.

Perhaps to a greater extent than Scottish historians, social scientists in Scotland are orientated towards wider academic networks and career opportunities at the British or international levels. While there are sociologists *in* Scotland, many of whom use Scottish material as part of an academic specialism (such as medical sociology and educational sociology, which are particularly well represented), there are, however, far fewer sociologists *of* Scotland, that is analysts of Scottish society as such. There are legendary difficulties in getting Scottish material published unless it can be shown to add purchase to a wider (usually British) problem. Not unnaturally, the market for Scottish research is smaller, more confined, and presumably less profitable.

The power structure of British academic life is such that 'Scotland', as an academic focus of study, does not have the clout in social science enjoyed by other analytical subdivisions of social science. To put it bluntly, studying Scotland is not a good career move.

In institutional terms, sociology came late to the Scottish universities. Like Oxbridge, the 'ancient' universities did not encourage its development as a critical social science. Consequently, when in the 1960s departments of sociology were founded north of the border, they were staffed mainly by non-Scots, who were mostly from England, but some from the United States and a few from continental Europe. On the face of it, then, the relative neglect of Scottish social analysis might be laid at the door of these incomers. In many respects, this is a limited argument, and secondary to the career structures and opportunities which provide the context for avenues for research. Closer inspection reveals that, in any case, many English academics–some of them contributors to this volume–have made a major contribution to our knowledge of Scotland, its history and society. It is as if, as classical 'marginal men' (and women), they have found Scotland's society intellectually curious, and in many respects different from the one in which they grew up, and in need of explanation. Those born and brought up here are perhaps more likely to treat it as largely unproblematic.

As well as this 'Englishing' of the study of Scotland, it is interesting to note the high proportion of writers on Scotland outwith Scottish academic institutions. Neither Tom Nairn nor Neal Ascherson, two foremost Scottish commentators, occupy academic posts. Christopher Harvie (West Germany) and Michael Hechter (USA) are commentators who view Scotland from afar. Of the writers in this volume, five (less than half) occupy permanent academic posts at Scottish institutions of higher education, and of these five only two are Scots.

The marginal status of the social analysis of Scotland within the academic community is in stark contrast with its centrality in current political debates in Scotland. The political prominence of the Scottish dimension tinges virtually every utterance about Scottish society with political significance. This is especially true of any analysis which aims at a characterization of Scottish society as a whole, which deals, for example, with Scottish nationhood, and its relations with England. Scottish sociology and social science has gained a particular salience in recent years by tackling issues which are at the very heart of the Scottish political agenda. We need only contrast this state of affairs with that south of the Border, where there has been a marked divergence between political issues and sociological debates in recent years, in contrast with the common ground which persisted in the two decades after the Second World War where political Fabianism and British sociology were considerably intertwined. The collapse of the 'welfare consensus' and the rise of the New Right appear to have fractured irretrievably this marriage of the political and intellectual realms.

Not so in Scotland, for the agenda of Scottish politics is about definitions of reality which generate political identities and political loyalties. Analysis of Scottish society by sociologists, historians or political scientists–by the social science community more generally–crucially affect these definitions. Thus, academic debate is also political debate at a crucial conjuncture in Scotland's history. Consequently, academic definitions of Scottish reality are frequently used in political debate, and in turn these political debates colour academic analyses. It is this interaction between the political and the intellectual agendas which gives Scottish social analysis its charge and its sense of relevance to today's issues and problems.

This conjuncture presents opportunities, but also difficulties for the sociologist of Scotland. It is part of the remit of sociology to demythologize social reality, and in Scotland there is much to demythologize. Scotland seems particularly prone to mythical ideas about itself, to mythical accounts of the past. In a society in which national consciousness has had few outlets for nearly three centuries, the creation of myths is perhaps an inevitable corollary. The truths which sociologists or historians attempt to unearth are often not what political contenders within Scotland want to hear. To take two examples: the belief that Scotland is somehow a more egalitarian society than England dies hard, for it is part of the self-image of Scots, and lends itself to radical, nationalist and even conservative accounts of the social order; secondly, considerable energy has been devoted to asserting that Scotland is a form of colony of England, despite the considerable academic controversy about using such a term of a relatively developed society such as Scotland. In many respects, comfortable myths are much more politically useful than unpalatable truths. This in turn produces pressures on the production of social knowledge in Scotland which are as much political as intellectual.

Of course, a debunking, or at least cautionary, note is the proper one for intellectuals to sound, rather than to collaborate in wholesale myth-making. Most societies are replete with myths, which act as an almost sacred set of values and definers of the national condition, but have adequate resources to place them in proper perspective. However, the constitutional status of Scotland means that few of the resources are available to confront these myths with proper social analysis. Scotland's constitutional and institutional subordination is reflected in the lack of resources devoted to the study of Scottish society. While there is a present blossoming of work on Scotland, we must ask how healthy the roots are. In the context of a general crisis of academic recruitment, the marginal sectors of academe are squeezed still further, including their younger members–responsible for much of the new work–who are confronted by a shrinking job market.

Undoubtedly there is a considerable need for social and political analysis of Scotland at the present time, yet it is hamstrung by the institutional and constitutional drawbacks which have produced that need in the first place. Judged as a body of work on a 'region' of Britain, analysis of Scotland looks impressive. Judged as a body of work on a nation of five million people, it leaves much to be desired. In Scotland we have a difficult row to hoe. To borrow the telling distinction made by the historian Christopher Smout–made about history not sociology-sociologists of Scotland have two obvious options open to them: 'us-too' sociology, which argues that much of Scotland's development simply parallels that of England; or, on the other hand, 'not-us' sociology, seeking to show that Scotland cannot be subsumed in this way, but follows a distinct trajectory of its own. The third option is the more likely and the more difficult: to show that Scotland is in crucial respects similar and in crucial respects different. That, we might say, is the challenge for the discipline at a time when political reality and social analysis are almost uniquely in alignment.

We have argued that the sociological study of Scotland suffers from major problems as a professional activity. These problems are, however, exacerbated by the extremely problematic nature of Scotland as an object of study. It just does not fit many of the taken-for-granted assumptions about what it is that sociology is supposed to be studying. Sociology conventionally examines regular and patterned social processes by means of the subspecialisms of the discipline–the sociology of work, urban sociology, political sociology, for instance–or by focusing on social institutions such as the family, the education system, or the welfare state. These specialisms have been generated, by and large, internally and theoretically by sociology as it has developed over two hundred years, as well as by accepting the taken-for-granted divisions of the social world we inhabit. The standard subdivisions of sociology are in large part the legacy of the discipline's search for generalizable theorems and laws based on the natural-science model. Analysing geographically defined 'societies' cuts across such academic boundaries.

But Scotland is in fundamental ways not like most other societies. It is, of course, a geographical area, a territory, partly defined by its climate, topography and natural resources, as well as economic factors deriving from considerations of geographical location. On a different level, Scotland is an administrative unit, a sphere of jurisdiction within which certain administrative structures operate, based on geographical definition. As such, Scotland can be considered as a governed system, and as such, it becomes politically meaningful. Most obviously, the remit of the Scottish Office helps to define Scotland politically and sociologically. Thirdly, Scotland exists at the ideological level: in the minds of people, reflecting in part the historic residue of Scotland as an erstwhile nation-state until 1707. At this level, Scotland survives as a taken-for-granted reference in so far as aspects of its culture (tartan, speech, anthem, flag) reinforce the sense of nationhood.

These common-sense ways of defining Scotland, however, are only the starting point for any sociological analysis. Conventional non-Marxist sociology does have ways of handling the 'national' or territorial level of analysis. The first way is to treat 'society' at a high level of abstraction ('Society', as it were). In this treatment, studying the specificities of 'real' societies–reflecting their historical and conjunctural features–gives way to focusing on broad, common patterns of development. Hence, 'industrial', 'capitalist' or even 'human' are general epithets applied to 'society' in common currency within sociology, reflecting those aspects which are judged to be driven by similar determinants of social structure. The implication of this mode of analysis, of course, is that one 'industrial society' is much like another, or that one 'underdeveloped society' is much like another, or, indeed, one region is much like another. To coin a phrase, society is society is society, and the particular society in question is irrelevant. Quite obviously, this kind of analysis has a great deal to do with Western, and especially

American, ethnocentrism. In other words, the society in which analytical models have been most developed so that they apply to any society – to Society – is the United States. In a British context, too, it has been all too easy to treat 'Britain' as a 'society' in which social patterns are largely uniform (at least in their urban forms), and for much of this century sociology in this country went along quite happily with this assumption. 'British society' had a resonance to it, and many writers addressed their work to what were assumed to be its common problems.

This view was reinforced by a second, and related, perspective on handling societies at the national level, and this was the commonsense assumption that the 'society' of which sociology was the science was the 'nation-state'. As Norbert Elias put it:

> Many twentieth century sociologists when speaking of 'society' no longer have in mind, as did their predecessors, a 'bourgeois society' or a 'human society' beyond the state, but increasingly the somewhat diluted ideal image of a nation-state. (Elias, 1978, p. 241)

Such a perspective allowed comparative work, because it permitted sociologists to compare one society with another according to abstract master-plans of 'Society'. If they differed from each other and from the ideal, that could be explained by alternative trajectories towards the same goal, or by blockages to 'modernization' erected by cultural or political factors. Certainly, Parsonian structural functionalists could easily reconcile this approach with their quest for the fundamental features of Society. Such an approach had much appeal to British sociologists also, because Britain was a unitary state politically, and there was a considerable degree of homogeneity in terms of key social structural variables across the country, or so it seemed.

The legacy of established forms of Marxist social science has been a similar set of problems in dealing with the national level of analysis. Whether it is a matter of more traditional approaches, stressing relations of production and an 'internalist' model of social development, or neo-Marxist approaches which stress exchange relations and an external dynamic to social development, the national level remains a highly problematic focus of study and never more so than in the case of Scotland.

It is a moot point whether the rigid application to Scotland of frameworks for the analysis of the national level developed elsewhere has been beneficial to the understanding of Scottish society. Perhaps it is inevitable that the study of Scotland should be a battleground for pre-formed theories. It has also often been their graveyard. It is perhaps the healthiest aspect of the social analysis of Scotland that Scotland's unique status as a society – in terms of its constitutional relation to the rest of Britain combined with its unique role as a spearhead of industrialization at the heart of a world empire – demands that we take it on its own terms. To a large extent, we have to make our tools.

In general terms, then, conventional sociological models can only be applied to Scotland with some difficulty, if at all. Equating 'society' with the 'nation-state' is particularly inappropriate in the case of Scotland which may be a nation, but which long since ceased to be a state. In many respects studying Scotland labours under intellectual as well as institutional difficulties. Scotland's peculiar constitutional status – a nation without representative national institutions, but with historic residues of law, education and religion – has led to difficulties for social scientists in dealing with it as an object of study. As a result, the links between sociology and related disciplines, such as history, have been especially important.

## Sociology and History: Understanding Scotland

The theme of the conference and this volume, sociology and history, is a particularly apt one to host in Scotland. One of the remarkable features of Scottish social analysis is that while the normal institutional demarcations apply – academics are employed as sociologists or as historians – in terms of the realities of academic debate and co-operation, such demarcations are often ignored. Thus, there is not, for example, a sociological debate about Scotland and a historical debate about Scotland, but simply a debate about Scotland's social development.

If there has been an adverse consequence of inter-disciplinary demarcation, it would be that the social history of the 1940s and 1950s in Scotland is relatively under-researched. This period is seen as too distant for the sociologist to tackle, predating as it does the existence of survey material on many important topics. On the other hand, these decades are too recent to be seen as a major focus of attention for historians. This is unfortunate in that they are crucial decades, without an understanding of which it is difficult to come to terms with what are seen as the more exciting social and political developments of the 1960s and onwards.

This temporal disjuncture apart however, relations between sociology and history in Scotland are generally fruitful. As John Brewer points out in his essay in this volume, sociology emerged out of history, and, especially in the work of Adam Ferguson, the making of sociology was bound up with the making of Scotland. Ferguson was interested in 'conjectural history' of civil society, by which he meant the application of theoretical principles about human nature and what he termed 'our external situation' (a whole range of factors including geography, climate, social circumstances and culture) in order to offer an interpretation of historical development and social change. Unlike the 'classical economists' – Smith, Hume, Millar – Ferguson took a negative view of the division of labour, highlighting its dehumanizing effects, a feature taken up by Marx. Why then, asks Brewer, did Ferguson not develop a separate discipline of sociology? Above all, his ideas were diverted into discourse on 'civic humanism', and Ferguson himself was subsumed under the dominant school of classical economy which became so influential in the Scottish Enlightenment and in the Scottish universities.

It has been the political forefronting of the national dimension in Scotland which has provided much of the dynamite for increased analysis of Scotland as a society and a polity. Not surprisingly, theoretical concern with the nature of the nation and nationalism has been a result. John Foster in his contribution to this volume explores both Marxist and non-Marxist accounts of nationalism, and argues that while liberal or 'bourgeois' accounts stress the manufactured nature of nationalism, Marxist accounts examine the substance, in particular the role played by ethnic social carriers of nationalism. Marx, he says, was not guilty of reducing nationality to class, and Foster urges us to study the ways national movements mobilize social and class opposition against dominant economic groups.

Sociologists like Tony Dickson and Steve Kendrick in their different ways have tackled the degree to which Scotland is different from England, and if so, why. Dickson takes issue with the argument propounded by Kendrick, Bechhofer and McCrone that Scottish economic and social development has not, in many major respects, been significantly different from the rest of Britain. He focuses on the particular features of historical change in Scotland, and especially its political and cultural aspects, and argues that in certain crucial ways Scottish development has been divergent from the rest of the UK. In reply, Kendrick reinforces his earlier point that occupational and industrial trends in Scotland have largely mirrored those elsewhere in the UK, and cannot be taken as the root cause of divergent political behaviour north of the border. Instead, he argues, since the 1960s there has developed an alternative Scottish frame of reference, an agenda which is amplified by the media in Scotland to present economic and social developments in an alternative way to that operating in the UK as whole. The debate between Dickson and Kendrick is a good example of how knowledge about Scotland as well as the analytical tools of sociology have been refined by focused disputation and argument.

The contribution of sociology to our understanding of Scotland has also benefited from the development of theoretical ideas in the discipline as a whole. Richard Smith, for example, has applied Wallerstein's world-system perspective critically to Scotland's own periphery, Shetland. He argues for a fusion of this externalist perspective with an analysis based on the social organisation of production, an internalist view. He rejects the conventional account of Shetland's development that the control of trade alone was the dynamic of its history, and points out that in the early nineteenth century there was even social and economic regression as conservative forces in the islands reasserted their control.

Similarly, Linda Mahood applies the social theories of Foucault to her analysis of prostitution in nineteenth-century Glasgow. She points out, following Foucault, that 'prostitution' is a historical construction not a social fact, that it was a political rather than a technical term, and that like Foucault's analysis of homosexuality, prostitution has acquired a 'personage, a case history, and a childhood'. Above all, it was a discourse of social control, a means whereby the local bourgeoisie controlled women who threatened to defy middle-class standards of sexual and vocational propriety.

It is one of the key distinctive markers of sociology in Scotland (compared for example with American and even English sociology), and one which it shares with sociology in Wales and Ireland, that it is heavily suffused with historical understandings. The 'making' of Scotland is very obviously a dynamic process, and a considerable legacy has been left by powerful institutions and dominant values deriving from the last century and before. Allan MacLaren makes the case, contra the historian Harold Perkin, that Scotland's liberal professionals – professors, clergymen, lawyers and doctors – did not form an important economic class, but were only loosely embedded in the capitalist middle class, and might even be considered pre-capitalist as late as the mid-nineteenth century, if Aberdeen was anything to go by. Ian Levitt looks at the role of the Board of Supervision for the Relief of the Poor in nineteenth-century Scotland, and finds it dominated by landed interests with quite different views from the emerging class of Scottish capitalists. The work of MacLaren and Levitt in their different ways indicate how valuable is the cross-fertilisation of history and sociology in understanding Scotland.

History, or rather, 'the past', also makes a major contribution to our analysis of modern Scotland in terms of its ideological significance: the past as retrospect, rather than as history. Steve Bruce and Stephen Yearley consider the case of the De Wet portraits of the Kings of Scotland to make a number of important points about the political uses of 'tradition'. They are concerned with the social construction of tradition for political purposes by the Stewart monarchy to legitimate their shaky hold on monarchical power. Max Weber's concept of charismatic authority provides an analytical lever on this rewriting, even invention, of history.

This theme of selectively mobilizing the past in the interest of the present is examined by Grant Jarvie in his analysis of Highland Gatherings. Culturally marginalized after 1746, they were reinvented and popularized after the 1840s to suit the ideological purposes of the British monarchy and landed classes (clans as composed of familial, but certainly not social, equals), and their gradual incorporation into the market-place of modern capitalist society. The selective use of traditions and rituals is explored by David McCrone, who takes issue with the pursuit by Scottish intellectuals of a Scottish 'national culture' in place of what they purport to be a deformed, subverted one. Such a pursuit, he argues, is increasingly meaningless in modern, pluralistic cultures, and condemns Scotland to the desert of history.

The business of selective remembering is the theme of Bert Moorhouse's contribution, in which he takes issue with the analyses of football by English sociologists, in which the primacy of class and masculine values is asserted rather than proved. As a consequence of growing violence associated with football south of the border, the annual Scotland-England game has been redefined by the English media and politicians as a 'violent' event. Academic accounts fail to perceive that the level of violence has changed little over the century, and fail to understand the trip to Wembley as a major cultural event, an assertion of national and ethnic identity. Ultimately, theirs is an Anglocentric view.

*Conclusion*

If sociology is concerned at all with the social preconditions for, and pressures on, its own production of knowledge – with the sociology of knowledge of sociology – then in Scotland we have a very special case. Sociology is closely embroiled with patterns of political change in Scotland which could well lead to constitutional change. The analysis of Scottish society is a classic case of the observer being closely involved with the observed. Social analysis has its effects on political reality, and in turn is crucially affected itself by that political reality.

As the old assumptions about the unitary nature of Britain decay, as Britain becomes, in the phrase Neal Ascherson borrows from Karl Miller, 'a country filled with anxiety and ill-feeling, and with a sense of a dishonoured public life' (Ascherson 1988), as Scottish politics diverge significantly from those in the south, as the sense of Scottishness grows in most sections of Scottish society, so sociology finds itself closely part of the Scottish 'project'. We would like to think that the (re)making of sociology and the making of Scotland are now more closely fused than they have ever been, and that this volume makes some contribution to both of these endeavours.

REFERENCES

Ascherson, N. (1988) 'Ancient Britons and the Republican Dream', John P. Mackintosh lecture, Edinburgh University, 1986, in, N. Ascherson, *Games with Shadows,* London, Radius Books.

Elias, N. (1978) *The Civilising Process,* Oxford, Blackwell.

Smout, C., (n. d.) 'An Agenda for Scottish History', Presidential Address to the Scottish History Society (mimeo).

# 1

## Conjectural History, Sociology and Social Change in Eighteenth Century Scotland: Adam Ferguson and the Division of Labour

JOHN D. BREWER

*Introduction*

The Scottish Enlightenment thinkers were among the first social and political theorists to write histories of civil society, or what Dugald Stewart, a lesser-known member of the school, called 'conjectural history', and in the process they shifted discourse toward the concerns of nineteenth-century sociology.[1] Interpretations of the origins of sociology in the nineteenth century are many and varied. For example, Gouldner (1970) represents sociology emerging in the nineteenth century as a counterweight to utilitarianism, challenging its view that society was rooted in individual need by demonstrating the existence of social and collective interests. Nisbet (1967) argues that sociology arose in the nineteenth century as a conservative reaction to rapid political, social and economic change in its emphasis on the communal nature of social order and stability, while Therborn (1976) presented it as a negative critique of the problems caused by the bourgeois revolution. Giddens described it as an encounter between the advances of natural science and the accomplishments of industrial society, in an attempt to understand the basic structure and developmental trends of modern society (1971, 1976). What is striking about these claims, and others like them, is the similarity in their portrayal of the discourse of nineteenth-century sociology, in that all show how it became dominated by references to the social structure, with social institutions and processes simultaneously furnishing sociology's topics of enquiry and its set of explanatory variables. The distinguishing feature of these characterizations is their account of the ideological framework within which this discourse operated, but the terminology associated with the notion of social structure is revealed as a common vocabulary.

This chapter leaves aside a consideration of the wider ideological context of sociology as it emerged in the nineteenth century, and identifies how its discourse on the social structure predates the transformations of that century and can be found in the writings of Adam Ferguson in eighteenth-century Scotland. While the argument that Ferguson was a founder, or at least a precursor, of sociology is not unfamiliar and has been made by successive generations of sociologists in modern times (for example, Barnes 1917; Brewer 1986; Bryson 1945; Kettler 1965; Lehmann 1930; MacRae 1969; Meek 1967; Pascal 1938; Salvucci 1972; Swingewood 1970), this claim is established here by means of a more unusual case-study; namely, Ferguson's analysis of the division of labour.

However, while the chapter shows that Ferguson provides the first sociological discussion of the concept, the primary intention is to demonstrate how this emerges out of his concern with writing conjectural history, although paradoxically this simultaneously restricted the extent of his sociological work in later writings. Further, Ferguson's analysis of the concept will be linked to broader processes of cultural and economic change occurring in Scotland at the time of his writing, which his remarks were an attempt to analyse and explain. I will argue that sociological discourse finds its origin partly in a special type of history and that it began to be deployed by Ferguson in eighteenth century Scotland because it enabled analytical discussion of social change in Scotland. Therefore, the 'making of Scotland' was also in part the 'making of sociology', for in placing Scotland's transformations within the wider framework of the history of civil society, Ferguson achieved a radical reconceptualization of the general features of society and social life. This shift in discourse and perspective was a prerequisite for the formal emergence of sociology in the nineteenth century.

*Conjectural History among the Scots*

Not only modern sociologists have appropriated the Scots as precursors or founders of their discipline. Reading from the present into the past, people have described the Scots as economists, political scientists, social anthropologists and psychologists. It is less well understood that figures like Adam Ferguson, John Millar and Adam Smith saw themselves at the time as writing history. But it was a particular form of history, and one which easily lent itself to the development of sociological ideas and discourse.

At a superficial level, the historical focus of their work is attested to in the titles they chose for their studies, many of which were presented as an 'enquiry', a term used interchangeably with 'history': a fact which is often obscured in the modern tendency to abbreviate the titles. In the content of their studies, the historical focus of the Scots shows itself in two ways. First, they wrote numerous studies which recorded and analysed concrete historical events, notably Millar's analysis of the English civil war, Robertson's study of the colonization of America and Ferguson's account of the decline of the Roman empire, a work which influenced Gibbon's more famous study. More significantly, the Scots believed that, by a process of deductive reasoning, theoretical principles which are observable in the present can be applied to understand the past and all historical development to this point. Aristotle, Vico and Montesquieu had done this before the Scots, and many have attempted it since. The problem facing them was the same: that of finding principles that simultaneously explained current circumstances and rendered the apparent chaos of history intelligible. Dugald Stewart used the term 'conjectural history' to describe this enterprise, although Millar and Smith, borrowing a term from Aristotle, described themselves as 'philosophical historians', a view of their enterprise which Comte shared, and which some modern accounts also employ (for example Trevor-Roper 1963), although Comte used it in order to devalue their contribution to the discipline he named and saw himself as founding.[2]

What distinguishes the solutions theorists have provided to this common problem, is the nature of the theoretical principles employed, for this largely determines the resulting vision of history. As used by Stewart, conjectural history is the application of theoretical principles about human nature and our 'external situation', in order to offer an interpretation of historical development and change. It has to be recalled that discussions of human nature were commonplace in the eighteenth century, especially of whether or not people are innately sociable, and, along with the notion of luxury, the concept of human nature usually provided the opportunity for a wide ranging account of human affairs, in much the same way as a discussion of agency and structure does today. Smith's theory of moral sentiment, for example, presaged an analysis of commercial life, while the first part of Ferguson's account of the history of civil society is devoted to analysing human nature. The remnants of this approach were still evident in the early Marx, who made 'species being' central to his account of alienation. 'External situation' was a short-hand description for a whole range of factors, such as geography, race, climate, social circumstance and culture. The Scots combined these factors with the general facets of human nature that they had identified, to produce a whole range of variables with which to structure their interpretation of history.

Despite the emphasis on the Scots as constituting a coherent school of thought, they were not agreed in their description of human nature, nor equal in the emphasis given to the sociological aspects of people's 'external situation'. There was not even concord on the aspects of historical development that needed to be explained. Hence the conjectural history practised by some Scots is less sociological in its direction, but for Ferguson, Millar and, to a lesser extent, Smith, the social structure was simultaneously both a topic whose origins and development needed to be explained and the source of an array of explanatory variables used in causal analysis. This is most clearly evident in the theory of the four stages, in which rests the claim that the Scots anticipated Marx's materialist conception of history (see Meek 1967; Pascal 1938; Skinner 1982). In the theory of the four stages, society evolves through four stages, each defined by its mode of subsistence, so that the way people have organized production becomes the central means by which other features of society can be understood: society's mode of subsistence makes the past and the present intelligible. There is some way to go from this point to Marx's historical materialism, as Sombart, at the beginning of this century, was the first to note, but the theory of the four stages does contain a version of technical-economic determinism through which is understood the diversity of institutions, customs and practices over time and space.

Conjectural history in Ferguson did not take this form, for he does not adopt the theory of the four stages, even though he is the only Scot singled out for special praise by Marx. Ferguson provided a history of civil society which makes no reference to the mode of subsistence but which Marx valued because it traced the historical evolution of institutions and processes which he held to be key elements in society (on the Scots' view of society see Frisby and Sayer 1986). The social institutions and processes which Ferguson discussed included private property, social class (see Calvert 1982; Rattansi 1982), exploitation (see Brewer 1986; 1987), alienation (see MacRae 1969), social change (see Bartolommei 1979; Slotkin 1965), political subordination and the division of labour (see Rattansi 1982; Swingewood 1970). Not only were these institutions and processes placed in a historical context, in order to understand their origins and development, they also became variables which in large part explained the changing forms of social structure across temporal and spatial differences. Hence, for example, private property and the division of labour were processes used to explain the emergence of exploitation, alienation and social regression. Therefore, from his concern to write a conjectural history of civil society, Ferguson was led into discussing institutions and processes, which became key terms in the discourse of nineteenth-century sociology. However, Ferguson fails to reify these as concepts and only considers them in the context of his historical account of the development of civil society to its present state. This can be demonstrated with a specific case by analysing Ferguson's writings on the division of labour. First, however, it is necessary to establish the state of knowledge that existed on the division of labour in the eighteenth century.

*The Division of Labour in the Eighteenth Century*

The person who is accorded first use of the term 'division of labour' is Mandeville, who notes in the *Fable of the Bees* that the 'division and subdivision of tasks' is crucial to material development, although the idea that there is occupational specialization and a division of tasks goes back to Plato and Xenophon (see Foley 1974; Rattansi 1982). Borrowed from the Greeks, the more usual term in the eighteenth century was the specialization or separation of arts and professions, and this terminology was in wide currency. Even Locke in the seventeenth century refers to the specialization of employments in the chapter on property in his *Second Treatise*. Myers (1967) shows that by the eighteenth century there were two images of the division of labour. The first is the orthodox economic image, in which the division of labour increases productivity and enhances material development. This positive view was associated with the writings of the Mercantilists, like William Petty and Henry Martin, and especially with Mandeville and Adam Smith; it was also a view held by the Greeks.

A much less common view was the socioeconomic image, in which the economic benefits of the division of labour were linked to the enhancement of social cohesion. In a remarkable anticipation of Durkheim, some eighteenth-century writers claimed that the division and specialization of labour created social solidarity. (Durkheim does not acknowledge their work, however.) Writers like Joseph Priestley, James Harris, James Stewart and John Maxwell used the idea of the division of labour to resolve the well-rehearsed debate between public and private interest, arguing that through the economic benefits of the division of labour the private actions of individuals aimed at pursuing their own welfare resulted in the enlargement of public welfare. Mercantilists mentioned the division of labour as a method of increasing efficiency and reducing production costs, which had overall economic benefits for the nation's competitiveness on world markets. Maxwell was the first to note that these economic benefits extended to promoting the public good. Although this was an innovation, Maxwell's argument amounts to only a lengthy remark, of little more than a page (see Myers 1967, p. 434). Later writers give the division of labour a central role in forming the type of society in which 'the sovereign good' will ultimately reign. The argument is Durkheimian, in that the division of labour increases economic dependence which in turn pulls people into society and connects and binds them together (see Myers 1967, pp. 436, 438). These sociological benefits are solely a product of the commercial economy, which is seen as creating a distinct society where economic dependence reduces social conflict and promotes cohesion. Their vision of commercial society is very similar to the much later classic liberal view, in which, in Mandeville's older terminology, private vices lead to public virtue: the selfish pursuit of personal benefit through the division of labour has unanticipated rewards for society.

However, there is a third image of the division of labour which comes to us from the eighteenth century, which is the more familiar sociological critique. Here the emphasis is upon the dehumanizing effects of this form of labour and its wider social costs. Such a view in the eighteenth century is associated exclusively with Adam Ferguson, and constitutes the first of two major advances he makes in his account of the division of labour.[3] The second was to link the concept with other features of the social structure of commercial society in a thorough analysis of the problems of modern society as it existed at that time, which took as its premiss his experience of socio-economic change in Scotland. Both innovations, however, are bound up with his interest in writing a conjectural history of civil society and cannot be separated from this intent, so that in his work conjectural history and sociology inseparably merge with a concern to understand changes occurring in eighteenth-century Scottish society.

Ferguson's earliest mention of the separation of arts and professions is in his first and major book *An Essay on the History of Civil Society,* written in 1767. The *Essay* represents Ferguson's only attempt at writing conjectural history, although he published a number of subsequent works, and successive sociologists have recognized this as his greatest contribution to the discipline, which is no coincidence given the arguments here. Conjectural history meant for Ferguson tracing the history of present commercial or civil society back to its most simple form in order to understand better its special features and how they developed. This inevitably lead him toward sociology, for he discussed the social structure of earlier stages of society, noting the emergence of such institutions and processes as class, class distinctions and inequalities, gender inequalities, language use, the rule of law, exploitation, political subordination, private property and the division of labour. In discussing how and why these institutions and processes emerged, Ferguson operates with an array of causal variables ranging from human nature and climate to elements of the social structure. With respect to the latter, there is something of the nineteenth-century conception of the social structure as an interdependent unit with causal relations existing between its parts, for Ferguson begins to give elements of the social structure explanatory status and to chart the causal relations that exist between them. But this use of sociological perspective and discourse arises only out of his intent in writing conjectural history, so that, once this history is written, the sociological perspective and discourse are not developed in later works, for Ferguson had an inability to conceive of them existing separately from conjectural history. While this type of history therefore encouraged Ferguson to write sociology, it also limited the extent to which he subsequently developed his sociological ideas and discourse; the failure to do so is a universal complaint against Ferguson made by modern writers who have seen him making a contribution to the development of sociology.

## Adam Ferguson and the Division of Labour

The concept is introduced in part 4 of the *Essay,* in which Ferguson addresses himself to the consequences of commercial growth, which is one of the features, he argues, that distinguish commercial society from earlier forms. His account begins with the orthodox eighteenth-century view that the division of labour emerges with the commodity-exchange economy and provides economic benefits that advance commerce (Ferguson 1966, p. 181, also see pp. 180, 230). Two more novel matters are then considered. First, Ferguson asks what causes the division of labour to emerge at this stage of social development. In a brief paragraph he lists inclinations derived from human nature, the accident of favourable opportunities and the unequal distribution of the means of subsistence, none of which is given further comment (1966, p. 180), although he does later point out how the division of labour was the result of unintended consequences (1966, p. 182). Ferguson makes no connection between a commodity-exchange economy and the unequal distribution of the means of subsistence, but the origins of the division of labour raise little interest because the focus is almost entirely on its harmful effects, an issue which was more central to his concern with a conjectural history of civil society.

Ferguson is at his most sociologically astute when discussing this issue, for it is here that he begins to use elements of the social structure as explanatory variables and to employ the discourse of nineteenth-century sociology. The first of these effects is the creation of a new distinction between manual and mental labour, a fact which Herder discovered only two years after the *Essay* was published (see Pascal 1939). According to Ferguson, those who labour with their hands lose control over decisions which affect their labour and, being no longer required to think for themselves, have difficulty in comprehending the system within which they are locked.

> Many mechanical arts require no capacity; they succeed best under a total suppression of sentiment and reason; and ignorance is the mother of industry... Manufactures, accordingly, prosper most where the mind is least consulted and where the workshop may be considered as an engine, the parts of which are men... In manufacture the genius of the master is cultivated, while that of the inferior workman lies waste. The statesman may have a wide comprehension of human affairs, while the tools he employs are ignorant of the system in which they are themselves combined... The former may have gained what the latter has lost... and thinking itself, in this age of separations, may become a peculiar craft (1966, p. 183, also pp. 181-2).

Those left performing manual labour are thus degraded. Both the object of their labour and the means by which it is produced dehumanize and degrade workers. 'The labourer, who toils that he may eat, the mechanic, whose art requires no exertion of genius, are degraded by the object they pursue and by the means they employ to attain it' (1966, p. 184). Were Ferguson to have used the term alienation here instead, he would have anticipated two of the four senses Marx gave to the term in the Paris Manuscripts, although many emphasize Ferguson's contribution to the development of the concept (Forbes 1966, p. xxxi; MacRae 1969, p. 19).

However, by far the greatest impact of the division of labour is felt in the subordination and inequality it helps to create, and an entire section of the *Essay* is devoted to this topic. As three factors which cause inequality and subordination, Ferguson lists the division of labour, private property and natural talents and dispositions (1966, p. 184). The division of labour therefore plays an important role in reinforcing the class system, although not in forming its origins, which Ferguson places in the development of private property at an earlier stage (1966, p. 96, *passim*). He is critical of the way the division of labour perpetuates and reinforces these divisions, and he gives the impression that the system works in concert against the poor. Ferguson perceptively described the legal system as a means of securing unequal private property and which thus ensures that power accrues to those people who may be feared to abuse it (1966, p. 157). Thus the legal system, the system of private property and the division of labour interact to create and reinforce subordination.

There is something here of the nineteenth-century notion of distributive injustice, the principle by which private property leads to differences in power, goods and rewards, differences which are maintained by other elements of the social structure. This anticipation of nineteenth-century sociological concerns is enhanced when these arguments are combined with Ferguson's discussion of conflict as a general feature of human nature and his outline of the specific conflicts which emerge under certain structural conditions, such as class conflict. This use of the division of labour as an explanatory variable is repeated in his account of the dangers facing democratic government in commercial society (1966, p. 187).

Here Ferguson is unlike other Scots, such as Smith, Hume and Millar, who believed that the commercial economy necessarily brought with it peace, stability, civil liberty and the rule of law, although all too often Ferguson is unthinkingly categorized along with them as a classic political economist. 'The boasted refinements of the polished age are not divested of danger. They open a door, perhaps, to disaster, as wide and accessible as any those they have shut' (1966, p. 231). Nor was his opinion of the modern economy positive (1966, p. 237). As Hopfl emphasizes, Ferguson was atypical because his conjectural history was not a celebration of the present (1978, p. 37). There is no blind belief in social progress, for social regression was a real phenomenon for Ferguson, and the division of labour played a central role in this process. Although in one passage Ferguson appears to endorse the eighteenth-century view that the division of labour enhanced social solidarity by drawing people into the social bond (1966, p. 188), he goes on to argue that commercial society has weak bonds and that the different classes are separate and estranged (1966, p. 191). In fact the final two parts of the *Essay* are completely given over to an account of how nations can decline, as he terms it. At the level of the social structure, the division of labour is one of several factors which interact to promote this regression.

> The commercial arts gain an ascendant at the expense of other pursuits. The desire for profit stifles the love of perfection. Interest cools the imagination and hardens the heart. But apart from these considerations, the separation of professions, while it seems to promise improvement in skill, yet in its ultimate effects serves, in some measure, to break

the bands of society and to withdraw individuals from the common scene... Under the distinction of callings, by which members of polished society are separated from each other, society is made to consist of parts, of which none is animated with the spirit of society itself... members can no longer apprehend the common ties of society. The members of a community may, in this manner, like the inhabitants of a conquered province, be made to lose the sense of every connection, and have no common affairs to transact but those of trade (1966, pp. 217–20).

*Conjectural History, Civic Humanism and Sociology*

For all Ferguson's ability to employ social structural variables in causal analysis of social phenomena and to use sociological discourse, there are constraints which limit his anticipation of nineteenth-century sociology. This is often overlooked by those modern sociologists who have enthusiastically appropriated Ferguson as a founder of the discipline.

Conjectural history was a source of limitation on his sociological perspective and discourse in two ways. First, it led to a concern with the prospects of civil society which easily encouraged the use of civic humanist discourse and ideas which interfered with the sociology. The central concern of civic humanism is with the political community, which is itself defined in institutional terms, such as a regular constitution and mixed government. Emphasis is placed on the obligations of citizens. They are expected to participate actively in the government and defence of the community, and this commitment requires a sense of public spirit or virtue. Only by doing this will they realize the political liberty which the institutional arrangements of mixed government make possible. Should citizens not devote themselves to the obligations of citizenship, but substitute private for public interest, the political community will be threatened by corruption, which is an endemic danger (for an outline of the tradition see Hont and Ignatieff 1983; Pocock 1975; Robertson 1983). The key notions in civic humanism are virtue, citizenship and corruption, and elsewhere I have shown how this tradition is woven with his sociological discourse in Ferguson's account of exploitation (Brewer 1986, pp. 471–5). Ferguson's conjectural history in the *Essay* was partly concerned with the historical fate of 'polished society' and the 'decline of nations', and with 'corruption' and 'the loss of virtue'. These concerns constitute his worry about the failure of people to participate in public affairs, the disintegration of the human personality and the curtailment of human autonomy, so that 'virtue' and 'corruption' form the context in which he discusses private property, the division of labour, class conflict, alienation and economic exploitation (for example see Forbes 1966; 1967). While this does not detract from his sociological perspective and discourse, and civic humanism takes a pronounced sociological twist in his writings, this alternative discourse pulls Ferguson back from expanding and developing his sociological ideas.

One other factor working in the same direction was Ferguson's failure both to recognize that he was using a new sociological perspective and discourse and to deploy it independently of his conjectural history. This was abandoned after the conjectural history was written, so that later works are a disappointment for modern sociologists who look for an extension of his earlier ideas. The concept of the division of labour, for example, is nowhere again given the same attention, nor are the insights taken further. The work published immediately after the *Essay* was noted for his lectures in moral philosophy, and the concept is referred to only in passing in his *Principles of Moral and Political Science* of 1792.

There is, however, an unpublished essay devoted to the topic. Although they are undated, the general consensus is that the essays were written late in life and represent mature reflection on a whole range of themes, although they are handwritten and close to note form. Winifred Philip, who has done most work on analysing the essays, considers them to be Ferguson's most philosophical work (Philip 1985), and they cover a range of conventional topics within moral philosophy. Sociological insights are made in the midst of moral philosophy (on the general relationship between the two disciplines, see Bryson 1932), but they are few and made with such brevity that the contrast with the *Essay* is striking. Essay 15 is on the division of labour, and while there is some new terminology, such as 'state' instead of 'government' and, remarkably, the term 'super structure', there are no fresh insights. In fact the civic humanist discourse on corruption, virtue and citizenship is more in evidence than before and nearly envelops the sociological themes. It appears that it was only within the framework of his conjectural history of civil society that Ferguson was able to conceive of the social structure as worthy of serious attention, although when he did so his sociological perspective and discourse was an impressive anticipation of nineteenth-century themes. His failure to engage in further conjectural history was thus a constraint on his sociological ideas and discourse.

*Social Change in Eighteenth-Century Scotland*

Considerable effort has gone into explaining why eighteenth-century Scotland should have experienced this intellectual effervescence in social and political theory, as well as in philosophy, natural science, and technical innovation (for an overview see: Campbell and Skinner 1982; Chitnis 1976; Rendall 1979). The factors identified include psychoanalytic theories emphasizing the early childhood experiences of the leading figures, which inculcated the values of independence and universalism (Camic 1983), and a whole range of political, economic and social circumstances. The latter include such factors as: a non-élitist education system and other educational innovations which opened up mass education and increased levels of literacy, especially in lowland Scotland (Bullough 1970; Bullough and Bullough, 1971, 1973; Morrell 1970); the ethos of liberal education at Scottish universities which linked natural and moral philosophy (Olson 1975); the payment-by-results system by which Scottish academics received remuneration (Morrell 1970); the scientific-mindedness of the landed gentry who supported intellectual and technical innovation, and wider institutional support from learned and medical associations (Christie 1974; Shapin 1974a, 1974b); political stability and economic growth, especially after the Jacobite Rebellion of 1745 (Phillipson 1973, 1975); and the development of an urban and commercial society, whose civic culture integrated commerce, industry and the universities (Emerson 1973; Pascal 1938).

It is this last factor in particular which explains why Ferguson began to use sociological ideas and discourse in a critique of modern society. The Scottish lowlands were a thriving commercial centre and after 1745 witnessed the introduction of machine industry, the key to which was Glasgow and its tobacco and linen trade with America. Linen production increased fivefold between 1728 and 1777, and this industry was the first to move to machine and factory production (on Scotland's economic progress see Lenman 1981; Smout 1983). Bank assets rose in Scotland by 856.5 per cent between 1744 and 1772, and home-produced exports rose by 18.7 per cent in the nine-year period from 1775 (Smout, 1983 pp. 52, 56). Even the Highlands were being enmeshed in the new trading economy, so that there was no split between the capitalist plains and the traditional hills (Smout 1983, p. 48). Technological change was also rapid: the annual number of patents granted in Edinburgh rose threefold in the nine-year period from 1760 (Kindleberger 1976, p. 2).

It would be inaccurate to call this an 'industrial revolution', although dating this transformation is notoriously difficult, with estimates ranging from 1760 to 1787. Smout refers to it as 'pre-industrial growth' (1983 p. 71), while Kindleberger uses the term 'proto-industrialisation' (1976 p. 24). But there were undoubted economic and technological transformations in Scotland in the middle of the eighteenth century, and with them came changes in established social patterns. The population grew and became more urbanized. Population growth in Scotland's five main cities between 1755 and 1775 was three times the national average, and in Paisley, a textile town, the growth in the same period was 121.4 per cent (Smout, 1983 p. 67). Flax did not grow well in Scotland, unlike in Ireland, and therefore linen production was progressively separated from farming. Ultimately there developed a proletariat skilled in linen production but divorced from the land and needing work in the towns. This population shift was reinforced by agrarian decline and politically forced depopulation of the Highlands, which produced a mass of unskilled labourers separated from their former livelihood. New social problems were created: problems of adjustment, of providing relief for the distressed, of human rights and of the effects of machine production. Ferguson's own position, as a former Highlander who had become socially and geographically mobile in moving to Edinburgh, added a special dimension to his concern with these problems (Forbes 1967, p. 41; MacRae 1969, p. 19).

Adam Smith, in contrast, was not in tune with the revolution in production and social life that was occurring around him. The only thing he has to say about 'large manufactures' is that they frequently corrupt the morals of workers, and before the *Essay* Smith's vision of the labour process was still one of independent craft workers owning their means of production (see Brewer 1987, p. 9). Kindleberger has claimed that Smith's *The Wealth of Nations* is the work of a literary economist because it draws on examples from books, not from the real industrial world (1976, p. 6): hence Asa Briggs's famous remark that Smith has insight but no foresight. Ferguson did have foresight, even though there is a dearth of specific examples taken from the Scotland of his time. However, the transformations occurring around him in Scotland permeate his work at the abstract level, for Ferguson focuses upon the negative effects of some features of industrialization, such as manufacturing production and 'mechanical labour', a term he borrowed from Francis Hutcheson. Moreover, he was aware that the labour process had fundamentally changed and that some people now sold their labour power and did not own their means of production, and that from this change arose specific problems in modern society. There are two references in the *Essay* to the forced character of mechanical labour, where Ferguson refers to the 'necessity' which drives some people to perform mechanical labour in order to have 'moderate enjoyments of life' (1966, pp. 259, 217). Elsewhere Ferguson refers to workers having no option but to toil for others (1966, p. 241), and to the 'ordinary race of men' being the 'property of persons' who are considered to belong to a superior class (1966, p. 254). Above all, Ferguson's discussion of the harmful human and social effects of the division of labour is evidence of his foresight, showing that he was taking his perspective and discourse in the direction of nineteenth-century sociology.

*Conclusion*

Ferguson's use of sociological perspective and discourse as critique arose out of his attempt to analyse and explain broader processes of cultural and economic change occurring in Scotland at the time of his writing. These changes were deliberately placed in the comparative framework of his conjectural history of civil society, so that the distingushing features of modern society could be defined, and the causal factors behind the process of social development and change identified. Therefore Ferguson, much more thoroughly than other Scots, undertakes a comparison of various forms of society, discussing a range of social structural variables which are given explanatory status, visualizing the social structure as an integrated unit with causal relations existing between its parts. The discourse of civic humanism is also employed to understand these changes, and limits the extent to which Ferguson anticipates nineteenth-century sociology, but this bifurcation of the two traditions provides one historical route through which nineteenth-century sociology emerged from seventeenth and eighteenth century social and political theory. The discourses of conjectural history, civic humanism and sociology are all therefore linked in Ferguson's work, and if Foucault is correct to say that the history of ideas is a succession of discourses, Ferguson marks the point where sociological discourse on the structure of society begins to emerge out of the discourse of civic humanism and conjectural history.

This new departure demonstrates that sociological discourse originated partly in a special type of history and then developed independently because it focused on questions of social change. The idea that sociology arose from an attempt to understand and conceptualize social change is a familiar claim with respect to the great transformations of the nineteenth century, which form the context to the development of sociology in that century.

The argument here is that the social transformations in Scotland which pre-date the nineteenth century were vital to this new perspective and discourse, and by placing them within the wider framework of the conjectural history of civil society, Ferguson achieved in eighteenth-century Scotland a radical reconceptualization of the nature of modern society and social life. This shift in discourse and perspective was a prerequisite for the emergence of sociology in the nineteenth century. The making of Scotland was, in this sense, also the making of sociology.

NOTES

1. I am grateful to Duncan Forbes and Ali Rattansi for their comments on the Edinburgh conference paper, of which this is a shorter and revised version.
2. In the third of his unpublished essays, Ferguson writes of history as the primary form of 'informative discourse' so that the past 'should be recorded with the most rigorous regard to reality'. However, in contradiction of this plea for accuracy, and in line with the arguments of this chapter, he drew a distinction between 'narrative history', being an accurate record of successive events, and 'descriptive history', whereby the past is classified and understood according to some theoretical schema. This latter type is what Stewart called 'conjectural history'. For an account of how popular conjectural history was in Scotland at this time see Hopfl (1978).
3. Elsewhere I have argued (Brewer 1986, p. 465, 1987, pp. 13–14), drawing on the work of Hamowy (1968), that Ferguson's work on the division of labour precedes Smith's in time and in sociological content, and that Smith's well-known charge of plagiarism against Ferguson only refers to Ferguson's reference to pins to illustrate the productive capacity of the division of labour, although Foley (1974) shows that Smith himself borrowed this from the *Encyclopedie*.

REFERENCES

Barnes, H.E. (1917), 'Sociology before Comte: A Summary of Doctrines and an Introduction to the Literature', *American Journal of Sociology*, vol. 23, pp. 174–247.

Bartolommei, S. (1979), 'Forzo del "Progretto", Potere della "Cirostanze", e Teoria de "Progresso" in *An Essay on the History of Civil Society* di Adam Ferguson', *Pensiero Politico*, vol. 12, pp. 344–60.

Brewer, J.D. (1986), 'Adam Ferguson and the Theme of Exploitation', *British Journal of Sociology*, vol. 37, pp. 461–78.

Brewer, J.D. (1987), 'The Scottish Enlightenment', in, A. Reeves, *Modern Theories of Exploitation*, London and Beverly Hills: Sage, pp. 6–29.

Bryson, G. (1932), 'Sociology considered as Moral Philosophy', *Sociological Review*, vol. 24, pp. 26–36.

Bryson, G. (1945), *Man and Society*, Princeton: Princeton University Press.

Bullough, V.L. (1970), 'Intellectual Achievement in Eighteenth Century Scotland: A Comparative Study of the Importance of Education', *Comparative Education Review*, vol. 14, pp. 90–102.

Bullough, V.L., and Bullough, B. (1971), 'Intellectual Achievers: A Study of Eighteenth Century Scotland', *American Journal of Sociology*, vol. 76, pp. 1048–63.

Bullough, V.L., and Bullough, B. (1974), 'Historical Sociology: Intellectual Achievement in Eighteenth Century Scotland', *British Journal of Sociology*, vol. 24, pp. 418–30.

Calvert, P. (1982), *The Concept of Class*, London: Hutchinson.

Camic, C. (1983), *Experience and Enlightenment*, Edinburgh: Edinburgh University Press.

Campbell, R., and Skinner, A. (1982), *The Origins and Nature of the Scottish Enlightenment*, Edinburgh: John Donald.

Chitnis, A.C. (1976), *The Scottish Enlightenment*, London: Croom Helm.

Christie, J.R. (1974), 'The Origins and Development of the Scottish Scientific Community 1680–1760', *History of Science*, vol. 12, pp. 122–41.

Emerson, R. (1973), 'The Enlightenment and Social Structure', in, P. Fritz and D. Williams, *City and Society in the 18th Century*, Toronto: Hakkert.

Ferguson, A. (1966), *An Essay on the History of Civil Society*, Edinburgh: Edinburgh University Press.

Frisby, D., and Sayer, D. (1986), *Society*, London: Tavistock.

Foley, V. (1974), 'The Division of Labour in Plato and Smith', *History of Political Economy*, vol. 6, pp. 220–42.

Forbes, D. (1966), 'Introduction', in Ferguson, A. (1966).

Forbes, D. (1967), 'Adam Ferguson and the Idea of Community', in, D. Young, *Edinburgh in the Age of Reason*, Edinburgh: Edinburgh University Press.

Giddens, A. (1971), *Capitalism and Modern Social Theory*, Cambridge: Cambridge University Press.

Giddens, A. (1976), *New Rules of Sociological Method*, London: Hutchinson.

Gouldner, A. (1970), *The Coming Crisis of Western Sociology*, London: Heinemann.

Hamowy, R. (1968), 'Adam Smith, Adam Ferguson and the Division of Labour', *Economica*, vol. 35, pp. 249–59.

Hont, I., and Ignatieff, M. (1983), *Wealth and Virtue*, Cambridge, Cambridge University Press.

Hopfl, H.M. (1978), 'From Savage to Scotsman: Conjectural History in the Scottish Enlightenment', *Journal of British Studies*, vol. 17, pp. 19–40.

Kettler, D. (1965), *The Social and Political Thought of Adam Ferguson*, Ohio: Ohio State University Press.

Kindleberger, C.P. (1976), 'The Historical Background: Adam Smith and the Industrial Revolution', in, T. Wilson and A. Skinner, *The Market and the State*, Oxford: Oxford University Press.

Lehmann, W.C. (1930), *Adam Ferguson and the Beginnings of Modern Sociology*, New York: Columbia University Press.

Lenman, B. (1981), *Integration, Enlightenment and Industrialization in Scotland 1746-1832*, London: Edward Arnold.

MacRae, D. (1969), 'Adam Ferguson', in, T. Raison, *The Founding Fathers of Social Science*, Harmondsworth: Penguin.

Meek, R.L. (1967), 'The Scottish Contribution to Marxist Sociology', in R.L. Meek, *Economics and Ideology*, London: Chapman and Hall.

Morrell, J.B. (1970), 'The University of Edinburgh in the Late Eighteenth Century: Its Scientific Eminence and Academic Structure', *Isis*, vol. 116, pp. 158-71.

Myers, M. (1967), 'The Division of Labour as a Principle of Social Cohesion', *Canadian Journal of Economics*, vol. 33, pp. 432-40.

Nisbet, R. (1967), *The Sociological Tradition*, London: Heinemann.

Olson, R. (1975), *Scottish Philosophy and British Physics 1750-1880*, Princeton: Princeton University Press.

Pascal, R. (1938), 'Property and Society: The Scottish Historical School of the 18th Century', *Modern Quarterly*, March, pp. 167-79.

Pascal, R. (1939), 'Herder and the Scottish Historical School', *Publications of the English Goethe Society*, vol. 14, pp. 23-42.

Philip, W. (1985), 'The Contribution of Adam Ferguson to Social Science' Ph.D., University of Surrey.

Phillipson, N. (1973), 'Towards a Definition of the Scottish Enlightenment', in, P. Fritz, and D. Williams, *City and Society in the 18th Century*, Toronto: Hakkert.

Phillipson, N. (1975), 'Culture and Society in the 18th Century Province', in, L. Stone, *The University in Society*, Princeton: Princeton University Press.

Pocock, J.G.A. (1975), *The Machiavellian Moment*, Princeton: Princeton University Press.

Rendall, J. (1979), *The Origins of the Scottish Enlightenment*, London: Macmillan.

Rattansi, A. (1982), *Marx and the Division of Labour*, London: Macmillan.

Robertson, J. (1983), 'Scottish Political Economy beyond the Civic Tradition', *History of Political Thought*, vol. 4, pp. 451-82.

Salvucci, P. (1972), *Adam Ferguson: Sociologia e Filosofia Politica*, Urbino: Argalia.

Shapin, S. (1974*a*), 'Property Patronage and the Politics of Science', *British Journal for the History of Science*, vol. 7, pp. 1-41.

Shapin, S. (1974*b*), 'The Audience for Science in Eighteenth Century Edinburgh', *History of Science*, vol. 12, pp. 95-121.

Skinner, A. (1982), 'A Scottish Contribution to Marxist Sociology?', in, I. Bradley and M. Howard, *Classical and Marxian Political Economy*, London: Macmillan.

Slotkin, J. (1965), *Readings in Early Anthropology*, Chicago: Aldine.

Smout, T.C. (1983), 'Where had the Scottish Economy got to by the Third Quarter of the 18th Century?', in, I. Hont and M. Ignatieff (1983).

Swingewood, A. (1970), 'Origins of Sociology: The Case of the Scottish Enlightenment', *British Journal of Sociology*, vol. 21, pp. 156-80.

Therborn, G. (1976), *Science, Class and Society*, London: New Left Books.

Trevor-Roper, H. (1963), 'The Historical Philosophy of the Enlightenment', *Studies in Voltaire and the Eighteenth Century*, vol. 27, pp. 1667-87.

# 2

## Nationality, Social Change and Class: Transformations of National Identity in Scotland

JOHN FOSTER

'The theory of nationalism constitutes Marxism's greatest historical failure'. Over the past decade this comment by Tom Nairn in his *Break up of Britain* (Nairn 1977, p. 1) has encouraged the belief that the Marxist tradition has little to offer on the subject. Here the opposite will be argued. As in Nairn, the argument will be based largely on the history of the Scottish people. Unlike Nairn, I will seek to show that this history can only be understood by relating the *content* of Scotland's nationality, and how it changes historically, to the dialectics of class struggle. This, I contend, is how Marx himself sought to understand the concept of the nation and nationality. First, however, in order to isolate the specific contribution of Marx and the Marxist tradition, I will examine the adequacy of some recent non-Marxist approaches to nationality.

*What is the Historical Status of the Nation?*

The last decade has seen the blossoming of a major debate about the historical status of the nation. It focuses on the question of whether there have 'always' been nations, or whether the nation, as we know it, is a very recent arrival. Ernest Gellner and John Breuilly have challenged conventional accounts of nationality by denying any necessary connection between the modern nation and previous ethnic formations. Both present the nation-state as the direct product of industrial society. Against this, A.D. Smith has sought to reassert the historical universality of national identity as a political form.

Gellner (1964, 1983) starts the debate with an ingenious paradox. The world possesses many thousands of ethnic and linguistic groupings. Yet only a small minority, a few hundred at the most, have emerged as the basis for national movements. Still fewer sustain active nationalisms at any particular moment. Accordingly, argues Gellner, it is very difficult to argue for any simple, direct causal link between the existence of an ethnic identity and the coming into being of a national movement. On the other hand, the nation-state is, almost exclusively, the typical political form of modern industrial society, unlike most pre-industrial societies. Hence, says Gellner, if this relationship is to be explained, the answer must derive in some way from the specific functional requirements of modern industrialism.

Gellner's elucidation of this problem draws heavily on Max Weber. He presents us with a model of pre-industrial agrarian society, where culture and power were kept distinct and organized on separate planes. An élite culture – military, legal, religious – was organized horizontally on a continental basis and was often sustained by a closed clericy (Catholic, Muslim, Brahmin) using its own separate 'international' language. Below this lay a landlord-ruled peasant society divided vertically into self-contained parochial communities with minimum communication. Neither level of this organization geographically corresponded to linguistic or ethnic communities. There existed, therefore, no space where the exercise of power could be posed in terms of linguistic culture and no basis for what we have come to call nationality as a form of personal and state identity.

Modern industrial society, in contrast, is organized in states where culture and power, force and legitimacy, are geographically fused together in ways that embrace the entire population. Gellner's explanation of why modern society should be organized in this 'national' way is closely linked to his understanding of how industrialism emerged. Like Weber he gives a key place to Protestant individualism. The Protestant doctrine of individual responsibility – for salvation and social conduct – is presented as eroding the basic structures of the old society. The assertion of the individual's right to full knowledge challenged the cultural authority of the clericy. The stress on an earthly measure of moral conduct demanded the application of this knowledge to the stewardship of resources. The result, he claims, was the emergence of a new type of rationality, instrumental, critical and innovative, which struck the shackles of custom from peasant production and provided the base for industrialism (Gellner 1983, p. 19–20).

Gellner derives two reasons from this as to why the resulting industrial society should be organized on national lines. The first is socio-economic. It refers to the way this new instrumental rationality was economically set in motion and reproduced. The economic success of the new society derived from its ability to generate a division of labour in which technologically-related skills were rapidly interchangeable and progressively enhanced. This demanded, says Gellner, cultural uniformity and progressively stronger central state-direction across territorially defined economies. Hence, in contrast to the mutually exclusive systems of culture within pre-industrial society, modern society demands a *state-sustained* commonality of education, language and custom, which gives it the character which has come to be called national.

Gellner's second explanation is socio-psychological. The symbolism of the nation fulfils a need for personal identity in face of a social system that is, to use his own word, entropic. The individualism of industrial society, the interchangeability of persons that sustains its division of labour, means that its members exist in a state of systematic randomness. Personal identification with the nation-state, its actual worship as Gellner sees it, meets this need.

It is also for these reasons that *new* nationalisms come into being. This process is analysed as a consequence of what Gellner sees as the uneven pace of industrial expansion. The populations of more backward regions, disadvantaged within the new division of labour by less than equal educational preparedness, will inevitably seek to achieve 'their own' separate linguistic state. The actual content of the new nation's identity is, for Gellner, somewhat arbitrary. He leaves no doubt that, although a mixture of ethnicity and religion is probably the most durable combination, it is social circumstance, and not anything which derives from the authenticity of the ethnic tradition, which causes the growth of new nationalisms.

John Breuilly (1982) has recently taken this analysis a stage further. Like Gellner, he sets nationalism and nation-building exclusively in the modern period and does so within the same Weberian perspective. Unlike Gellner, he does not conceive nationalism in socially functional terms. On the contrary, Breuilly's nationalism is solely political: a vehicle for the acquisition of state power which takes advantage of the space created by the emergence of 'civil society'. This is defined as the existence of a sphere of economic and social activity independent of the state, and not prescribed in detail by those holding political authority. As such, it is seen as the hallmark of the modern state and as the necessary condition for economic individualism. But the very separateness of this private vernacular culture inevitably provokes demands that the identity of the 'state' be made the same as that of the 'people'. Hence the development of movements in the early modern period that attempted to secure – either by separation, unification or by internal national revolution – an exact match between the linguistic character of the state and the geographical area inhabited by a particular people. Breuilly takes a fairly sceptical view of what constitutes a 'people' and of the justifications offered. The criteria chosen may be linguistic, religious, physiological or simply imagined historical constructs. He is also sceptical about the social functionality of the resulting nationalism. For every nation-state that can be claimed as creating an optimally sized division of labour, it is possible to point to at least two others that might be considered to have impeded, balkanized and disrupted a region's economic advance. Modern industrial society creates the occasion, not the reason, for national movements. Nationalism itself is a purely 'parasitic' phenomenon, an ideological product created by politicians seeking to occupy vacant political territory.

It is for this reason also that Breuilly sees such national movements as being self-limiting. As the modern nation-state penetrates all aspects of social life, so the space once accorded to civil society is once more squeezed out. This is particularly so for totalitarian national states which by definition demand the rigorous elimination of all non-national cultural pluralism. Accordingly, while the formation of the modern state system saw the activation of nationalist movements, its further development progressively limits the ground on which new movements can operate.

These two contributions, both fairly characteristic of the modernist school, have the merit of taking discussions beyond the simple assumption that some form of national identity is an inevitably accompaniment of all human societies. But there are also obvious weaknesses, and A.D. Smith (1986) notes at least some of them. Political structures with recognizably ethnic national identities can be found quite readily in ancient and medieval periods and to a large extent constitute the norm there also. They may not have incorporated the precise social functions indicated by Gellner, but in the ancient Middle East and classical Greece a close relationship was seen to exist between linguistic and ethnic cohesion and the political and economic strength of particular states. Moreover, not all the modern political leaders who sought power on the basis of strengthening the nation did so in societies that were notably pluralistic. Against what he sees as Breuilly's purely instrumental view of nationalism, Smith makes the telling point that he fails to account either for the power of national ideology or its specific limitations. National ideology is notable for the fact that it cannot be exploited purely at will, and that it places considerable constraints on its practitioners.

In reasserting the claims of ethnic continuity, Smith does not deny that new developments took place in the early modern period. The Western nation-state is seen to represent a specific phenomenon resulting from the convergence of three separate transformations: the creation of the new economic division of labour in the sixteenth and seventeenth centuries (common trading and labour conditions across political territories); the military and administrative centralization characteristic of eighteenth-century absolutism; and the emergence of national educational systems in the early nineteenth century. But while such nation-states were new as political forms, the national identities around which they crystallized were not, and cannot be explained simply by citing their role in the new system. Smith writes: 'nations are not fixed and immutable entities "out there" (not even the nationalists thought so); but neither are they completely malleable and fluid processes and attitudes, at the mercy of every outside force. To interpret them as masks and channels of "real" social forces or the cultural surface of anatomical structures beneath is to miss the independent role and originating force of ethnic identities and ethnic cleavage' (Smith 1986, p. 211).

For Smith the nation is a shared community of mythic values which supplies a universal 'need for immortality through the memory of posterity'. He adopts the French term 'ethnie' to stress that nations are communities based on a cultural (and not physiological) distinctiveness and defines them as 'human populations with shared ancestry myths, histories and cultures, having an association with a specific territory and a sense of solidarity' (Smith 1986, p. 57). In these terms nations and nationalities can be identified for all periods.

*Some Anomalies of Scottish History*

The debate between modernists and their opponents has undoubtedly helped to clarify issues. Yet methodologically both perspectives present difficulties. Their coherence depends at least partly on definitions that are self-limiting, and this makes them less than helpful as tools of historical analysis. This can be fairly readily seen when we examine some of the theoretical problems posed by Scotland's history as a nation.

These include the following.

*The origins of Scottish nationality.* All historians agree that ethnically the Scottish land-mass was occupied by at least five linguistically separate and distinct groupings in the early Middle Ages. Most historians also agree that by the eleventh to thirteenth centuries at least four of these groupings had fused together into a nation that identified itself as Scottish; long before any moves towards modernization and at a time when Scots society was decidedly uncivil.

*The ending of Scottish statehood.* After securing its independence in the fourteenth century, Scotland possessed sovereign statehood for three centuries. Then, in precisely that era when modern industrial society was emerging, the Scottish state, with, it appears, the support of its commerical and merchant élite, abandoned its own independent sovereignty and was politically integrated into another nation-state.

*The survival of Scottish nationality.* Despite Scotland's short history as a nation-state, and despite being itself bisected by language and other subethnic allegiances, it has sustained some form of testable national consciousness into the late twentieth century.

*The duality of Scottish and British national allegiances.* A majority of those considering themselves Scottish, including most of those supporting some form of internal self-government, also profess forms of allegiance to British institutions, either to the British state itself or to the Labour Party and its legislative programme. Polls over the past decade have repeatedly indicated support for a Scottish Assembly exceeding that for independence from Britain. A subset of this problem is the oscillation of support for the SNP and the Labour Party. The strong variation of support for the SNP (from a peak of 30 per cent in 1974) appears to derive – as happened both in the 1960s and again in the 1970s – at least partly from switches in voting preference among working-class voters who would otherwise have voted Labour. The SNP victory in the 1973 Govan by-election (and the subsequent general-election reversion to Labour), and the 1988 by-election in the same constituency would be examples of this phenomenon.

*The timing of demands for greater Scottish self-government.* Little significant demand appears to have existed in the eighteenth and nineteenth centuries; although some, not very easily measured, support for home rule did arise in the thirty years before 1914. There was apparently no significant mass support for such demands during the First World War or between wars. The major surges of support for the SNP came in the mid-1960s and the mid-1970s. The Labour Party's position of support for a Scottish assembly with tax-raising powers emerged in the course of the 1970s. Yet in terms of regional differentials (whether one looks at wage levels or real income per head) Scotland's position was no worse in the 1960s and 1970s than it had been in the 1930s (or the 1840s) and better than that of Wales (where the demand for national institutions has been much less widespread) or, for that matter, of a number of English regions.

None of these anomalies are easily explained by Breuilly or Gellner. Both would find it difficult to explain how it was that Scottish nationhood emerged in the pre-modern period (long before any of the social and political processes which they cite could be even remotely perceived). Nor would be it easy for them to explain the converse: why, in the early modern period, those Scots most closely identified with modernization and the new institutions in a series of unions with England. Breuilly's model provides no way of explaining the timing of subsequent demands for the restoration of national institutions. Scottish civil society and the British state existed in mutual counterposition in 1830 and 1930 as much as in 1970. Finally, Gellner does not appear to have an easy answer to the phenomenon of two apparently coexisting and overlapping national identities (are the Scots perhaps particularly entropic?); or to the problem of why Wales, which has at least some linguistic base to its nationalism and suffers a greater regional differential, has so far possessed a much weaker national movement.

Smith, at least by analogy with his treatment of Switzerland, would probably explain the origin of the Scottish nation as an example of 'frontier nationality': as stemming from a fight for joint freedom by different linguistic groups living in the same territory against external economic control. He might also adequately explain the survival of a nation without sovereignty. But it is difficult to see how he would tackle the question of apparently dual national allegiances and the timing of recent demands for self-government within the multinational British state.

Nairn (1977) builds his thesis around this phenomenon. He utilizes Gellner's concept of uneven development but in a different way: applying it not to the period of industrial capitalism's development but to the era of its decline, in particular to the end of empire. While previously the Scottish élite had been well-rewarded clients of the British state, drawing benefit from the empire and the union, this was no longer the case, and the crisis of imperialism and reactivation of rationalism now portended the 'break-up' of Britain. Like Gellner, therefore, Nairn gives a central role to the economic interest of the élite. First, this is used to explain the disablement of Scottish culture during industrialization – its alternation between romantic antiquarianism and derivative enlightenment rationality – and then, much later, the emergence of a combative nationalism in the 1960s. Hence, Nairn does provide answers of a kind to at least two of the questions posed. But it is more difficult to claim that he enables us to *evaluate* the character of Scottish nationality or explain the riddle of the dual allegiance. Hobsbawm, in a somewhat disapproving review, argued that Nairn's use of uneven development would, taken logically, lead to an infinite nationalist regress. He also queried what he felt was a more basic assumption of Nairn's thesis: that separatist nationalism is necessarily anti-imperialist. The balkanization of the existing state system might just as easily lead to enhanced external manipulation: giant companies, little states. Using an important if somewhat unfashionable term, he concludes by warning against seeing nationalism as inherently 'progressive' (Hobsbawm 1977). In dealing with Scotland's history, therefore, none of these approaches seem to provide us with a totally satisfactory solution.

*Marxist and Non-Marxist Perspectives Compared*

Let us start by looking more generally at what the non-Marxist approaches fail to do.

None of them, neither Gellner, Breuilly nor Smith, provide any way of explaining the specific *content* of national ideologies. Smith and Breuilly provide typologies. Smith stresses the limits which such ideology imposes on those who wish to use it. But none explain how the content of national ideology evolves, and what determines the specific character of the constraints which make it such an unpredictable political force.

No less important, none of them provide any method of *evaluating* national ideology. Smith ultimately poses nationality as an issue of political legitimacy (a justification for self-determination). Gellner sees himself as delimiting the scope of nationality to a particular social functionality. Breuilly presents nationalism as parasitic. But when it comes to evaluating particular national ideologies or trends within them, none of these approaches takes us beyond relativism. Each ideology or trend is seen to possess equal legitimacy as the chosen identity of a particular national group.

These gaps are important in leading us to the intellectual closure, or conceptual self-limitation, by which the definitions are generated and sustained. Gellner achieves his definition by sharply sundering nationalism from ethnic nationality (which is not defined) and then anchoring nationalism within a particular model of modern industrial society. Breuilly does much the same. The resulting explanations depend on reducing nationalism to a functional product of this model. In Gellner's case it is its requirement for social reproduction and identity. In Breuilly's it is, more negatively, the initial lack of fit between state and civil society and the power vacuum which this creates. In neither case are the models of industrial society, which ultimately validate these explanations, themselves subject to sustained scrutiny. In contrast, Smith does not operate by limiting his definitions historically. Instead it is given significance by allocating it a universal character, but this is a character that has, ultimately, a static rationale. Nationality is a mythic identity that satisfies a universal human need for immortality.

All the explanations, therefore, exist, in a sense, 'outside' history. National identity is either conceived on a trans-historical plane (and to this extent is unaffected by history) or is a phenomenon that emerges, as if programmed, in line with a specifically conceived stage of historical development and takes its role and character from its particular conceptualization. It would of course be quite wrong to say these approaches are without historical elaboration. Naturally, this forms the substance of their typologies and of their general argument. But it does seem fair to claim that history is not examined in a way that might infringe the integrity of the original definitions. In so far as the *content* or ideological function of national identity is discussed by Gellner or Breuilly, it derives from their concepts of 'industrial' or 'civil' society rather than the analysis of actual historical struggles within a particular society. In contrast, one of the reasons why Marx is sometimes accused of not treating the issue 'systematically' is because he approached nation and national identity in precisely this way.

It is, therefore, all the more difficult to provide a brief summary. What follows should be read with this in mind. It is not what Marx said, but what commentators have constructed from a massive corpus of wider social analysis. It will inevitably be schematic.

First, ethnicity is a basic and continuing – though not invariable – feature of human society. The belief, of Nairn among others, that Marx saw nationality as a phenomenon somehow anchored to rise of capitalism, and to be therefore a facet of bourgeois ideology, derives from a somewhat tendentious reading of *Capital* and the *Communist Manifesto*. When, however, we turn to other of Marx's writings there is no scope for misinterpretation. In texts that do not focus specifically on capitalist production, Marx stresses the presence of ethnicity throughout all stages of human development. In both the *Grundrisse* (1857) and in the *Ethnological Notebooks* (Krader 1972) Marx presents ethnicity as an originating feature of the communality of human society. In this sense it is somewhat akin to language. Ethnicity was an expression of the basic social identity needed to permit a sharing of skills and resources that could be historically cumulative: 'the naturally evolved tribal community... is the first precondition for the appropriation of the objective conditions of life' (Marx 1857, p. 400).

Second, ethnicity is a social construct. It is not, in essence, physiological or biological, even though it may have physiological consequences. The Soviet scholars Bromley (1974), Alexayev (1974) and Zagladin (1975) have recently sought to clarify this relationship. They distinguish two interacting forces.

On the other side, there is the 'ethnic formation', representing the basic continuity of cultural identities. On the other, there is what they call the 'ethnic social carrier', the historically transitory social or state form within which the ethnic formation exists at a particular moment. The ethnic formation is defined as a 'historically established community of people, characterized by common, relatively stable cultural features, certain distinctive psychological traits and also by an awareness of their identity and distinctiveness from other similar communities' (Bromley 1974, p. 36). Its 'relative stability' is defined by how far it is able to maintain its identity in face of major disruptions, such as migration. The ethnic social carrier, on the other hand, is the 'specific historical carrier of the ethnic at a particular moment'. It may or may not be in the form of a state, depending on the stage of social development. In the life of any 'relatively stable' ethnic formation its social carrier will often be transformed or changed, merged or fragmented many times. And the ethnic formation itself will also change. It may indeed at particular points – and over long historical periods – contain within it physical or genetic traits. But even such characteristics will (over periods of time) themselves be subject to change. The historically very stable Han Chinese identity, for example, had physiological traits that were the result of socially determined mixing of previously ethnically distinct peoples over two or three thousand years. The creation of a new ethnic social carrier can combine and merge within a single cultural-political relationship previously separate ethnic formations. In these circumstances, new ethnic formations, developing their own distinct physiological features, may emerge, and then in turn be intermixed with others. The active force is the political economy, in the broadest sense, of the ethnic social carrier.

This brings us on to the third element of the Marxist approach. For all post-communal periods, the content of national identity will be mediated by class forces, and its development will be determined by class struggle. This is not to reduce nationality to class but to pose a relationship. Like any language, a nationality has a continuing, though neither static nor necessarily permanent, existence that spans different politico-economic systems and is independent of any particular class. On the other hand, the significance given to a national identity, like the class-inflected meaning ascribed to particular words, will depend on class position and ultimately on class power. The state form, which acts as an ethnic social carrier, will define and represent the interests of a particular class and a particular mode of production. It will need to define (or redefine) ethnic identity on its own terms. Correspondingly, those who have opposing class interests, whose aspirations are expressed in class struggle against the existing order, will contest this meaning. There will always be different class trends within any national identity. In dealing with the modern period, Lenin put it as follows:

> the elements of a democratic and socialist culture are present, if only in rudimentary form, in *every* national culture, since in *every* nation there are toiling and exploited masses, whose conditions of life inevitably give rise to the ideology of democracy and socialism. But *every* nation also possesses a bourgeois culture (and most nations a reactionary and clerical culture as well) in form not in 'elements' but of the *dominant* culture (Lenin 1913, p. 24).

The fourth element follows on. Nationality is a social construct. It gives form and significance to linguistic, psychological and sometimes physiological traits. But its power is *ideological,* and there is nothing *inherently* progressive about it. This power drives precisely from its assertion of 'equality' within a national community. As ideology it incorporates a species of false consciousness which is, in a sense, the reified double, of Marx's primitive communality. It reinstates in a class-divided, exploitative society a totality of social relationships which are not exploitative. Hence, it is neither, as an ideology, directly conducive to class awareness, nor totally manipulable by the ruling class. It holds a double-edged position which derives from the fact that, as with any other cultural identity in a class society, it is materially rooted in a mass of rights and expectations which themselves reflect, even if inexplicitly, a particular balance of class forces, the achievements of past struggle and the overall level of development of production relations. At the same time, its assertion of 'equal membership', while potentially progressive, has historically been subject to profoundly reactionary manipulation. In so far as it can be used to assert equality 'in the nation', *with* the dominant, exploiting class *against* those exploited 'outside the nation', national ideology has always been the basic component of chauvinism, fascism and racism. It was for this reason that Marx, and later Lenin and

Dimitrov, were so emphatic about the need for the working class to take up the issue of nationality and national self-determination, not in terms of abstract rights, but critically on the basis of a specific historical analysis. Marx was convinced, for instance, that 'the English reaction in England has its roots (as in Cromwell's time) in the subjugation of Ireland' and consequently that 'the English working class will never accomplish anything' until the issue of Irish self-determination had been resolved (Marx, 1869). English workers had to be won to see their national tradition not in terms of a classless chauvinism that divided and disabled them but in terms of its real history.

The fifth and final element concerns the character of this 'progressive' response, which may come not only from the working class but from any class that represents, in its time, a historically progressive force. In order to assume state power, and indeed in the process of doing so, a class has to make its own objectives universally relevant to all forms of class oppression in the old society. This universalization lies at the heart of the revolutionary process. It is intrinsic both to the creation of a revolutionary alliance and the organic destruction of the old order. For the working class, it demands, as Marx put it, that 'it must rise to become the leading force of the nation, must itself constitute the nation, [be] itself national, though not in the bourgeois sense of the word' (Marx and Engels 1848, p. 485–8). It is, therefore, these periods of revolutionary redefinition that are crucial for the development and sometimes transformation of an ethnic formation. They represent the breaks in continuity when an ethnic formation and its specific social carrier part company, and where on some occasions, the new state system will define its citizenship and what it is to be national, in a way that creates a new nation.

Examples of such class alliances as the basis for a new nation might be the transformation of England and Scotland into Britain, and the creation of the United States. The political revolutions that created these new state forms demanded revolutionary alliances that encompassed much broader forces than the class that achieved power. Each demanded a sharp break with the preceding order and established territorial limits that defined a new citizenship. The fact that they were class-based societies, and that they changed the boundaries of exploitation, both geographically and in terms of production relations, also meant that new definition of the 'nation' was double-edged and contested. It could not simply be promulgated. The 'freeborn English' who formed the foot-soldiers of the anti-feudal revolution were forcibly deprived of full citizenship. The new ruling class might represent them in national terms as 'free' in contrast with the enserfed peoples of feudal Europe, and, still more potently, with the subject and enslaved peoples of the multi-national British state and empire. But this redefinition was not automatically accepted. Cromwell's army, when refused citizenship in 1647-9, vocally challenged this chauvinist sleight of hand, opposed external conquest and revived the universal aspirations of the original anti-feudal alliance. Later, of course, this counter-definition was reinforced by a direct perception of the material contradictions of the new social order and the state power struggles they generated. Hence, to sum up, the Marxist approach does not reduce nationality to class. On the contrary, nationality is seen as a continuing and separate feature of human society. It is associated with the setting of politico-economic boundaries for productive sociality. But at the same time, while supplying the cultural bonding for particular divisions of labour, it is not specific to any particular mode of production, nor is it static or unchanging. If it is, it dies. Rather, it is a developing phenomenon, whose changing content is determined precisely by how people respond to the class character of that society and its politico-economic contradictions. As an ideology that culturally bonds a system, nationality asserts a classless equality which gives it a particularly powerful ideological status within any class society. This is why it also becomes so important in periods of basic social change. Any change in class relations, which at the same time redefines the nation, will demand a revolutionary alliance with universalized aims powerful enough to combine potentially antagonistic class elements. These will remain, whatever the class character of the state, to inform the new class dialectic about the nature of the nation.

Accordingly, in Marxist terms, if the 'nation' is not to be imposed as a static justification for the existing order, its content must be related, critically and historically, to the class forces which moulded it. The acceptance of a definition which ties a population to the external plunder of its ruling class will, for instance, be incompatible with any successful working-class challenge. Any historical reconstruction has to go beyond just describing the two class trends to an analysis of the key politico-economic turning points which 'made' the nation, specifying the character of the class alliances used to redefine it and how new modes of production changed relations with other nationalities. It is necessary to ask the following questions. How far, within a multinational state, did the relationship between the state and component nationalities involve national oppression or colonialism? How far did it prevent the further socio-economic development of other nations? By what stages, through what alliances, was the identity of the dominant nation defined? In so far as this identity incorporated 'common' progressive aspirations, what was their original material base and how had they been subsequently redefined? Without this information no effective intervention can be made. This is why such stress is laid on content. But, to return to our earlier argument, it is also the contention here that without an effective analysis of content – the blind spot of Breuilly, Gellner and Smith – there can be no adequate conceptualization of nationality either.

*The Development of Scottish Nationality: Some Marxist Comments*

Scotland's national identity poses, as we have seen, some particularly tricky problems. Its origin, transformation and ambiguous continuity do not correspond to any available model. How far, then, can a study of its class dialectics – within a wider politico-economic perspective – provide the explanation we are looking for?

The first challenge is the actual creation of the nation out of several separate ethnic groupings in the early Middle Ages. We need, even for this distant period, to identify the class forces that took the lead, and define the circumstances in which they could create an alliance that was both progressive (in its production relations) and universal (in bringing to an end the manifold oppressions generated by existing forms of class rule).

Historically, the changes in this match the wider transition from Roman slave society to early feudalism. It is the contention here (developed in Dickson 1981) that the Scottish land-mass was not isolated from this process, and that it is within the transition from slave society that we find the relevant class forces.

Scotland was for four centuries the border region of a Roman province: transformed first by systematic slave trading and then later by its cessation and replacement by settled agrarian clan lordships. In the fourth and fifth centuries these border lordships became economically and culturally harmonized with those south of Hadrian's wall. Rome's military collapse left a collection of British statelets which spanned the border, Pictish princedoms further north and, on the west and east flanks, intrusive princedoms of the Irish Scots and North Angles. Though ethnically all very distinct, they were in politico-economic terms quite similar: part tribal but also with important elements of proto-feudal lordship, and all of them, by the seventh century, definitively Christian. In the ninth century all faced destruction by the Vikings. For the settled peasant communities of Lowland Scotland this Viking threat did not mean simply the substitution of one lord for another. It meant subordination to an economically retrogressive slave-trading empire. This was the crucial class-issue.

To this extent, the century-long struggle against the Vikings did, it is argued, have the progressive and universal character required for nation-building. The military form of this struggle was feudal. It was based upon allegiance – by Britons, Picts, North English and Gaels – to lords holding land for military service within an increasingly centralized kingdom. At the same time, it defended the relative freedoms of the settled agrarian peasantry. Its Christian and increasingly national ideology represented the new balance of class forces: symbolizing – against slavery – the sanctity of the family, and reaffirming – against the blood-kin subordination of the clan – an understanding of mutual reciprocity and independence in relations between the peasant community and the feudal lord.

This strand of national identity, representing in part the aspirations of the subordinate class in feudal society, was, it is contended, of continuing and determining importance for the next redefinition of national identity and class power in the 1300s. The historical occasion was the war of independence against England. The outcome was, of course, to consolidate the sovereignty of a separate Scottish ruling class. Yet it also changed the character of that rule. The war increasingly took on the character of a struggle against the recent imposition of a far harsher and more rigorous form of feudal rule (including what was seen as the 'non-Scots' institution of formal enserfment). The faction of the Scottish aristocracy which led the fight had to accept, as a condition of military victory, quite unfeudal modes of warfare: guerrilla tactics which were effectively the same as those used in peasant revolts on the Continent. Something like half of all the feudal landlords in Scotland were expropriated for supporting the English, and victory left the political economy of Scottish feudalism chronically weakened: serfdom ended, the basis of military service changed and peasant land-purchase common. No less important it brought direct commercial relations with the Continent. Agriculturally, Scotland was opened up for the export of cash crops, especially of wool, financed from the Low Countries and Northern Italy, organized through the merchant élite and conducted, on a non-feudal basis, through peasant and laird-gentry land-purchase and clearance. Hence the introduction of a Roman law system of absolute property rights. The fifteenth century therefore saw, within a redefined Scottish identity, a particularly strong anti-feudal trend, secular, commercial and, as in the poetry of John Barbour and the Makars, celebrating the independence of the Scots laird and peasant. It was this trend that erupted in the sixteenth century to provide the materials for the Scottish reformation.

If this series of revolutionary class alliances determined the creation and development of a Scottish national identity, what caused its eclipse? Why were the origins of industrial society so closely bound up with the creation of a new 'British' identity? Here there would seem to be a discontinuity not just of content but of form and the emergence, in Bromley's phrase, of a new multinational ethnic social carrier.

Again, it is argued, this transformation can only be understood by returning to the very special course of Scotland's earlier national development and its relation to the politico-economic needs of the new capitalist order. Specifically, Scotland's experience encompassed (directly as a result of a class dialectics its own nationhood) an early weakening of feudal institutions, the premature development of commercial and anti-feudal forces (strongly embedded in, and redefining, national identity) and an economically marginal position on the periphery of Europe. The new presbyterian state, created by a classic class alliance of populist and propertied interests, was too weak – internally and externally – to survive by itself. In the struggles of the seventeenth century both trends within the class alliance, those with capitalist property and those without, came to espouse alliance and then union with similar class forces in England.

Accordingly, in nice contrast with the theorization of Gellner and Breuilly, we find the eighteenth-century Scottish philosophers who popularized the concepts of civil society and the division of labour, Smith, Hume and Millar, also the most enthusiastic champions of British, not Scottish, state institutions. A dual alliance involving both class and national dimensions now crossed existing ethnic boundaries.

The basic question for the Marxist approach is, however, to evaluate the class significance of the results. We need to know that the new British national identity signified in terms of politico-economic subordination. No less important is the task of identifying how far the emerging class trends within the post-feudal Scots identity were transferred, and how far a separate Scottish identity was maintained. It is the argument here that, in contrast to Ireland, the key significance of the new British identity in Scotland was precisely the exercise of economic and political power over other nations. Its dominant trend was intrinsically imperialist. The Union with England, negotiated between 1704 and 1707, had one objective above all: access to the markets of the English empire (which then became British). Parliamentary sovereignty was exchanged for the external economic power essential for continued capitalist accumulation in Scotland. It was, moreover, negotiated on terms which gave Scottish capital the power to continue its own internal reproduction. In Breuilly's terms, it would be difficult to find a more striking contrast than that between the character of the eighteenth-century British state and the institutions of Scottish civil society. Scotland retained a separate university system, its presbyterian institutions of social control (worship, poor relief, education and sexual conduct) as well as separate legal and banking structures, every one of them the relatively recent creation of anti-feudal struggle in Scotland.

All this, however, was only possible because the new structure rested on a broader class alliance. The Union was not simply a matter of the narrow interest of one class. It was made to represent the universalization of class objectives that had been intrinsic to the revolutionary transformation of Scots society over the previous century. It is difficult to see how it could have been otherwise. Unless the Union incorporated what were seen as the progressive and quasi-democratic institutions of presbyterian social organization, there would have been little chance of developing any wider base of support. This seems to have been essential to its success and to the two centuries of its political consolidation.

However, if this was the case, if a new British national identity did emerge, how do we explain the ultimate redevelopment of a Scottish identity and in particular its peculiar class dialectics? In the twentieth century the leading force for this redevelopment was certainly not provided by Scottish capital. Large-scale capital strongly opposed it. Small business and the professional strata did have some role. But for the last twenty years it has been the Scottish Labour Movement, representing the subordinate class trend in Scottish society, that has been the most effective proponent of Scotland's national development, and its main demand has been for a Scottish parliament, not for independence. Is this simply a transitional stage or does it represent something more stable? This question is a central one for the future of the national movement in Scotland, and is closely linked to another: the apparent duality of Scottish and British allegiances.

Given our assessment of the dominant 'British' trend of identity in Scotland, how do we account for the fact that for a century and a half those who built the working-class movement in Scotland were also, in the great majority of cases, committed to some form of unity at British level? It could simply be that this is one more example of the imperialist corruption. The Orange Order did indeed express just this. It combined a populist assertion of personal and religious freedom with the celebration of external conquest and power in a profoundly reactionary way. Yet such a diagnosis does not really match evidence. Only a small fraction of Scots were Orangemen, while the great majority identified with at least some elements of a British nationality. Even those who took an explicitly anti-imperalist political stance, including those who supported Irish self-determination, defended a perspective of class unit at British level. This applied not just to those who built the trade-union movement in the nineteenth century and the ILP and the Communist Party in the twentieth but to the Scottish Chartist movement and the Radicals of the 1790s. The most ambitious public challenge mounted by the early radicals of England and Scotland was the British Convention held in Edinburgh in 1793 and 1794.

The alternative explanation is that British state did indeed represent a new ethnic social carrier, of a specifically capitalist type, and that we are dealing with the development of a subordinate, anti-capitalist, trend of British national identity. This is the interpretation that is argued here: that there did emerge in Scotland an anti-capitalist trend of British identity that was generated by the particular material contradictions of Unionist Scotland. The Union underwrote the power of large-scale landed and mercantile capital. This class could compete only by exploiting Scotland's lower labour costs and needed to carry out wholesale clearances to secure its agrarian base. Culturally and ideologically the battle against it demanded new forms of class unity that linked British and Scottish national traditions. In the same way that the Orange Order incorporated directly Scottish (populist and anti-feudal) elements within the imperialist British ideology, so also was the converse true. The poetry of Robert Burns, for instance, enjoyed immense popularity in the nineteenth century. It attacked the *class* use, by Scottish capital, of Scottish presbyterian institutions, and lampooned the cant and hypocrisy involved. It invoked, both directly and through its use of Scots dialect, the traditions of freeholder independence, and did so to justify wider and sometimes revolutionary aspirations for liberty and brotherhood. For the smallholder and labourer it was *Scottish* capital manipulating these Scottish institutions that was perceived as the immediate enemy. In their defence they sought to combine the populist and anti-absolutist traditions of the past with the strength of the British labour movement. Trade unionists had to face attempts by Scottish capital to isolate Scots workers from those south of the border and defeat the very active efforts to exploit ethnic divisions *inside* Scotland. The creation of working-class organization directly demanded the creation of a new transethnic British unity. Accordingly, the 'British' identity of the Scottish labour movement developed a quite different significance from that of its Unionist employers. It was not about external power, of Scots over other nations, but about being united within Britain *against* capital.

This is the crux of our argument about the transformations of Scottish national identity in the twentieth century. It is that the contrasting content of these two trends of 'British' identity in Scotland meant that they were affected in quite different ways by what has happened to Britain's world role over the past sixty years. The essence of the capitalist trend was imperialist. Its ability to dominate ideologically, to penetrate and hold a base among the petty bourgeoisie and indeed among workers, depended on the material reality of Scottish power through Britain over other economies. The history of the twentieth century reversed this. In so far as large-scale Scottish capital was able to survive, it has been by alienating itself from Scotland and merging itself with British capital. Scotland's experience has been transformed. It is now dominated by external capital through Britain. On the other hand, the logic of the subordinate class trend, of a unity of national contingents within Britain *against* capital, has taken a new and potentially universal siginificance. Capital concentration in the city of London, its international alliances and the sharply uneven accumulation of capital within the British Isles now directly threatens the productive economy of all regions. In this way a material base has been created for a national alliance, on working-class terms, that embraces other strata including small-scale capital. Moreover the decline of one trend and the rise of the other has not happened in isolation. The waning influence of imperialist Britishness within the working population has itself helped to open the way for a non-reformist leadership able to universalize its class objectives. To conclude, therefore, with some brief comments about timing.

If we are dealing with the mutual disintegration and development of class alliances, it is essential to see the process as a whole. The interwar years, for instance, saw the first cracks in the base of Scottish Unionism. Administratively, the establishment of a Scottish Office in Edinburgh returned some of the levers of governmental power. The Scottish Economic Committee was created. Initiatives were taken to develop electricity production, industrial estates and film-making at quasi-state level within Scotland. The patrons of this process, which is sometimes described as the Scottish planning movement, were the men who controlled large-scale capital, Colville, Lithgow, Bilsland, Collins. Politically they were Unionist, opposed to any form of nationalism. Economically they had to contend with the consequences of Britain's inability to continue as world banker and the resulting decline, by almost half, in the demand for Scottish steel, ships and engineering. Their response was one of fierce cartellization. Greater Scottish control over the political framework of economic activity was a natural consequence, not least to discourage incursions into Scotland by external capital. The planning perspectives of these men were, of course, not democratic but authoritarian and corporativist (although perhaps within the tradition of paternalist presbyterianism). They relied on the support of their friends in the City of London and saw themselves as sustaining the political base of Unionism in Scotland. Yet by taking this road they also introduced a basic contradiction within it. Their actions amounted to a visible trade-off between the decline of external power and the restoration of internal control.

Once the governmental influence of Scottish big business had been eroded during and after the Second World War, it was comparatively easy for Tom Johnston and his successors at the Scottish Office to take over the mantle. The perspectives of the Labour Party at this period were also firmly Unionist and entirely reformist. But it was able to create the initial basis of a new class alliance which saw the existence of a British Labour government as the best guarantee of Scotland's ability to control and plan its future. On this basis, although still electorally in a minority position, Labour was able to detach significant sections of the professional and semi-professional strata from allegiance to the Conservative and Liberal parties. Conversely, to the extent that the Conservative Party was able to maintain its base in the 1950s and 1960s it was by contesting the new territory of regional planning developed by Labour.

The key change, however, came in the 1960s and early 1970s. These years delivered decisive blows both to the credibility of traditional Unionism and Labour reformism. Large-scale Scottish capital detached itself from the productive economy, and, in so far as it maintained a separate existence, did so as broker for external capital. British and overseas firms moved in to grab markets, labour, natural resources and local savings, to the obvious detriment of Scottish small business and without providing any stable base for economic growth. The following decade saw an unprecedented disintegration of the political base of the Conservative Party in Scotland (Foster and Woolfson 1986). The economic crisis of the 1970s was no less fatal for Labour's reformist unionism.

As mixed economy Keynesianism showed itself to be unable to deliver the goods, so the balance of influence shifted within the Scottish Labour Movement and the Labour Party. This occurred quite dramatically in the sharp class struggles of the early 1970s. The Communist and Socialist leaders of the non-reformist Left found little difficulty in demonstrating the conflict of interest between monopoly capital – at the level of British state power – and the further development of the Scottish economy. They were, moreover, able to lead mass struggles in which new class alliances were actively called into existence. The year-long action to save Clydeside's shipyards, for instance, successfully challenged the state power of monopoly, and visibly did so on the basis of class alliances assembled at both British and Scottish level. The subordinate trend within Scottish national identity, that of a unity of national contingents against capital at British level, now demonstrated its potential to become the basis of a new dominant class alliance. Reflecting this change, the Scottish Trades Union Congress and then the Labour Party committed themselves in the course of the 1970s to the establishment of a Scottish parliament with legislative power.

Tom Nairn, looking at these developments in the mid-1970s, saw them as the first stage in a wider rekindling of regional nationalisms across Europe. Both he, and the Scottish National Party, had expectations that from 1974 the path of nationalist mobilization would be relatively speedy and cumulative. This did not happen. The Labour Party and the Scottish Trades Union Congress, not the SNP, became the accepted exponents of Scottish interests for the following fifteen years (and no doubt for longer still depending on the emerging political balance of power inside the Labour Movement). The weakness of Nairn's analysis was that it focused on only one element in the situation: the crisis of empire and the impact of uneven development on the élite. Nairn was not able to analyse the class dialectics, the two class trends, within either Scottish or British national identities or their mutual interaction. Marx's treatment of the national question does, it is argued, provide us with a way of doing this.

REFERENCES

Alexayev, V. (1974), 'Modes of race formation' in, I. Grigulevich (ed.), *Races and Peoples*, Moscow: Progress.

Breuilly, J. (1982), *Nationalism and the State*, Manchester: Manchester University Press.

Bromley, Y. (1974), 'The term "ethnos" and its definition' in I. Grigulevich (ed.), *Races and Peoples*, Moscow: Progress.

Dickson, T. (1981), *Scottish Capitalism*, London: Lawrence and Wishart.

Foster, J., and Woolfson C. (1986), *Politics of the UCS Work-in: Class Alliances and the Right to Work*, London: Lawrence and Wishart.

Gellner, E. (1964), *Thought and Change*, London: Weidenfeld.

Gellner, E. (1983), *Nations and Nationalism*, Oxford: Basil Blackwell.

Hobsbawm, E. (1977), 'Some reflections on the "Break-up of Britain"', *New Left Review*, no. 105.

Krader, S. (1972). *The Ethnological Notebooks of Karl Marx*, ed., L. Krader, Assen: Van Gorcum.

Lenin, V. (1913), 'Critical remarks on the National Question', *Collected Works*, vol. 20, Moscow: Progress.

Marx, K. (1857), 'Economic Manuscripts of 1857-8', *Collected Works*, vol. 28, London: Lawrence and Wishart, 1986.

Marx, K. (1869), Marx-Engels, 10 December 1869, *Collected Works*, vol. 43, London: Lawrence and Wishart, 1988.

Marx, K., and Engels, F. (1948), 'The Manifesto of the Communist Party', *Collected Works*, Vol. 6.

Nairn, T. (1977), *The Break-up of Britain: Crisis and Neo-Nationalism*. London: New Left Books.

Smith, A.D. (1986), *The Ethnic Origin of Nations*, Oxford: Basil Blackwood.

Zagladin, V. (1975), *The Revolutionary Movement of our Time and Nationalism*, Moscow, Progress.

# 3

## Scotland is Different, OK?

TONY DICKSON

The results of the 1987 General Election in Scotland, when the Conservative Party was reduced to holding only ten seats, have given a renewed impetus to attempts to explain what makes Scotland different from England. My main intention in this chapter is to take issue with certain of these recent analyses that have been advanced in relation to developments in Scotland, and to show how they repeat the mistakes of earlier accounts. In particular, I wish to question what seem to me to be quite mistaken assumptions that underlie accounts given by some academics, politicians and media commentators. These accounts have in common a belief that events in Scotland can be explained, or explained away, solely in terms of either regional variations or regional similarities when comparing the Scottish economy with other areas of the UK. Such explanations seem to me to suffer from two major defects.

First, however much they are dressed up in complex terminology or statistical techniques, they all are examples of a fairly simplistic economism. Second, they are almost always profoundly ahistorical, thereby neglecting a critical element in attempting to account for beliefs and actions in Scotland. My principal objections are not, however, to the materialist base on which such explanations are erected, but rather to the crude manner in which it is assumed that cultural and political forms can be imputed from a description of the economy. Whilst agreeing that the nature and performance of the Scottish economy is the essential starting point for a proper account of behaviour, the argument that follows is an attempt to show that we need to locate our explanations in a more sophisticated analysis of the ways in which economic relations have been reflected in, and influenced by, the particular circumstances of historical change in Scotland. It is this analysis of the developing relationship between the economic, political and cultural levels that should constitute an adequate materialist account.

## Economism: An Example

The limitations of space preclude a systematic analysis of all the explanations of developments in Scotland which have fallen within this category. However, a very brief look at one such account may illustrate both the problems they contain and enable me to point to other factors that need to be included in any attempt to understand what is different about Scotland.

Kendrick, Bechhofer and McCrone (1985) have argued that an examination of occupational and industrial structure in Scotland over the last hundred years reveals that, in most essential respects, there is no significant reason for explaining developments there by reference to differences in these structures. On the contrary, in terms of the statistically based 'index of dissimilarity' they construct, it is claimed that Scotland is shown to have largely mirrored the changes occurring at a wider British, and international level. This information is used to attack those explanations of Scotland which Kendrick *et al.* characterize as hingeing around notions such as dependence or core-periphery relations. As they put it:

> An influential strand of argument concerning Scotland's economic, social and political development has in recent years been shaped by a set of framing assumptions centred on such terms as 'core' or 'centre' and 'periphery', and 'dependence' or even 'underdevelopment'.
>
> It would be pushing it too far to call this set of assumptions as applied to Scotland a theoretical framework in the sense of a set of propositions which define what 'dependence' or 'peripherality' is and would allow an empirical check as to whether or not Scotland does in fact satisfy the criteria of 'dependence' or 'peripherality'. What has happened instead is that Scotland is compared with England on a range of socio-economic indicators, and whatever differences, or more precisely deficits, are found on the Scottish side are taken as evidence that Scotland is indeed peripheral to, or dependent on England. (Kendrick, Bechhofer and McCrone, 1985, p. 63)

Kendrick *et al.* then proceed to plough their way through an impressive-looking set of statistical indicators so as to dismiss the claim that Scotland is different from the rest of the UK. Having done this they conclude:

> In this chapter, then, we have been critical of attempts to explain industrial and occupational change in Scotland by exaggerating certain distributional differences, and by linking these to some version of 'dependency' theory. The tendency has been to focus on those aspects of the Scottish social and

economic structure which are different, in order to explain Scottish phenomena (such as the rise of the Scottish National Party). Thus factors which are specific to Scotland (and these often include cultural specificities) or which express Scotland's differential position in a wider structure tend to be given greater prominence than they analytically deserve. It is important to stress in contrast that there are processes operating which are nothing to do with Scotland's particular experience, but more to do with the fact that Scotland is part of Britain. In a wider sense processes are at work within Scotland which are to some extent common to all industrial societies – the shift in the balance of the working population from the primary to the secondary to the tertiary, from the extractive to the manufacturing to the service sector. (Kendrick, Bechhofer and McCrone 1985, p. 99-100)

In a longer work it would be instructive to focus on the many problems of this approach even on its own terms, such as its neglect of the differences between occupational and industrial sectors between regions, Kendrick *et al.* for instance, seems to assume that a category like 'shipbuilding', as a category, can be assumed to be precisely the same kind of activity wherever it occurs in Britain. This is an assumption that, at the very least, should require investigation and, as in the case of Clydeside compared with Tyneside, may be shown to be extremely suspect. This kind of simple-minded empiricism, which assumes that a statistical index constructed by the observer self-evidently describes exactly the same underlying actions and events, is surprising when advanced by sociologists!

However, for the sake of brevity, the purposes of this chapter are best served by focusing briefly on one of the accounts attacked by Kendrick *et al.* They use the following quote to illustrate what they see as the deficiencies of 'Scotland is Different' accounts:

In relation to Britain as a whole, what were to emerge in Scotland were *complementary* rather than *competitive* forms of capitalism, their interdependence being regularised under the political domination of Westminster. Such were the roots of the dependent or *client* status of the Scottish bourgeoisie. (T. Dickson (ed.) 1980, p. 90)

In retrospect I would agree that the interpretation given to our concept of client capitalism by Kendrick, Bechhofer and McCrone, and their attack upon it, has some justification, albeit limited. In order to illustrate this concept we did, I think, tend to over emphasize the extent to which most forms of capitalist development in Scotland were complementary rather than competitive.

On the other hand, the simplistic indices used by Kendrick *et. al.* commit greater sins in the opposite direction by reducing all differences to nil. By focusing on categories in the macro-economy they uncritically assume that the economic activities that they have placed within each category are the same wherever they are found. Moreover, they neglect both regional specialization within Scotland and those cases where English and Scottish development was obviously different. Shipbuilding is one small example; jute and some forms of textile specialization are more substantive illustrations of complementarity.

More important, however, is the way that, in their desire to emphasize the similarity of Scotland to the rest of Britain, Kendrick *et al.* misunderstand the central intent of the concept of client capitalism and thereby remove any basis in their own work for explaining the real differences in Scotland, which are illustrated later in this chapter. It was never our intent to propose a simplistic economism in which Scottish development could be explained solely in terms of the difference between its economy and that of some metropolitan centre. Rather, we were attempting to stress the crucial importance of the articulation in Scotland between the economic, political and cultural levels *based on the particular pattern of historical development.*

Especially important to our explanation was the manner in which Scottish economic growth was inextricably tied to the fact of political domination from Westminster. What is neglected in the analysis by Kendrick *et al.* is the extent to which our arguments were not merely about capitalism as a disembodied economic process. Their reading of the quote reproduced above demonstrates this nicely. Instead of trying to explain change solely in terms of economic differences, we were pointing to the relationship between forms of capitalist production and their development within a quite specific set of political arrangements. For this reason, the rather crude economism which characterizes their own analysis of why Scotland is not different was never intended to underlie our own arguments.

Furthermore, if, according to Kendrick *et al.,* the specific features of the Scottish economy and 'cultural specificities' are 'given greater prominence than they analytically deserve', the logic of their own position, as the conclusion to their chapter implies, must be that Scotland is in no way different from other areas of the UK and does not justify any status as a focus of separate investigation. The discussion below is intended to show that Scotland is different and that any attempt to explain the origins and nature of this difference must avoid a single-minded concentration on the Scottish economy. Instead, economic relations must be placed within the context of their effects on political and cultural change in Scotland's history and their implications for contemporary beliefs and actions.

## Scotland and the 1987 General Election

Since the 1987 General Election Scotland has found itself at the centre of national political debates. Its centrality was indicated when the Government took the unusual step of allowing one of the debates following the Queen's Speech to be focused on 'Divided Britain'. This has been followed by a succession of visits by senior Conservatives (including both Margaret Thatcher and Nigel Lawson) to Scotland; a wholesale re-organization of the Conservative Party in Scotland; the continuing importance of Scotland as the guinea pig for the introduction of the Poll Tax; and the publication, by the Labour Party, of a draft Bill to establish a Scottish Assembly with revenue-raising powers. The language of British politics has become tinged with tartan as the 'West Lothian Question' (Scottish MPs having control over Scottish affairs through an Assembly but still having a Westminster vote on English legislation), and the 'Doomsday Scenario' (a massive Labour majority in Scotland but a Conservative dominance in Westminster) have become standard features of political debate.

The immediate cause of this interest is, of course, the fact that in the 1987 Election the Conservative Party in Scotland was humiliated, emerging with only ten of the 72 seats, whilst the Labour Party has 50 Scottish MPs. The Scottish Office Ministers Michael Ancram and John Mackay were swept away by a tide that appeared to run directly contrary to the pro-Conservative waves of English voting. For the Parties, and for other commentators, this has raised the question: 'What happened in Scotland in the 1987 Election?' The explanations offered have been, in the main, immediate, surprisingly uniform and, in a fundamentally important sense, mistaken. In their different guises they parallel the kind of reasoning that underlies the approach by Kendrick *et al.*

These explanations have mainly revolved around an analysis of the economy and the policies of 'Thatcherism'. For the Labour Party, the election result demonstrated a decisive rejection by the Scottish electorate of the appropriateness of Thatcherite economic doctrines in Scotland, together with an opposition to the proposed Poll Tax, though why the Scots should be so enlightened is never explained. The Conservatives have responded by arguing that Scotland is lagging behind the rest of the UK in realizing the benefits of an 'enterprise culture'. As Nigel Lawson put it: 'Large areas of Scottish life are sheltered from market forces, and exhibit the culture of dependence rather than that of enterprise.' *(Glasgow Herald,* 24 November 1987). The message is that Scotland needs more, rather than less Thatcherism. Malcolm Rifkind expressed this view in a slightly different way immediately after the election when he claimed that 'the recession bit deeper in Scotland and recovery has been slower'. The implication is that it is merely a matter of time before Scotland falls into line with the rest of the UK.

The SNP and the Liberal/SDP Alliance took the same economic theme and argued that Scotland has realized the damage done by Conservative policies. In their view, Scotland, in this sense, was ahead of, rather than behind, the rest of Britain! A related theme has characterized the explanations given by most non-party commentators. They have widened the analysis to make the rejection of Thatcherism a phenomenon of the older industrialized areas that have been worst affected by the decline of traditional manufacturing sectors. According to this view, these peripheral/urban/industrial areas (Scotland, Wales, the North and North-West) form the basis of a clear north/south divide. Thus, Glasgow, Newcastle and Manchester now share the common feature of having no Conservative MPs.

Apart from the similarities they share, in seeing the performance of the Scottish economy as the factor which has determined the actions they seek to explain, the crucial issue that all of these existing accounts neglect is the nature of 'Scottishness' and its implications for political action. This can only be understood by reference to the way in which economic change has been reflected in political and cultural developments. They have thus failed to grasp how what happened in Scotland was different from elsewhere. A brief sketch of the development of Scottish society, and its cultural and political dimensions, is necessary before the 1987 Election can be seen in context as merely one kind of expression of more persistent underlying features of Scottish identity.

*Cultural Nationalism and the Issue of Control*

By the Act of Union in 1707 Scotland became a strangely hybrid society. The primary reason for the Union was economic, with Scotland gaining access to markets hitherto controlled by the English, and then finding the course of its own capitalist development inexorably altered as a consequence (Dickson *et al.* 1980). At the same time, however, Scotland retained the body of its civil society but ceded political control to a Parliament based at Westminster. The major social institutions which structured the experience of Scots, and through which they defined their identity, remained specifically Scottish. The legal system, with quite different antecedent traditions and unique procedures, continued to develop separately from its counterpart in England. Although of course the overall British framework operated via Westminster, and latterly through the EEC, has affected Scots law, the system is still very different, with its own specific features, such as the pivotal role of the Procurator Fiscal and the operation of Children's Panels.

Similarly, the education system in Scotland has maintained a separate form and development. In schools children pursue a broader curriculum, leave for higher education a year earlier than in England, and the structure of Scottish degrees is different, with a three-year ordinary degree and four-year honours degree. One reflection of the significance of these differences was in the separate education legislation proposed in 1987 for England and Scotland. Such features as 'opting out' by schools were not included in the Scottish legislation as they were felt to be inappropriate to the Scottish system.

At the same time, religion in Scotland developed its distinctive traditions. Despite the many fissures from the mainstream, and the strong tradition of dissenting sects, the Church of Scotland has always maintained its role as a national church. This view of itself is reflected in its major committee, the Church and Nation Committee. Its organizational form, with democratic control exercised by congregations through the Kirk, not only emphasizes its distinctively Scottish nature, but has also been a fiercely guarded aspect of its history.

These three major social institutions are an illustration of the way in which Scottish society has retained a core of distinctive everyday life that has helped to define the image that Scots have of themselves. But this has taken place alongside the fact of political control exercised through Westminster. This was at its most extreme in the eighteenth and early nineteenth centuries, when patronage meant that political managers, like Henry Dundas, effectively controlled enough Scottish MPs to be able to deliver their votes to whatever Westminster régime needed them. The gravy train operated through Westminster ensured that aspiring Scots had to channel their ambitions through the English-based controllers of the favours that could be dispensed from the metropolitan capital in London. One result of this was that, despite the staggering flowering of Scottish talent and intellectualism in the period known as the Scottish Enlightenment, these achievements had to be couched in a political language that accepted the reality of political domination in Westminster, i.e. through an English Parliament. Even when the aggressive success of Scottish industrialists in the nineteenth century sparked a campaign by the Scottish middle classes for Home Rule, its result was the establishment of the office of Secretary of State for Scotland and what has come to be known as the Scottish Office. In other words, control of Scottish affairs remained firmly mediated through Westminster.

The legacy of this pattern of development is a sensitivity by most Scots to the extent to which key decisions are taken outside Scotland. This feeling has been reinforced in recent years by changes within the Scottish economy. The strength of Scottish industry in the latter part of the nineteenth century was built on the foundations of heavy industry in such areas as shipbuilding, engineering, coal and steel. However, the long-term weakening of this base from the 1920s onwards resulted in a trend towards a double pattern of external dependence. First, the State became a key element in debates about the economy as it effectively controlled central parts of the economy. For example, the revival of the Scottish economy in the 1930s was largely brought about through expenditure on munitions and armaments needed by the Government. Similarly, as the British economy has gone through recurring crises from the 1960s onwards, the role of government has been crucial in such areas as shipbuilding, steel and coal. One illustration of this is, the continuing debate over the long-term viability of the Ravenscraig steel complex. Thus, the dependence of Scots on decisions taken in Westminster is continually apparent.

The second feature of the Scottish economy that reminds Scots of their lack of control is the extent to which, as the traditional heavy industries have declined, a large proportion of new industrial development has come from non-Scottish companies. This is particularly true in the 'sunrise' industries in electronics and computing. This 'branch factory' syndrome only serves to increase the perception that control lies elsewhere. For example, one recent assessment (which excluded the biggest multi-nationals, such as IBM and ESSO, who do not disaggregate their accounts to show a Scottish dimension) argued that over 50 per cent of the 200 largest companies in Scotland were externally owned *(Glasgow Herald,* 7 December 1987). It was these twin features, of external political and economic control, that were so successfully fused together by the SNP in the 1970s in their campaign around the slogan, 'It's Scotland's Oil'.

One further aspect of Scottish social development can be added to this pattern. Nigel Lawson talked, during his visit to Scotland in November 1987, of the 'culture of dependence' on the state. If he had talked instead of 'reliance', he might have been more accurate. Particularly in housing and health and in other crucial areas of everyday life, many Scots do rely on government expenditure, either at national or local levels. A far higher proportion of housing in Scotland is publicly owned (49 per cent, as opposed to 31 per cent in England). Historically, Scots have also experienced poor-quality housing and social conditions, and these are reflected in mortality rates for such diseases as heart disease, bronchitis and lung cancer far above the European norm. These factors are, in turn, translated into a special reliance on government spending. For example, for every £100 of government spending in England in 1986/87, Scotland received £122. In health the comparative figures were £97 in England and £122 in Scotland.

The effects of this pattern of development have been to product a Scottish identity which, whilst fiercely proud of its 'Scottishness', is acutely aware of the country's dependence on the outside world. (Discussions of the development of Scottish society and its cultural and political consequences can be found in Nairn (1977) and Dickson (1978)). This helps to explain what is often seen as the almost schizophrenic nature of many Scots: aggressively asserting the superiority of their country whilst hiding a deep-seated feeling of inferiority. Over the years this cultural identity has developed, as part of its self-definition, a caricature of the 'English' that functions as a target for the resentments implicit in the notion of external control. To be Scottish is, to some degree, to dislike or resent the English. This ritualized (but none the less real) animosity expressed by the players and supporters on the occasion of the annual England–Scotland football matches is one illustration of this.

This resentment swirls around the caricature of the archetypical English: a Home Counties accent, a natural arrogance, a taken-for-granted superiority, an uncaring disregard for others, and some degree of affluence. Thus, whatever the historical origins of the phrase, the 'Auld Enemy' for Scots has long since been the English.

These factors illustrate how the concept of client capitalism remains especially appropriate to an understanding of the effects of capitalist development in Scotland. Unless the particular features of Scottish society, and their implications for cultural identity, are understood, there is a danger of misunderstanding the significance of what happened in the 1987 election in Scotland. We can now return to a brief examination of the election within this overall context.

*Thatcherism and Scotland*

Explanations of the election result in Scotland in 1987 that see it either as merely another example of a regional trend, or as something that can be explained solely in terms of that election itself, are mistaken. Scotland had certainly experienced, in common with other areas of Britain with a concentration of heavy industry, a major loss of jobs consequent upon the de-industrialization of the economy. This may help to explain the reluctance of voters in such areas to support a Conservative Party seen to have operated economic policies that encouraged, or did not seek to mitigate, this trend. However, on various economic measures, such as the level of unemployment, Scotland in 1987 was not faring as badly as some other regions, notably the North of England. Such economic factors, then, by themselves, do not explain why Scottish voters acted differently from those elsewhere. The real difference in Scotland was the extent to which its voters were specifically anti-Conservative and, in particular, anti-Thatcherite. This can be illustrated by comparing the Conservative vote in different regions of Britain as shown in Table 1.

Table 1: **1987 Election: Conservative Vote by Region**

| Region | Conservative Vote (%) |
| --- | --- |
| South-East (excluding London) | 55.8 |
| East Anglia | 52.0 |
| South-West | 50.5 |
| East Midlands | 48.6 |
| London | 46.4 |
| West Midlands | 45.6 |
| North-West | 38.0 |
| Yorkshire and Humberside | 37.5 |
| North | 32.0 |
| Wales | 29.5 |
| Scotland | 24.0 |

*Source:* The *Independent,* 13 June 1987.

Right across Scotland voters supported whichever party was most likely to oust the Conservative candidate. In the urban areas the Labour Party was the main beneficiary. But elsewhere the SNP and the Liberal/SDP Alliance gained seats at the expense of Conservative candidates. It is, therefore, important to appreciate how far this was a specifically anti-Conservative vote. Although the Labour Party increased its share of the poll compared to its 1983 performance by over 7 per cent, its gains and its overall support were bettered in other regions of Britain. For example, Labour's share in Scotland (42.4 per cent) was exceeded in the North (47 per cent) and in Wales (45 per cent).

## Scotland is Different, OK? 63

Why, then, was Scotland so unique in its rejection of Margaret Thatcher's brand of Conservatism? The answer to this question lies in the factors described earlier. It is the specific features of Scottish society, its economic development, and the effects on the cultural identity of Scots which explain this result. A brief indication of their particular relevance to 'Thatcherism' can be given. At the same time, some illustration of the attitudes of Scots is given through comments deriving from a recently completed study of employees in different sectors of the Scottish economy.

The main objectives of this study were to examine variations in attitudes to employment and government policy. The study focused on different cohorts of workers in Scotland, in an attempt to examine variations in attitudes between the public and private sectors. (For a preliminary analysis of the results see Dickson, McLachlan, Prior and Swales (1988)). No questions were asked which would explore 'Scottishness' or elicit any specifically Scottish dimension. The comments used below were, therefore, views that emerged as a by-product of more general questions. The study was undertaken between the latter part of 1984 and the beginning of 1986. Comments from those respondents who indicated an intention to vote for the SNP have been excluded, so as to avoid the suggestion that these views represent those individuals who are, by definition, nationalists (at least in the narrowly political sense). The views, then, are those of individuals who did not at the time, see their 'Scottishness' as best represented by an overtly nationalist party.

What is apparent is that the policies of the Thatcher governments since 1979 have been perceived by Scots as especially inappropriate to the particular circumstances of their country and its economy. The Conservative attack on public spending was hardly likely to be applauded in Scotland where, as indicated earlier, social need has historically dictated a higher level of government spending. The Poll Tax, which originated as an attempt to appease a threatened revolt by middle-class rate-payers in Scotland facing their second property revaluation in ten years, is nevertheless guaranteed to be unpopular in a society where there are comparatively few payers of high rates!

Thatcher's economic policies have been especially unpopular. In the 1980s there has been a long list of highly publicized plant closures in Scotland, with consequent large-scale job losses. These include the Rootes/Peugeot car plant at Linwood; British Leyland trucks at Bathgate; a succession of coal pits; the steel plant at Gartcosh; and a number of shipyards on the Clyde. There continues to be a long-running uncertainty over the Ravenscraig steel complex. Even the post-election assurances on Ravenscraig by the Government have been received sceptically by most Scots, being seen, at best, as a heavily qualified commitment to the plant's future. In many of these cases (e.g. coal, steel, the shipyards) the Government was the direct employer and was therefore seen to be responsible for the job losses.

In addition, a large section of the Scottish population is sensitive to the issue of closures and sympathetic to action to resist them. It was the workers' occupation of UCS to protect jobs that forced the famous 'U-turn' on the Conservative government of Ted Heath. Since then there have been many other similar campaigns of resistance by work-forces in Scotland to oppose threatened closures, such as those of Lee Jeans, Plessey and the Caterpillar plant at Uddingston. The latter occupation took place shortly before the 1987 election, thereby highlighting the issue of job loss and the government's unwillingness or inability to act.

The systematic distmantling of Regional Aid has added to this perception by Scots that Margaret Thatcher does not care about jobs in Scotland, and that her economic policies have positively contributed to the growth in unemployment north of the border. For example one of the respondents in our study commented: 'It seems anyway that the United Kingdom at the moment stops at the Border anyhow, or North of England, you know – north of London maybe.' Another said: 'We always seem to get the rough end of the stick in Scotland. We always seem to be forgotten about. That's still true today. I think even more so to do with the Thatcher Government.' A more pointed explanation came from the individual who said: '... they don't seem to care about any social aspects, or what's happening in this country. As far as I'm concerned they've done nothing for Scotland. They don't carry any weight here, so why should they bother? ... so, I think they're prepared to keep Scotland just as an industrial wasteland.'

These perceptions, deriving from the historical development of Scottish society and its reflections in the cultural identity of Scots, are particularly focused on the personality of the Prime Minister. The public persona of Margaret Thatcher appears to many Scots to capture all the worst elements of their caricature of the detested English: uncaring, arrogant, always convinced of her own rightness ('there is no alternative'), possessed of an accent that grates on Scottish ears, and affluent enough to afford a retirement home costing around £500,000. She is also associated with the conspicuously yuppie/affluent South-East, and the City. These are bitter images for Scots, well aware of the stark contrasts offered in Scotland by high unemployment, pockets of appalling social deprivation in the major urban areas, and reared in a culture where Scottish Protestantism, whilst not denigrating the accumulation of wealth, has always emphasized its distaste for the flouting of its manifestations. One reflection of this has been the way that, in its reports on social conditions in Scotland, the Church and Nation Committee has increasingly come into conflict in the 1980s with the Conservative Party in Scotland.

Our respondents clearly reflected these perceptions. One said: 'I wouldn't say that Britain is a united country. You've got the North and you've got the South. The South is prospering and the North is practically a desert land.' Others echoed similar views: 'Some of the houses are in a terrible state in Scotland, a lot worse than England. In the South-East of England – that's all Maggie's interested in.' . . .'she is strong-willed, doesn't listen to anybody, is uncaring, goes her own way, and only in extreme cases will she ever change her mind. A bully, and has all millionaires – surrounded by millionaires who are the same, uncaring.' 'I don't think she worries about Ravenscraig because it's so far north and she's not relying, in all honesty, on the votes in Scotland. The votes she relies on are really in the South-East of England where, you know, there's no problem for the likes of people working there.'

That these perceptions are widespread in Scotland is illustrated not just by the strongly anti-Conservative swing that differentiated Scotland from other regions in the 1987 Election. An opinion poll in October of 1987 showed that only 9 per cent of Scots rated Margaret Thatcher as a good/very good Prime Minister for Scotland. Even amongst Conservative voters in Scotland only 43 per cent described her as good/very good for Scotland. A massive majority (84 per cent) thought she was not very sympathetic/not at all sympathetic to the needs of Scotland *(Glasgow Herald,* 1 October 1987). Another poll in November 1987 found that 77 per cent of respondents felt that the government did not care about Scotland. The same poll, on specific policies, found that 75 per cent favoured some form of devolution, whilst 68 per cent thought that the Poll Tax would be less fair than the existing rating system *(Glasgow Herald,* 30 November 1987).

*Thatcherism and Cultural Nationalism*

It is clear then that the personality and the policies associated with Margaret Thatcher have focused important elements within Scottish cultural identity in a way that has generated special hostility towards the Conservative Party in Scotland. Of particular significance is the feeling by Scots that control of many aspects of decision-making lies outwith the country. Together with a long-standing resentment towards domination of political life through Westminster, these features reduced the Conservative Party to a rump at the election.

Equally important, however, are the possible consequences of the failure, by Margaret Thatcher and her advisors, to recognize the real origins of Scottish anti-Conservatism. This is apparent in the post-election insistence that the problem in Scotland was a failure to get the message across properly. The remedy, therefore, lies in more Thatcherism, rather than less. The re-organization of the Party in Scotland has been designed to achieve the better delivery of the gospel. Nigel Lawson, in his visit to Scotland in November 1987, proclaimed: 'The attitudes of some Scottish people are wrong, and that is sometimes reflected in the Scottish media.' There is certain delicious irony in the comments by Lawson and Malcolm Rifkind that the Party face a hostile press in Scotland, when they were so massively supported by the press in England. Yet, of the authentically Scottish press (rather than English-based newspapers who produce 'Scottish' editions), only the *Daily Record* and *Sunday Mail* could be described as consistently pro-Labour. It would be difficult to see the *Scotsman, Glasgow Herald,* or *Sunday Post* as instinctively or traditionally anything other than conservative papers.

The point generally missed by the government is that as Scottish papers they had become increasingly unhappy at the inappropriateness of Government policies to the special characteristics of Scotland. The editorial comment by the Glasgow Herald on Nigel Lawson's November comments illustrates this perfectly: 'The puzzling thing is that Ministers can so persistently misunderstand their critics and the message of the polls. What is at issue is not the necessity of industrial change but the way in which it is being managed, with inadequate regard to the social consequences or to the particular economic needs of Scotland.' *(Glasgow Herald,* 24 November 1987).

This misunderstanding derives from a failure to grasp the ways in which Scotland is different. The potential for further exacerbating deep-seated hostilities amongst Scots can be shown by the way in which Lawson's comments were treated by two English newspapers most ardently in support of Thatcherism. The *Sun's* headline, referring to the higher levels of public spending in Scotland, was 'Will ye stop your snivelling, Jock?' The *Sunday Times,* on the same theme, led with 'Canny Scots scoop the pool but just can't stop moaning', and went on to explain anti-Conservatism by arguing that 'Scottish voting patterns have become rather unreal . . . It is safe to vote for any opposition party, including Labour, on the quiet understanding that the Tories will rule Britain with a prudence which the Scots themselves would inwardly approve... Safe in the assurance of Conservative government where it matters, her middle classes are free to play radical. There is no harm in it, but not much meaning either.'

Both the responses of these papers, and those of the government, not only demonstrate a profound misunderstanding of Scotland, but also that arrogant disregard for Scottish perceptions of behaviour that Scots believe is so typical of the English. No matter what Scots say or do, it will be interpreted as confirming the government's view of their own correctness! For example, despite the many opinion polls indicating very widespread support for devolution, one spokesman for the Conservative Party in Scotland was still claiming, in November of 1987, that 'There was no evidence of any support for devolution at the last election. Whilst the party in Scotland will continue to address itself to all issues, it does not believe there is any serious support for devolution at the moment.' *(Glasgow Herald,* 30 November 1987).

## Towards the Break-Up of Britain?

Given the government's unwillingness to recognize that anything really untoward has happened in Scotland, and its determination to press ahead even more strongly with the policies that have already proved so unpopular, there is a real possibility of the extinction of the Conservative Party in Scotland. Of the ten seats that they still hold, four have majorities of under 2000! The severity of their position was illustrated by the loss of Bearsden and Milngavie to Labour: the equivalent, in the words of the Sunday Times, of 'Ruislip going Labour'. Equally, George Younger, the Defence Secretary and the former Secretary for Scotland, hung to to his seat in Ayr by just 182 votes. Yet the defence issue was stressed by Margaret Thatcher in the election campaign since she regarded it as Labour's Achilles' heel. Once again, Scotland, with its large number of military bases and installations which are perceived to be under two kinds of external control (i.e. an English government and the USA) was different. As one of our respondents put it: 'I don't like the idea of having American missiles based here ... especially as we don't seem to have the power over them. It's not going to be a joint button-pushing exercise. It's going to come and we're not going to have any say in anything. I think that's quite frightening... instead of being a country, we're just another star on that flag."

With just ten Scottish MPs the Conservative Party faces a crisis of legitimacy. Its failure, by the end of 1987, to secure agreement on the membership of a Select Committee for Scotland, is one illustration of the problems it will continue to experience. In addition, there are already cracks appearing within the Party in Scotland as some members recognize the underlying sources of opposition. Just before the election, Iain Lawson, a prominent Scottish Conservative, defected to the SNP, angered by his Party's failure to protect jobs in Scotland. Alick Buchanan-Smith, one of the remaining ten Tory MPS, refused to accept a Scottish Office post after the election due to his disenchantment with policy in Scotland. In November of 1987 a number of leading Scottish Conservatives announced the formation of a pro-devolution group, the Conservative Constitutional Forum.

Unless there is a dramatic upsurge in the economy, which results in significant benefits for Scotland, it is difficult to see how the Party can revive its fortunes north of the border. The present worries about a world recession, as the US grapples with the problem of bringing its budget deficit under control, do not suggest grounds for much optimism in this direction.

On the other hand, the Labour Party, the apparent beneficiary of the anti-Conservative vote in Scotland, may find itself supping from a poisoned chalice. The 'Doomsday Scenario', of English-based Conservative control at Westminster, now looms large. The SNP have already christened the Scottish Labour MPs the 'feeble fifty'. Although these Labour MPs can harry and obstruct the government, the size of the Tory majority is such as to nullify effective challenges to its parliamentary control. By the end of 1987 there were already clear signs of English Conservative MPs making play of the futility of opposition by Scottish Labour members. In these circumstances, some of the more radical and nationalist – inclined members of the Scottish Labour contingent are likely to begin to articulate demands for more effective non-parliamentary action, thus opening divisions within the group. Such divisions were already apparent by the early months of 1988, with some MPs announcing that they would refuse to pay the Poll Tax in defiance of agreed Party policy.

These potential developments raise the longer-term possibility of a swing towards a more explicit nationalism in Scotland. The issue of external (especially English) control is a festering historical sore in the Scottish psyche. In the right circumstances, as in the 1970s, the frustrations of Scots can be channelled into political support for a nationalist party, the SNP. One of our (non-SNP) respondents commented that: 'I mean, here we are with this government, North-Sea oil, right – we've had that for ten years now; it's been on tap for ten years. Now, we must be the only country in the world who ever discovered oil and the people in the country are worse off after we discovered it than before:' Faint indications of a nationalist breeze may already exist. In October 1987, the SNP overturned a Labour majority of 1,213 in a Regional Council by-election in Fife to win the seat. An opinion poll at the beginning of December showed support for the SNP up by 4 per cent with a concomitant drop in support for the Labour Party. Throughout the first half of 1988 the opinion polls were showing support for the SNP at over 20 per cent.

These indicators are, as yet, merely straws in the wind. But, the continuing failure of the Conservatives to recognize the distinctiveness of Scottish society and its cultural assumptions, together with the inability of the Labour Party to force through policies more appropriate to Scotland, could yet turn that wind into a nationalist hurricane that might presage the 'Break-Up of Britain' (Nairn 1977). The peculiarities of the Scots could prove a potent force in a next five years.

## Conclusion

My objections to the explanations offered both by certain academics and by politicians is that they amount to a very crude form of economism which ignores the need to situate our analysis of the economic level within an understanding of the particular features of Scottish history that have led to a deep sensitivity to, and resentment of, external control (or dependence). The concept of client capitalism was advanced to help focus on this crucial aspect of Scottish history and seems to me to be more relevant than ever to Scotland in the 1980s. My plea is, therefore, not for less materialism, but for a more sophisticated and historically rooted materialism!

REFERENCES

Dickson, T. (1978), 'Class and Nationalism in Scotland', in *Scottish Journal of Sociology,* April.

Dickson, T. (ed.) (1980), *Scottish Capitalism,* London: Lawrence and Wishart.

Dickson, T., McLachlan, H., Prior, P., and Swales, K. (1988), 'Big Blue and the Unions: IBM, Individualism and Trade Union Strategy', in *Work, Employment and Society,* December.

Kendrick, S., Bechhofer, F., and McCrone, D. (1985), 'Is Scotland Different? Industrial and Occupational Change in Scotland and Britain', in, H. Newby *et al.* (eds.) *Restructuring Capital: Recession and Reorganization in Industrial Society,* Explorations in Sociology 20, London: Macmillan.

Nairn, T., (1977), *The Break-Up of Britain,* London: New Left Books.

# 4

## Scotland, Social Change and Politics

STEVE KENDRICK

*Introduction*

The immediate trigger for the form this chapter takes was a peek at a draft of the paper Tony Dickson was to present at the 1988 British Sociological Association Conference (see his chapter in this volume).

Tony Dickson's paper in turn appears to have been provoked by a paper delivered at the 1983 BSA Annual Conference in Cardiff, 'Is Scotland Different?' (Kendrick, Bechhofer and McCrone 1985), and is a welcome response albeit in the form of a fairly savage attack.

Essentially we stand accused of simple-minded economism in suggesting that an empirical comparison of patterns of change in industrial and occupational employment over the long-term in Scotland as compared with the rest of Britain shows that in terms of these parameters Scotland has long been a highly typical region (in the statistical sense and with no implications for Scotland's status as a nation) of Britain. The paper did have an economic focus in that it concentrated on the industrial and occupational structure of employment, and this focus provided an argument with which to refute an influential body of analysis based on the imagery of 'centre and periphery' or 'uneven development' to account for the general pattern of Scotland's economic, social and political development. As we concluded

> an intellectual atmosphere pervaded by the notions of core-periphery, dependence and the like had led to an over-emphasis on the differences between the pattern of social development in Scotland and that in the rest of Britain. In a form of circular reasoning, the existence of such differences is seen either as evidence for the operation of mechanisms akin to dependence or as demanding that such mechanisms be invoked to explain them. The message of the present chapter is that in terms of industrial and occupational structure,

differences sufficient to justify the invocation of such mechanisms do not exist. Or, in other words, the differences which do exist are sufficiently small to make the circular process of argument not only wrong but superfluous. (Kendrick, Bechhofer and McCrone 1985, pp. 98-9)

In that paper we made very little direct reference to the task of integrating the social and economic parallels we had outlined into an explanation of recent political divergences between Scotland and England. If we were economistic it was only as a reflection of the economism of the frame of reference we were criticizing and as a corollary of the particular area of social reality which was under direct consideration.

The implications of the analysis contained in our paper for an understanding of political divergence between Scotland and England are the opposite of economistic and must be so in a obvious sense. If patterns of industrial and occupational change in Scotland have long paralleled those in the rest of Britain then nothing is more certain than that political differences cannot be economistically read off from differences in the structure of employment.

However, we must not throw the baby out with the bath water. It is equally certain that long term changes in industrial and occupational structure are important in explaining patterns of political change; whether we are talking about the long-term rise and decline of the Labour Party in England or political divergence between Scotland and England over the last thirty years.

If we accept that long-term changes in industrial and occupational structure are important to an understanding of changing electoral behaviour – and I do not think that such a claim is necessarily economistic – then any overall explanation of electoral change in modern Britain and of political divergence between Scotland and England must incorporate such factors.

Of course, such parallels cannot constitute the whole of the explanation. At some point we must deal with the role of national specificities. However, the fact that we are explaining electoral divergence does not have quite the implications for the relative role of parallel and differentiating factors in the explanation as might at first be thought.

*Points of Logic*

What are we trying to explain? We are interested in explaining electoral divergence between Scotland and England over approximately the last thirty years. This has been a sustained and systematic process with the most constant factor being the decline of the Conservative share of the vote in Scotland relative to that in England. In the post-war general elections of 1945, 1950, 1951 and 1955, the Conservative share of the vote in Scotland was within one per cent of the Conservative share of the vote in England. Since then the Conservatives have steadily slipped behind in Scotland. In the 1987 general election, their share of the vote was only 24 per cent in Scotland compared with 46.2 per cent in England, a shortfall of 22.2 per cent (Kendrick and McCrone 1988). It has been the main beneficiary of this Conservative decline that has varied. In the first phase, the early 1960s, Labour was the main beneficiary. Then came the period of the SNP surge up until the late 1970s. Since then Labour has again reaped the advantage.

The task then is to provide a framework for understanding this electoral divergence on the basis of the general pattern of development of modern British society. I want to outline the logic of an account which will anchor our understanding of electoral divergence in an interpretation of patterns of parallelism and divergence at the economic, social, political and ideological levels of change.

Here I want to make a very general point about the causal logic involved. Suppose one had identified ten causal factors at any of these levels whose combined effect provided an explanation for the nature and timing of electoral divergence. It cannot be stressed strongly enough that not all these causal elements necessary to the explanation need to be differentiating factors. The nature of social reality is such that nine of the ten factors could be present in both Scotland and England, with only the tenth specific to Scotland, in order to produce massive differences at the electoral level due to powerful interactions between the one differentiating factor and the nine parallel factors. In addition, not all of the factors involved, whether common or different, need involve change. They could be relatively stable factors activated by change at other levels.

Causal explanation in social science is not simply an additive affair. If our hypothetical situation were the case, and only one differentiating factor combined with nine parallel factors were necessary to understand political divergence between Scotland and England, then in order to understand the dynamics of this political divergence it is not enough to attempt to read off the characteristics of the electoral divergence from the one differentiating factor. The dynamics and characteristics of the electoral divergence must be read off from the explanatory totality made up of the parallel and differentiating factors.

It is in part because of a lack of appreciation of this logic that many Marxist and more generally left-wing accounts of the emergence of the Scottish political dimension have felt a desperate need to identify a level of economic differentiation which can be directly linked to political differentiation in order to provide a self-evidently 'materialist' account. This produces precisely the kind of simple-minded economism which Tony Dickson is quite rightly so keen to root out.

However, the logic of my argument is that it is quite possible to produce an explanation of electoral divergence which is rooted in the changing material realities of everyday life – and if we cannot do that then there is something seriously wrong – without having to postulate any great differences in the material reality of everyday life between Scotland and England. The differences necessary to the explanation could be largely ideological without the explanation as a whole necessarily degenerating into an idealist one.

Just for illustration, a gross over-simplification can be made which has sufficient elements of truth in it to help make sense of some of the contradictions of attempts on the part of the Left in Scotland to make sense of recent political developments. If we take a fairly simple division of social reality into economic, social, political and ideological levels, then the further up the structure and into the superstructure we proceed in this progression, the greater and more obvious are the differences between Scotland and England. As we will see, parallelism or even convergence has far outweighed divergence at the economic and social levels. At the political level there is long-standing administrative and institutional differentiation. Finally at the ideological level there is a deep-rooted sense of national difference on the part of the Scots. Any explanation of electoral divergence which is couched solely in terms of differences between Scotland and England is inevitably pushed towards the superstructure. Nationalists are happy there. Marxists and the Left in general are not. Hence, there has been a series of attempts to push the explanation back down towards the base, to find an economic differentiating mechanism. It was our suspicion that this was what Dickson *et al.* were trying to do in positing that Scottish capitalism was forced to develop along lines which were 'complementary to' rather than 'competitive with' English capitalism (Dickson *et al.*, 1980 p. 90) which led us to suggest that at the level of economic development they were employing a superfluous distinction.

*Social Parallels*

Before moving on to outline a framework for explanation which will hopefully avoid these pitfalls. I would like to draw out some further implications of the kind of parallelisms which were traced in the 'Is Scotland Different?' paper.

Differences between Scotland and England in the long-term development of industrial and occupational structures can be presented as evidence of a structural relation of economic dominance between England and Scotland which can then be presented as an objective basis for a national or nationalist political expression. A parallel with the Third World is often drawn here. This is the kind of argument which 'Is Scotland Different?' originally aimed to refute and, indeed, make redundant.

However, we can also draw out the implications of the kind of analysis contained in 'Is Scotland Different?' in another way. Long-term differences and parallels in industrial and occupational structures have major implications for the material circumstances of daily life. These material circumstances in turn influence people's interests and identities, and thus the way they vote.

We can also widen the argument by looking at developments since the Second World War in other fundamental structural parameters which work to determine the material circumstances in which people live their everyday lives. The point to be stressed is that in terms of social change in this sense – social change as change in the material circumstances of everyday life – the dominant relationship between social change in Scotland and in England has been parallelism or even convergence. 'Is Scotland Different?' made the point that in the long-term development of the industrial and occupational structure, what Scotland has shared with the rest of Britain as a whole far outweighs what has differentiated it (see also Kendrick 1986). The same holds true for a wider range of structural parameters throughout the thirty-year period of electoral divergence. This can be briefly illustrated in terms of patterns of social mobility, women's employment patterns and the birth-rate.

Shared patterns of industrial and occupational change have done a good deal to determine the overall patterns of social mobility in Britain and in Scotland. A comparison of the results of the Oxford Mobility Study and the Scottish Social Mobility Study, both undertaken in the mid-1970s, shows that patterns of social mobility had been highly similar in the previous thirty years. Scotland shared with England and Wales a high level of upward inter- and intra-generational mobility from manual to non-manual occupations fuelled largely by a swing from manufacturing to service employment and from manual to non-manual jobs (Goldthorpe 1980; Kendrick 1983 p. 208).

Moving on to another dimension of employment change, one of the most massive shifts in patterns of economic life since the war has been an increase in the proportion of married women going out to work and the increase in the proportion of women working part-time. Historically, Scotland seems to have had a lower proportion of married women going out to work and of women working part-time. The last twenty-five years have seen a sustained convergence in these parameters between Scotland and England. (Kendrick 1984)

Finally we can look at a set of trends which are not often regarded as being relevant in a political context: trends in the birth-rate. Trends in family formation are important not only because they are major determinants of the material circumstances of everyday life, but because they are increasingly the result of decisions on the part of couples as to how they will shape their own circumstances.

Throughout the century, the birth-rate in Scotland has moved up and down in parallel with that in England. Earlier in the century, there was a difference of the order of two births per thousand, but all the major trends in the English figures, the post-war baby boom, the fall in fertility rates in the late 1960s and early 1970s have been faithfully and almost uncannily paralleled in the Scottish experience. More recently the gap has narrowed to become tiny. In terms of this crucial aspect of reaction to and shaping of the circumstances of their family lives, the decisions of Scottish couples have closely mirrored those made by couples south of the border, reflecting the same kinds of change in economic circumstances and aspirations. (Kendrick, 1983, p. 230)

The most important differences in the circumstances of everyday life which now remain can be directly related to the role of the state: Scotland's higher level of employment in the state sector and most importantly Scotland's higher proportion of public-sector housing. These are 'social structural' differences with powerful political effects, effects which can only be understood in the context of the discussion which follows.

*Relating to the Political*

Now this complex of change in the structural parameters shaping the material circumstances of everyday life is highly relevant to understanding long-term patterns of political change in modern Britain. The relationship between social change in this sense and electoral change has defined the agenda for political sociology in Britain for the last thirty years, from the 'Must Labour Lose?' debates of the early 1960s, through studies of the Affluent Worker (Goldthorpe *et al.* 1968, 1969) to the work of the Marshall, Newby, Rose and Vogler team at Essex (see for example Marshall, Rose, Vogler and Newby 1985; Newby, Vogler, Rose and Marshall 1985). Psephological analysis has had increasingly to come to terms with underlying patterns of social change in modern Britain, as evidenced in the increasingly 'sociological' nature of recent election studies. The studies of the 1983 general election by Heath, Jowell and Curtice (1985) and Dunleavy and Husbands (1985) both embodied the imperative to embed electoral analysis in an analysis of long-term patterns of social change.

If one theme has dominated the more self-consciously sociological literature on this topic it is that of 'privatism'. From this perspective the key aspect of social change in modern Britain has been the growth of increasingly privatized life-styles centred on the nuclear family rather than wider neighbourhood, community or kinship ties. This is associated with the break down of 'traditional' and sometimes class-based forms of voting behaviour and the growth of more volatile and instrumental patterns.

The point I want to stress again in this slightly different context is that in terms of aspects of social change which are generally held to be crucial for an understanding of long-term patterns of political change in modern Britain, I have yet to come across any evidence that Scotland has experienced such changes to a lesser degree than the rest of Britain. Similarly, no evidence has been put forward which would suggest that such aspects of social change are any less important for an understanding of political change in modern Scotland than they are for an understanding of political change in modern England.

However, in terms of understanding the divergence in political behaviour between Scotland and England, these parallels have implications which are the very opposite of 'economistic'.

Most obviously, the electoral divergence between Scotland and England of the last thirty years cannot be explained by any divergence in patterns of social change at the level of everyday life.

## The Experience of the State

So where do we go from here? How do we deal with differential expressions of the national dimension in British politics on the basis of common patterns of social change in Scotland and England.

I'm increasingly coming to the conclusion that the key to understanding these processes lies in what could be called the changing experience of the state. By this I mean quite simply how individuals or electors experience the state that they live in.

To begin with a truism. Politics is about the state. It is about who will run the state, about what the state will and will not do.

To add another truism. The single most important fact about the electors, whose voting decisions constitute electoral trends in

Britain, is that they are citizens of the British state. Their voting decisions are grounded in their experience of this fact, their experience of living in Britain, their experience of being governed by the British state: in short their experience of the state.

What the state does to make a difference in the real world is the basis for understanding the national dimension in British politics. To understand how that national dimension expresses itself in voting, we have to understand how voters experience the actions and decisions of the state.

How can we map changes in such a broad swathe of social reality as is encompassed by the phrase 'the experience of the state'?

A preliminary step is to break down this rather vague totality, the changing experience of the state, into three levels: the level of everyday life, the level of the communications media and the level of what the state does. It is the interaction of these three levels of change, each with its own determinants and periodicity, which can be seen as the generative matrix for many of the broad patterns of political change in Britain since the Second World War and in particular for the timing of the electoral success of the SNP and the general process of electoral divergence between Scotland and England.

The first of these three levels is the one which is closest to what is meant in conventional accounts of 'social change'. It is change at the level of everyday life, change in the real circumstances in which people live their lives. It is precisely the level of social change discussed above as exhibiting parallelism between Scotland and England, ranging from objective aspects such as change in the occupational structure to the more subjective aspects which cluster around the privatism debate.

We can introduce the third level next, since the second level, being that of the media of communication, mediates between the other two. The third level of the explanatory framework is that of the state. Change at this level consists of changes in the form and activities of the state: changes in the extent to which and the ways in which the state intervenes to make a real difference in the world. When we say we are talking about the 'experience of the state', it is important to accept that there is something real which is experienced, such experience is not just fantasy or false-consciousness. The state does make a difference. However, how 'what the state does' is translated into people's experience of the state is an extremely complex process and here the second level must be introduced.

The second level is that of the media of communication, which make the link between everyday life at the level of the home and the work-place on the one hand, and the state on the other.

Now such mediation is not always necessary. The relation between the level of everyday life and that of the state may be direct or indirect.

In certain contexts, such as signing on for benefit or paying one's tax bill, the contact between the individual and the state is direct. Here, the state directly intervenes to shape the circumstances of the individual or the household. This form of direct experience of the state, the experience of the unmediated effects of state action on personal circumstances, has had increasingly important electoral consequences. This view has been put forward in particular by the proponents of the consumption sectors approach to electoral analysis (see for example Dunleavy and Husbands 1985). In addition, a good case can be made that the politicization of the housing issue along the public *versus* private dimension has made a considerable contribution to electoral divergence between Scotland and England due to Scotland's higher proportion of local-authority housing. (Kendrick and McCrone 1988).

However, in this discussion I want to concentrate on more indirect forms of the experience of the state. In terms of the overall image of state action at the national level the individual is reliant overwhelmingly on the national media for information on state activity. In this sense, general beliefs about the state and the nation are shaped by the contexts in which information about the state and the national level of politics are transmitted and received.

Perhaps this formulation sounds somewhat strange because 'the state' is not a concept which often enters into everyday conversation. It is doubtful whether many people are conscious of the fact that they have an 'experience of the state'. Such generalized self-consciousness is not necessary for the concept to play a useful role. In many ways, the experience of the state consists of a set of taken-for-granted assumptions which underly the rhetoric of the national political game. It is the transmission of the images and messages which embody and transmit these assumptions which is the crucial mediating factor.

Defining these three levels does not imply that they are in any sense ultimately determining. They each have their own set of determinants, and a full analysis would describe these determinants. In the present analysis they are a heuristic device for gaining some purchase on the intractable issues of the experience of the nation and the state in the modern world.

The aim is to understand how people's perceptions of and feelings towards the nation and the state in which they live are shaped.

The method is to embed such orientations into the realities of everyday life, the realities of the modern nation-state and the realities of the forms of communications which relate the one to the other.

To define the totality comprised of these three levels is not to isolate a particular slice of social reality and say 'This slice matters, nothing else does'. It is rather to suggest a particular perspective on the social totality, a particular way of looking at its articulations.

Most importantly, it allows us to gain some purchase on the paradox at the heart of this discussion. On the one hand, we have close parallelism between Scotland and England in precisely the types of social change which are held to be crucial for understanding long terms patterns of electoral change at a British level. On the other hand we have sustained a systematic divergence in voting patterns.

The paradox is overcome precisely in terms of the articulation between the three levels of change which can be said to generate the experience of the state.

## *The Experience of the State in Scotland*

All this has been couched at a highly general level. Now I want to give a brief sketch of how I see changes at these different levels of social reality having interacted to produce the ever-widening electoral gap between Scotland and England. First I will look at the changing experience of the state from the point of view of dominant assumptions about what the state is about.

The starting point has to be the assumptions underlying the political consensus which framed British politics in the thirty years after the Second World War.

British politics from the Second World War onwards were predicated on an implicit relationship between the individual and the state. The economic fate of the individual was assumed to be to some extent contingent on the economic fate of Britain which itself was assumed to be to a certain extent under the control of the government of the day; the government was to a certain extent held responsible. Politics was about the management of the national economy. It is the national dimension to this dominant set of assumptions which must be stressed. In a strange way, self-conscious management of the national economy was implicit in the Keynesian consensus, yet there was little consciousness that Keynesianism is in fact a form of economic nationalism.

In Scotland's case what was crucial was the partial transfer of this national dimension of economic management and political relevance from the British to the Scottish level. This is a very hard process to pin down but I think we can point to the late 1950s and early 1960s as being the crucial years. These were the years in which developments in ideas and institutions relating to the management of the *Scottish* economy were transmitted from the levels of élites and the state to the level of the electorate.

We can point to two crucial agents in this process: the Labour Party and the arrival of television.

Playing a subsidiary role was the Labour Party. As Keating and Bleiman put it, Labour between 1959 and 1966 based its electoral appeal in Scotland on

> its ability to gain material benefits for Scotland. This would be achieved partly through the beneficial effects which Labour's overall U.K. strategy would bring, but partly through the ability of Labour's Scottish representatives to gain special concessions (Keating and Bleiman 1979, p. 153).

Miller makes an even stronger case in saying that 'Between 1959 and 1964 Labour made much of the case for a reviving S.N.P.' (Miller 1981, p. 35).

Labour was a major vehicle for the simple transfer of the dominant mode of discourse: government policies will deliver economic goods at the national level, from Britain to Scotland.

Playing perhaps a more fundamental role however was a transformation in the dominant form of political communication: the arrival of television. It is generally accepted nowadays that television is the most important form of political communication. There has been very little analysis however of the impact of the arrival of television as a historical event, in terms of the political implications of the media matrix before television compared with the media matrix after television (to use the term introduced by Meyrowitz 1985, in one of the few studies of the impact of television to avoid this stricture).

The political impact of television in Scotland can be seen at several levels. Scotland was a couple of years behind England in the pacing of the arrival of television, with 23 per cent of households having licences in 1956 increasing to 67 per cent in 1962. Coverage of regional, economic and current affairs was stipulated in STV's contract, and the arrival of STV prompted the BBC in 1957 to broadcast its first specifically Scottish news bulletin. Coverage of Scottish affairs soon settled into the pattern it has maintained ever since: a Scottish news magazine-programme on both channels following the British 'national' news as well as other Scottish news bulletins and current-affairs programmes. Current-affairs coverage in Scotland in addition had a strong economic and industrial focus (Kendrick 1983). Taking the arrival of television, its strong current-affairs bent and the focus on economic and industrial affairs together, we can talk about a qualitative shift in the degree of exposure of the Scottish people to the 'Scottish economic dimension'.

Direct proof of the degree of impact of the arrival of television on the Scottish political scene would be hard to come by, but the kind of effect which is being hypothesized is precisely the kind of effect which recent paradigms of media research would regard as being most likely. Effects are likely not in terms of a changing of attitudes or opinions but rather in terms of the reinforcement of frames of reference (see for example Blumler and Gurevitch 1982; Curran, Gurevitch and Woollacott 1982). In this case we are talking about the frame of reference which accepts Scotland as the national unit which national economic management and national politics are about.

It must be remembered that what is involved here is not a case of television conjuring up a version of political reality out of thin air. We need only see television as accepting, transmitting and reinforcing a framework of assumptions, already established and taken for granted, that politics was all about the economic management of a national unit. The only framing assumption that specifically Scottish television news and current-affairs coverage did not share with national (British) television news and current-affairs coverage was the identity of the national unit in question. This equivalence of national unit, which made the transfer all the more plausible, can itself be seen as grounded in certain obvious forms. First, the media does not primarily contain its ideological effect in the content of its news coverage, but rather in the form, in the way categories of news are organized. On television in Scotland, fundamental categories in the organization of news coverage are the national units of Britain and Scotland, and the forcefulness of the distinction between these categories is evident in the nightly switch from national British news to national Scottish news.

Second, the most obvious grounding is the sense of Scottish national identity shared by the audience. The 'strength' of Scottish identity is not at issue here. We have no evidence on trends in such 'strength' in the period in question (other than as expressed politically), and it is questionable whether indeed the 'strength' of Scottish identity is measurable in the abstract. What is at issue is the political relevance of a sense of Scottish identity. The process which made Scottish identity relevant to politics and politically effective is the same process which made Scotland an economically significant unit. The relevance of the Scottish dimension to politics is dependent upon the relevance to the economy of the Scottish dimension. The inferences drawn here are admittedly indirect. We do not have direct evidence that the arrival of television in Scotland and its soon acquired 'Scottish economic perspective' influenced the way people looked at politics in Scotland. All that can be said is that the framework through which television presented Scottish political and economic affairs was increasingly likely to be the framework in terms of which they interpreted Scottish political and economic affairs. After all, we are talking quite literally about a change in the way people saw Scotland.

However, here we must introduce an important proviso. The processes we have been discussing are likely to have been most important for those people lacking solidly grounded alternative frameworks through which to perceive and judge the political world.

*Privatism and the Nation*

Here we can approach the problem from the other end, from the first of the levels of the generative matrix: the level of everyday life. It is precisely the groups most affected by the set of processes going under the rubric of 'the growth of privatism' which are most likely to be influenced by the definitions of reality beamed into their living rooms: those moving away from older community and occupationally based loyalties. In general the kind of identity 'interpellated', to use Althusser's useful term, among the audience of television news and current affairs is a national one. Such national interpellation is mostly likely to be effective among those lacking alternative forms of social identification. A good case can be made that it was precisely those groups who responded most strongly to the appeal of the SNP: the young, the upwardly socially mobile, the more affluent members of the working class, the inhabitants of the new towns.

We can place this point in the context of discussions at a British level of the political implications of the growth of privatism. The logic of the argument has tended to run as follows. A major aspect of the growth of privatism has been a break down of traditional forms of embeddedness in the occupational community, the local community and kinship networks. This break down has in turn been seen as weakening forms of identity based on such traditional forms of embeddedness. Such forms of identity have been seen as having direct political implications. Most importantly the break-down of the traditional working-class community brought with it a withering of Labour voting as an expression of class-based, solidaristic identities. Such communally embedded forms of identity have tended to be replaced by much more fluid forms based on a more isolated, privatized nuclear family. These less fixed forms of identity, based increasingly on life-style and a family-based consumption project, have less rigid political implications. In particular orientation towards political parties takes on a much more instrumental, calculating and volatile form. Loyalty to party fades away to be replaced with voting on the basis of which party is perceived to be most likely to bring economic benefits. Such an orientation chimes very nicely with the bedrock assumptions of the post-war consensus of British politics outlined earlier.

When the argument is couched in these terms, there is almost a sense of what could be called an identity vacuum among the privatized, post-solidaristic citizenry. With whom do they identify, apart from themselves and their immediate family?

However, if we look at the process, not in terms simply of a decline in certain forms of face-to-face interaction which went to make up more traditional forms of community but rather as a change in the form of public sphere in which orientations towards politics, the state and the nation are formed, then a different picture emerges.

The growth of privatism is often talked of as a process whose political implications can be derived primarily and directly from changes at the level of face-to-face interaction, from changes in the forms of sociability. However, a link in the explanatory chain is being missed out here. A major aspect was precisely the arrival of a transforming medium of communication at the heart of the privatising process; and again we return to the arrival of television. To caricature the process somewhat, people have not been retreating from participation in face-to-face forms of embeddedness with all their political implications into a sealed-off private world of the family, but have rather been putting themselves into a position of increased exposure to information about the outside world inside their living-rooms via the television.

Several factors have been identified as providing the impetus behind the growth of privatism. Among the more important are: the development of the welfare state, reducing the need for kinship and community-based support systems; increased geographical mobility and the dispersal of occupationally homogeneous communities. Perhaps most central however was simply an increase in the relative attractiveness of the home both in terms of space (better housing and fewer children) and amenity (a widening range of consumer durables) compared with more traditional and communal sites of sociability. The television set, in this context, is a particularly important form of consumer durable, both in terms of its effects on patterns of sociability and as a medium of mass communication.

Raymond Williams puts television at the heart of the process of privatization, going so far as to see its social form as being heavily influenced by the growth of privatized life-styles:

> Yet this privatisation, which was at once an effective achievement and a defensive response, carried, as a consequence, an imperative need for new kinds of contact. The new homes might appear private and 'self-sufficient' but could be maintained only by regular funding and supply from external sources, and these, over a range from employment to prices to depressions and wars, had a decisive and often disruptive influence on what was nevertheless seen as a separate 'family' project. This relationship created both the need and the form of a new kind of 'communication': news from outside, from otherwise inaccessible sources...
>
> The full investment in (television) transmission and reception facilities did not occur until the late 1940s and early 1950s, but the growth was thereafter very rapid. The key social tendencies which had led to the definition of broadcasting were by then even more pronounced. There was significantly higher investment in the privatised home, and the social and physical distances between these homes and the decisive political and productive centres of society had become much greater. Broadcasting, as it had developed in radio, seemed an inevitable model: the central transmitters and domestic sets. (Williams 1974, pp. 27–9)

In terms of our general framework of elements which work to determine how the state is experienced, television is the most important of the media for providing and shaping perceptions of what is happening at the 'national', state level. It provides a direct link from the level of the activities of the state to the level of everyday life.

It is by means of the assumptions in terms of which the world 'out there' at that national or state level is presented that television has its deepest effects.

Perhaps the most fundamental level of such assumptions consists of assumptions about who the audience is. Television news and current-affairs output is broadcast with an implicit conception of the identity of the audience, and the audience is implicitly invited to share in that identity. Television coverage of the political and economic scene assumes a national identity on the part of the viewer and invites the viewer to share a national perspective. The assumption of any other form of identity, for example a class identity, is likely to run into trouble. The only unproblematic identity which mainstream news and current-affairs coverage can assume on the part of the audience is that of citizens, or members of a national community.

Perhaps the most crucial aspect of television's assumption or interpellation of this kind of identity on the part of the audience in its relationship with the national level of the state or politics in general is that it dovetails perfectly with the forms of identity in everyday life which the growth of privatism, the essence of which is the erosion of old identities, encourages. It is the aspect of this process which does most to provide and reinforce the newer forms of identity that are generated.

Those who have become most detached from older forms of social embeddedness will be those most open to having their relevance-structures and even identities shaped by the framing assumptions – the national framing assumptions – of the national media and in particular television.

At a fundamental level we could say that the electoral divergence between Scotland and England is in part a consequence of the forefronting of the national frame of reference on the part of new national media with a particular impact on those for whom older forms of identity are weakening.

*Electoral Divergence and the National Dimension*

We can make these general points rather more concrete by looking at certain aspects of the electoral divergence between Scotland and England in the light of the preceding discussion.

As pointed out earlier, the most systematic and sustained aspect of electoral divergence between Scotland and England has been the increasing shortfall in the Conservative share of the vote in Scotland as compared with England. Perhaps the most puzzling aspect of the Conservative decline has been not the dipping of Conservative performance in Scotland below its English level but rather the fact that the Conservatives began the decline, in the 1950s, from a higher share of the vote than would have been expected from Scotland's proportionately larger manual class, most famously when they received just over 50 per cent of the vote in Scotland at the 1955 general election.

The most plausible explanation for Tory strength in mid-twentieth-century Scotland is the Protestant connection. The tendency of the Scottish Protestant working class to vote Conservative was simply one expression of an ideological complex embracing Protestantism, Orangeism and Unionism with a strong sense of British national and imperial identity. In turn the sense of identity engendered by this complex was embedded in a network of associations at the community level which formed a Protestant working-class sub-culture providing an alternative focus to that based on the labour movement (Kendrick and McCrone, 1988).

In England sociological discussion of political change has tended to focus on the weakening of occupational and community-based class loyalties to the detriment of Labour. In Scotland, we can see the electoral trends of the last thirty years as being in part a reflection of the effects of growing privatism on a different form of social embeddedness – embeddedness in Protestant working-class culture – and in this case to the detriment of the Conservative Party. In Scotland, the close association between religion and electoral politics in the earlier part of this century has meant that the effects of the processes we have been talking about the growth of privatism have been supplemented by the effects of the secularization of Scottish politics.

In the context of the view that the Conservative vote in Scotland was dependent on decaying forms of social embeddedness, it is interesting to look at the ages of those who supported the Conservatives and the SNP at the October 1974 general election. There are very powerful age effects, which are almost exact mirror images, with SNP support being concentrated among the younger age-groups and Conservative support being concentrated among those who are older. For example, among the 18–24 age-group, only 10 per cent voted Conservative compared with 42 per cent voting SNP, whereas among the over-65s, 38 per cent voted Conservative with only 16 per cent voting SNP (Kendrick 1983, p. 42).

We can perhaps see here an indication of an early phase of a process whereby the Scottish framework was capturing the kind of younger voter in Scotland, who later on in the 1970s and in the 1980s would have been attracted to the Thatcherite Conservative Party in England on the basis of the same kind of, but English or British rather than Scottish, national interpellation.

At various levels, what we have seen at work in Scotland are the implications of the Conservative Party's self-image and presentation as the national, British party (see in particular McKenzie and Silver 19680.

In this sense the role of Margaret Thatcher as a personal embodiment of the Englishness of the Conservative Party is only the icing on the cake of a much more fundamental process, a process involving the national dimension itself. The British national aspect of the Conservative Party has become more explicit under Thatcher than it had been for a good while but it has always been operative. From this point of view, the regularity and consistency of the Conservative Party's decline in Scotland is to be seen as the systematic result of the taking root of the Scottish frame of reference, the assumption that politics are to be judged by their effects on Scotland. This taking root of the national dimension is in itself dependent on the kinds of process which have been outlined in earlier sections.

*Conclusion*

Where does this leave us in terms of the more general set of issues introduced at the beginning of the paper? I have suggested that electoral divergence between Scotland and England, although reflecting a national difference, must be explained, in terms of its timing and its form, to a large extent on the basis of aspects of social change which have been shared by both nations. In particular I have highlighted three levels of social reality which would seem particularly important to an understanding of how the state is experienced. First was change at the level of everyday life focusing in particular upon the growth of privatism. Second was the arrival of television which constituted a transformation of the matrix of political communication. Third was the taken-for-granted role of the state in taking responsibility for the national economy. It has been the mutual interaction of these levels and the interaction between them and the national material which was available – whether in the form of a sense of national identity, national symbolism or institutions – which has been crucial.

In the space available, the account has obviously been sketched in very broad outline. I have been trying to illustrate the logic of the kind of explanation which is required to account for electoral divergence.

In trying to counteract an imbalance of emphasis in existing accounts, I have probably presented a picture which tilts too far towards stressing the role of parallel developments.

However, to stress the role of parallels between Scotland and England is not to belittle the importance of studying Scottish society. It has been the incessant stress on difference which has trivialized much analysis of modern Scotland, a stress on difference which has sometimes kept the discussion marginalized in terms of its benefit from and contribution to what we know about the dynamics of advanced industrial society in general.

If the logic of this chapter were to be pressed into its smallest compass, it would be this. It has been profound changes at all levels of social development which Scotland has shared with England, and indeed much of the advanced industrial world, which, in their mutual interactions and in their differing reactions with the national level, have given political dynamism to the sense of Scottish national identity and are exposing the anachronism of Scotland's present constitutional status.

REFERENCES

Blumler J.G., and Gurevitch, M. (1982), 'The Political Effects of Mass Communication' in, M. Gurevitch, et al. (eds.), *Culture, Society and the Media,* London: Methuen.

Curran, J., Gurevitch, M., and Wollacott, J. (1982), 'The study of the media: theoretical approaches' in M. Gurevitch, et al. (eds.), *Culture, Society and the Media* London: Methuen.

Dickson, T., et al. (1980) *Scottish Capitalism: Class, State and Nation from before the Union to the Present,* London: Lawrence and Wishart.

Dunleavy, P., and Husbands, C. (1985), *British Democracy at the Crossroads,* London: Allen & Unwin.

Goldthorpe, J.H. (1980), *Social Mobility and Class Structure in Modern Britain,* Oxford: Clarendon Press.

Goldthorpe, J.H., et al (1968), *The Affluent Worker: Political Attitudes and Behaviour,* Cambridge: Cambridge University Press.

Goldthorpe, J.H., et al (1969), *The Affluent Worker in the Class Structure,* Cambridge: Cambridge University Press.

Heath, A., Jowell, R., and Curtice, J. (1985), *How Britain Votes,* Oxford: Pergamon Press.

Keating, M.J., and Bleiman, D. (1979), *Labour and Scottish Nationalism,* London: Macmillan.

Kendrick, S. (1983) *Social Change and Nationalism in Modern Scotland',* Edinburgh University Ph.D. Thesis.

Kendrick, S. (1984), 'Women's Economic Activity in Post-War Scotland, Social Change in Scotland and the 1981 Census Working Paper', University of Edinburgh.

Kendrick, S. (1986), 'Occupational Change in Modern Scotland' in D. McCrone (ed.), *Scottish Government Yearbook 1986,* Edinburgh: Unit for the Study of Government in Scotland.

Kendrick, S., Bechhofer, F., and McCrone, D. (1985), 'Is Scotland Different? Industrial and Occupational Change in Scotland and Britain' in, H. Newby et al. (eds) *Restructuring Capital: Recession and Reorganization in Industrial Society,* British Sociological Association Explorations in Sociology 20, London: Macmillan.

Kendrick, S., and McCrone, D. (1988), 'Politics in a Cold Climate: The Conservatives in Scotland', Edinburgh University, mimeo.

Marshall, G., Rose, D., Vogler, C., and Newby, H. (1985), 'Class, Citizenship, and Distributional Conflict in Modern Britain', *The British Journal of Sociology,* vol. 36, no. 2.

McKenzie, R.T., and Silver, A.M. (1968), *Angels in Marble,* London: Heinemann.

Meyrowitz, J. (1985), *No Sense of Place: The Impact of Electronic Media on Social Behaviour,* Oxford: Oxford University Press.

Miller, W.L. (1981, *The End of British Politics?: Scots and English Political Behaviour in the Seventies,* Oxford: Clarendon Press.

Newby, H., Vogler, C. Rose, D., and Marshall, G. (1985), 'From Class Structure to Class Action: British Working-Class Politics in the 1980s' in, B. Roberts *et al.* (eds.), *New Approaches to Economic Life,* Manchester: Manchester University Press.

Williams, R. (1974), *Television: Technology and Cultural Form,* London: Fontana/Collins.

# 5

## Shetland in the World Economy: A Sociological Perspective

R.J. SMITH

The history of Britain's periphery has been neglected by sociologists for too long. Few have taken Ian Carter's (1974) lead and become actively involved in the writing of the historical sociology of the periphery. This is important because some of the most contentious issues in the sociology of development are to be found in the study of the peripheral areas in what was once the most 'advanced' capitalist state in the world, in particular the existence of unfree labour relations and limited economic development. This raises central issues over the nature of capitalist development and the processes of social and economic change. Sociologists are required to be at the forefront in the writing of a new history of the development of capitalism in Britain, part of which must be the history of the periphery.

In this chapter I present a sociological interpretation of the history of the Shetland Islands from their first integration into the world economy in the mid-sixteenth century until the late nineteenth century. I concentrate on the way in which production was organized, in particular the labour organization of fishing tenures known as the Zetland Method. What is interesting from a sociological point of view is that early integration into the world economy did not lead to the development of free labour. My aim in this chapter is to answer the following questions: why did a form of unfree labour survive for so long; what effects did this have on the long-term social and economic development of Shetland, and in particular why did social and economic stagnation of the mid-nineteenth century occur after a period of rapid growth and change in the 1820s and 1830s? To do this it is necessary first to explain the historical conditions within which a distinctive form of social organization of production emerged and came to dominate, and then to outline the complex articulation between the organization of production at the local level and exchange of commodities within the context of a world economy.

The first point is that the history of Shetland is not one of isolation from the external world and the lack of a relationship with capitalism, but it is the history of the very nature of its relationship with the capitalist world economy. Shetland has been integrated into the world economy longer than many areas of 'developed' capitalist states, the so-called 'core'. To understand this relationship it is necessary to locate my work within the context of the existing historiography on Shetland and on more general sociological arguments.

There is a very rich local historiography, too extensive to discuss here. The most important figure is Dr. Hance Smith, and his main work is *Shetland Life and Trade, 1550-1914* (1984). In this, as in his earlier works (H.D. Smith 1969, 1977), he emphasizes the central role of trade in the history of Shetland. His argument takes the form of progressive evolution, where at each stage a different social group controls the external trade, an explanation that has correctly been deemed 'whiggish' and which accepts (at least implicitly) that opiate of conservative development theory, modernization. Theoretically there is no a priori primacy for trade over production. Indeed, the reverse is the case. An evolutionist argument is unable to explain the social stagnation of the mid-nineteenth century, which was revealed to the rest of Britain in the second report of the Truck Commission (Shetland 1872). After centuries of neglect the British state was finally prepared to criticize the social organization in Shetland. Furthermore, conflict is identified by Wills (1975) and Hance Smith (1984) as being between lairds and merchants over the control of trade, especially at the important transition periods between social groups. This is an incorrect identification of the problem. The conflict was over the control of labour, and between the capitalist, who wished to introduce 'free' labour conditions (or the supplier of labour to external capitalists i.e. the whaling industry) and laird (any anyone else), who wished to maintain unfree labour conditions.

As a sociological explanation of the development of Britain's periphery, Carter's (1974) interpretation of the historical development of the Highlands of Scotland, using Gunder Frank's model, was an important advance, but it suffered from the problems associated with the emphasis on 'exchange' relations rather than relations of production (Laclau 1971). Since then, two heuristic models have come to the fore: Wallerstein's world-systems theory (1974, 1980); and the perspective of the articulation of modes of production (Althusser and Balibar 1977), Taylor 1979, Wolpe 1980). Although Wallerstein has been criticized on similar grounds as those on which Frank has been criticized (Brenner 1977), the world-systems theory has become a major paradigm for understanding social change. This is part of the awareness that the 'nation-state' is no longer an adequate unit of analysis in itself. However, it is clear that there are dangers of providing a functionalist analysis of the social and economic structures of peripheries within the world-system, and that there is not an adequate elaboration of the processes that sustain this unequal relationship, or, more relevant to the concern of this chapter, of the maintenance of unfree labour in the periphery.

The concept of articulation has proved attractive especially to those at home with Althusserian language, but Wolpe (1980) has shown that there are disputes over the definition of mode of production, and he makes a distinction between restricted and extended versions. The 'restricted' includes the forces and relations of production, and the 'extended' adds to this a theory of reproduction and laws of motion of the mode of production. This confusion over the definition of the mode of production arises because in Marx's own writings there is no clear statement of what a mode of production is (Shaw 1978, pp. 31–2), although it is certainly a theoretical construct, an abstraction of social relations rather than a description of concrete social relations. This does not help us to explain how it is that within any social formation (in any given historical situation there will be more than one mode of production) one mode of production (capitalist) is able to reproduce another (non-capitalist) and vice-versa. There is the danger that this will itself become a functionalist analysis, that non-capitalist relations are seen as functional for the maintenance of capitalism at the level of the system. It is, however, an attempt to understand the complexity of any social formation. Furthermore, there have been calls for a synthesis of the world-systems and mode-of-production analysis (Munck 1982). There already exists the basis for this. Bettelheim (1972) argues that there is reproduction of productive forces and relations at both national and international level which have conflicting tendencies, the former to maintain the national level, the latter to undermine the national. For the purposes of this paper we could substitute the local (Shetland) for the national level and the world economy for the international level. Furthermore, since at any given level of forces of production there can be different social relations of production, social relations must have primacy over forces of production in any analysis; and as Miles (1987) has recently reminded us, we must locate any articulation analysis within the specific historical conditions of the social formation being studied.

It is difficult to see the value of one form of analysis without the insights of the other, and my work is sympathetic towards a fusion of the perspectives. The debate over which concepts are more 'marxian' is self-defeating; the point is to provide a sociological understanding of processes. If we cannot explain the development of parts of the world with the old conception of what is or what is not 'capitalist' then we much be prepared to create new concepts.

I have attempted to address my work to these problems in relation to the social and economic development of Shetland. To recap, in this chapter the starting point of the analysis is the form of labour organization, and this cannot be separated from the process of integration into the world economy. Then I will deal with the roots of the system, the failure to develop capitalist social relations, and finally with the reasons why the Zetland Method broke down in the late nineteenth century.

## *The Zetland Method*

The dominant way of organizing production in Shetland up until the late nineteenth century was the fishing tenure system (or Zetland Method). This is related to the main form of production; line fishing. Until the early nineteenth century stockfish was the most important export of Shetland, and its production was the main economic activity around which all other economic activity was organized. From at least the sixteenth century Shetland became a specialized producer of stockfish for European markets, and thus found its niche in the international division of labour.

Basically the fishing tenure system meant that a tenant had to fish for his laird as part of the lease, in effect to pay his rent. Rents were not related to the agricultural productivity of the land, nor were they set in specified amounts of goods or labour (although there were a series of 'taxes' that were paid in kind), but, instead, were given monetary values. Likewise, any produce of the tenant's land or labour was given a money value. These were not related to market prices for the goods and were slow to change. The important point is that the laird did not make his money through rents directly but by the selling of the produce of the tenants' labour. The system was maintained through debt-bondage; the laird, or his factor/tacksman, advanced the tenants the goods they required, which included materials for the fishing, and these were paid back by the fish (and some agricultural produce such as butter) the tenant caught. The tenant was in debt for much of the year, reinforcing his subordination to the laird. There was a tendency for these debts to be carried over from one year to the next, partly because the tenant had the cost of his share in a boat to pay off, partly because the holdings were small and the land so poor that there was not enough food to feed a family all the year. It was also in the interest of the laird to maintain his control over the tenant by allowing some of the debt to be carried over until the following year. The tenant could only fish for his laird or someone appointed by the laird and he could only receive his goods from the laird's shop, or a merchant's shop allowed by the laird. On the ground this system was maintained by a number of intermediate factors and tacksmen who had direct control of much of the daily lives of the people. Since the tenant was liable for his share in a boat and for the fishing materials, there was no separation of the tenant from the means of production. There was very little chance for the tenant to be able to pay his rent in any other way, as there were no external labour markets until the end of the eighteenth century.

This system was directly related to the main form of production, the distant hand-line fishing in summer called the *haaf* fishing (*haaf* means ocean). The traditional dates for the fishing were between 20 May and 12 August. The main catch was ling but also cod and to a lesser extent tusk (also coalfish in the most southerly parishes). At the height of its fishing industry Shetland produced some 1000 tons of stockfish for continental markets. The vessels used were small open boats with a crew of, by the mid-eighteenth century, six men. To reach the more distant banks they needed to sail up to thirty miles from shore. The fishing stations were sited on stone beaches necessary for the drying and curing of the fish and were as close to the banks as possible. They were concentrated in the northern parishes since these were nearest the main fishing areas. The *haaf* fishing was part of the great international cod fishery that crossed the North Atlantic from Norway to Newfoundland.

The origins of this fishery are related to the integration of Shetland into the world economy. It was German merchants from the old Hansa cities of Hamburg and Bremen that broke Shetland's reliance on the traditional trade with Norway. The first record of a German merchant visiting Shetland is for 1415, at a time of crisis in the organization of the Hanseatic League. By at least the mid-sixteenth century the German merchants controlled the internal production and the external trade of Shetland. They built up what had been a subsistence fishery into the *haaf* and organized it along the Hanseatic *ausreedsystem,* of advances in one year being paid off in produce the following year, which was the basis for the fishing tenure system. It is almost certain that they and not the tenants cured the fish. The merchants dealt directly with the tenants. The lairds played no part in these exchanges, although they did make charges on the merchants for the use of beaches for curing, trading booths and rights of access to tenants. They also established the markets in northern German towns for Shetland fish. The tenants remained in control of the means of production, which meant that the fishing could have developed into a form of petty commodity production if it had not been for the social changes at the turn of the eighteenth century.

In the eighteenth century there were several crucial developments in Shetland society. The first was a social revolution: a group of 'new men', mainly of petty-laird and mercantile origins, replaced the Germans (B. Smith 1979) and integrated the fishery into the form of landholding, a process which was completed by the end of the second decade. These merchant lairds controlled both internal production and external trade, and pursued the development and expansion of the fishery ruthlessly. The fishery became even more dominant and the number of boats rose to a maximum of 500 by the latter part of the century. The boats used were larger, with a shift from four-man to six-man vessels. The total average catch more than doubled from 400 tons to roughly 1000 tons by the end of the century. There were other changes. The most important was a change in markets for Shetland produce from Hamburg to the western Mediterranean markets centred on Barcelona. This also saw important structural changes in the organization of trade. Previously the lairds had carried out the trade at their own risk; now southern British merchant-houses placed orders for fish acting through a local middleman. This is a grey area in Shetland's history, and it remains unclear whether these changes were due to push factors in the German markets or pull factors from the southern markets. There is no evidence presented for conflict over this reorganization of trade which meant that local merchants were able to play a more prominent role in the economy. We can only speculate that the lairds were prepared to give up the risk of trading the fish themselves in return for greater security. They remained in control of production, and indeed it could be argued that the greater security enabled them to intensify further the *haaf* fishing. What can be said is that there was greater specialization of economic function, not that one social group was replacing another as the innovators within the economy.

As early as the 1740s one of the visitors to Shetland recognized the tyranny of the fishing tenure system:

> in the Summer, the men are obliged to go to Sea a fishing Cod and Ling for the lord of the Manor . . . Compelling their

tenants to go to sea for them ... those masters are so absolute as some Princes, for if these poor People do but murmur in the least of their Orders, they and their families are banished for ever out of their Territories. (Campbell 1970, pp. 13-14)

The system came in for increasing criticism towards the end of the eighteenth century, primarily from the clergy, who concentrated on the moral effects on the people. However, within a society where the landed interest still dominated, the state was not prepared to oppose the system:

Your Committee think themselves bound to observe, that no particular Reflection can, in their opinion, justly be cast upon the Land Owners of Shetland; as from everything that has appeared to your Committee, their conduct towards their Fishers and Tenants is such as naturally arises from the actual State of the Islands, and is probably such as their present Situation who ever had the property, would unavoidly require. (PP 1786, p. 142)

In the 1780s criticism was being made of the Zetland Method based on the need for free labour. The main advocate of this within the Islands was James Hay (R. Smith 1986). Hay believed that the only way to expand production in Shetland was through the introduction of free labour relations. He felt that the existing system limited the development of the forces of production (my terms not his), in particular the use of larger vessels and preventing Shetland from taking full advantage of the resources around its shores. Hay, along with some merchants from Great Yarmouth, tried to break the system by setting up a herring fishery in 1787, which was unsuccessful and ended in 1789.

The fishing tenure system allowed one social group to have near total control over the labour of the mass of the Shetland population. This structure could only continue to exist given Shetland's position within the world economy, the unity of the ruling élite, and the continued neglect by the British state. We can perhaps understand the existence of this system in the eighteenth century, but what of the bourgeois world of the nineteenth century when capitalism was victorious and dominant?

*The Truck Commission*

One of the most important social documents on Shetland in the nineteenth century is the second report of the Truck Commission (1872), which dealt solely with labour conditions in the Islands. The truck system was seen as an evil that prevented the proper operation of the labour market. What the commissioners discovered in Shetland was a whole community where the free market for labour by and large did not exist. Conditions in Shetland were only revealed as a problem on this scale in a document submitted in the first report (1871), from the Board of Trade on truck in the employment of men in the Greenland whaling. In this 'remarkable document' it was stated that the organization of labour for the whaling was only an extension of a more pernicious system that covered all forms of labour in all areas of production and which reached virtually everyone, male and female, of working age:

> To make this part of my report intelligible, I ought to mention that the truck system in an open or disguised form prevails in Shetland to an extent which I believe is unknown in any other part of the United Kingdom, and makes its depressing influence felt in all the ramifications of the industrial and social life of the natives ... while the men employed are not *free agents,* however fair an employer might desire to be, he cannot treat them as if they were, and if on the other hand the employer wishes to make all he can out of those he employs, and to take every advantage of their dependent position, he has unlimited opportunity of appropriating to himself all the result of their labour, leaving to them only so much as is absolutely necessary to prevent them from starving (PP 1871 vol. I p. xciv; my emphasis).

The first report concluded that a separate investigation on Shetland was required.

In the second investigation (1872) it soon became clear that the Commission was dealing with more than truck but with the total social organization of Shetland society which had its roots in the organization of production which itself was related to the form of landholdings:

> It is impossible to separate the question of Truck in Shetland from the land question—(1) Because Truck, in the form in which it chiefly exists, has arisen out of the old relations between the landlords and tenants in the times when the landlords were the principal or the only purchasers and curers of fish; and (2) because, to a very material extent the relations between the fish-curer and the fishermen are still subservient and ancillary to the landlord's security for his rent (PP 1872 vol. I p. 4).

The commissioners interviewed nearly 300 individuals from the whole spectrum of Shetland society. Their evidence reveals a system of labour control that tied the tenant to his laird and fish-curer, whose cod vessel or whaling vessel he could sail on, or determined which merchant a woman knitted for; in short the internal labour market did not operate. This was seen as necessary by those that ran the system, be they laird, or factor, or companies who held tacks of land, because it secured labour to pay off debts. The tenants fatalistically accepted their lot. Some were afraid to give evidence fearing that they would be evicted; others did not know whether they were free to fish for whom they wished. The largest company in Shetland, Hay & Co., owned or managed much of the Islands, to the value of one quarter of the Islands' gross rental. They ran these estates on the same lines as any laird. After discovering the number of estates where fishing leases had been made explicit, the Commission concluded that on the rest of the Islands:

> On other estates the tenants are nominally free, although it may sometimes be doubtful how far they are able to exercise any choice (**PP** 1872 vol. I p. 6).

How was it that Shetland was still organized in this way in the 1870s? Hance Smith has argued that a 'New Class of Men' had taken over Shetland society at the turn of the century and that it was now under 'The Rule of Capitalists' (1977 pp. 27, 35). We need to clarify some points of terminology. He is arguing for a transition of control from 'lairds' to 'merchants'. The latter are equated with 'capitalists'. This is a confusion between individuals and the structural position that they are in. It does not matter what we call the individuals who 'control' any social system. If their structural relationship to production is the same, then they fulfil the same role. Hance Smith believes that there are real and opposed differences of interests between a 'merchant' and a 'laird'. It is clear that 'merchants' are not 'capitalists' unless they act as 'capitalists'. 'Merchants' are only people that carry out specific economic functions in relation to trade. In any peripheral social formation there will be a strong tendency for a greater variety of economic functions to be carried out by any individual. It is much more precarious to specialize. Therefore, it was common for a 'merchant' to be a landowner and a factor and a fish-curer. Marx argued that 'merchant' capital is basically conservative, reinforcing existing forms of social organization rather than revolutionizing such relations. 'Merchants' had as much commitment to maintaining the system of unfree labour in Shetland as any laird did. I agree with Hance Smith that there were changes of personnel and that many of the lairds no longer directly ran their estates. The point that I am making is that this does not lead in itself to changes in the nature of that society. To put the problem more straightforwardly, what difference did it make to the Shetland tenant? As the Truck Commisson showed, there was very little difference at all. How can we explain the continuation of this system into the late nineteenth century?

## The Failure of the Capitalist Challenge: Social and Economic changes from the 1770s to the 1840s

Shetland experienced great social and economic changes from the 1770s up to the late 1830s, which I describe briefly below. The points that I want to emphasize are the two crises in production: the first was in the late eighteenth century, after which there was a 'freeing' up of social relations and a diversification in the economy, which, itself, was related to Shetland's changing position in the world economy. The second was in the late 1830s and early 1840s, precipitated by the collapse of the herring fishery. This led to a return to the 'old system', although, within the context of a more diversified economy, all the advances did not end, and there was not a total return to the *haaf*, but there was a general period of social and economic stagnation.

From the 1770s the system was coming under increasing pressure both internally and externally. Internally Shetland suffered from a Malthusian subsistence crisis: rising population had outstripped agricultural resources which had become increasingly marginalized as holdings were subdivided to make room for more tenants. This was to such an extent that by the late eighteenth century the plough had virtually disappeared and Shetland had become one of the main areas of spade cultivation in Scotland. There was also a major depression in fishing catches which meant that there were less exports to pay for the importation of foodstuffs. All this came to a crisis point in the dearths of the 1780s (R. Smith 1986 ch. 4). External changes included the Islands becoming a major source of labour for the Greenland whalers, and during the French wars as a supply for the Royal Navy. External employment is an interesting and distinctive example of the articulation between different forms of social organization; but first I want to deal with the economic developments that took place in the early nineteenth century.

The Zetland Method – a total system carried on throughout the Islands – survived in the eighteenth century because of the strength of the indigenous ruling class, and also because of the neglect by the British parent state. However, matters changed towards the end of the eighteenth century. The general crisis led to dissent in the ranks of the local élite. This took two forms: one was the emancipation of tenants in certain parts of the Islands; the second was the attempts to develop the economy along new lines. Divisions within local élites were important for creating the conditions for the penetration of new forms of organizing production where direct political and economic control was not the issue. Shetland operating under its own control was able to exist as a society closed to external control although depending on world markets for its continued existence. Emancipation only took place within the context of the general crises, and even then only in the areas where the *haaf* fishing was of lesser importance (R. Smith 1986, pp. 126-8). Diversification failed: a linen industry was established in the 1780s but was bankrupt within a few years, and the lairds' plan to control the supply of labour to the Greenland whalers never got off the ground.

There were only a few within Shetland society that argued for the introduction of capitalist social relations and only two men (that we know of) that were prepared to develop industries based on free labour: James Hay and Arthur Anderson. As early as the 1780s Hay was going beyond criticizing the existing system and attempting to develop a herring fishery. Later he and his son William were instrumental in laying the foundations of the herring and cod fisheries in the 1810s and were the main agents for the Greenland whalers. In 1814 Hay retired from active business and was replaced by his son, who, being able to operate within the context of the old system, never showed the same commitment to replacing it. Arthur Anderson (co-founder of the P. & O. shipping company) set up the Shetland Journal in 1837 and used its pages to attack the lairds and merchants who operated the Zetland Method. He set up a fishery for 'free fishers' on the island of Vaila, though we know almost nothing about this company besides that it failed. These men stand out for their attempts; their failure highlights the difficulty of indigenous capitalist development in Shetland at this time.

One of the most important developments was Shetland's changing position in the world economy during this period. This was its new role as supplier of labour to the Greenland whalers. There was a conflict of interest between the whaling agents and the lairds over the control of labour. In 1780 - there had been a plan by the lairds to rationalize supply of labour to the whaling vessels and remain in direct control of the tenants' labour (R. Smith 1986 pp. 194-8). Nothing came of this plan and the whale shipowners dealt with agents based in Lerwick. The conflict between agent and laird came at times of labour shortages. At these times the whaling was seen as a direct threat to the *haaf* fishing. There were either specific occasions where certain areas experienced a shortage of labour; this happened to Thomas Mouat in 1793 (Wills 1975, pp. 430-1) and on Arthur Nicolson's lands in Fetlar in the 1820s (R. Smith 1986, pp. 201-3). Or more generally there was a labour shortage in the war period (Edmondston 1809, p. 69). In terms of numbers of Shetlanders sailing, the industry reached its height in the 1810s and 1820s with some 1000 men sailing annually. One of the most important features of the whaling industry was that it was a source of significant capital, which was then used to develop the economy by investment and new industries (see below).

There was a growth of capitalist relations of production in the first three decades of the nineteenth century in the cod and herring fisheries. The cod fishing was mainly organized along the semi-capitalistic half-catch system, similar to sharecropping, where the value of the catch was divided between the owner of the vessel and the crew. Up to half of the vessels were individually owned which made it more comparable to simple commodity production than to wage labour capitalism. However the fishing depended greatly on state subsidies in the from of bounty and debenture. Sixty per cent of final income came from these, and when they were ended in 1829 the industry went into rapid decline until the 1840s. There is no evidence for this earlier period that the fishing was organized as part of the fishing tenure system. The later cod fishery reached its peak between 1863 and 1874 (in 1871 there were 817 men at the fishing, approximately a third of those at the *haaf*), but this was organized by the owners of the vessels as part of their wider economic interests in the *haaf*, as lairds or agents etc.

The most important development was the establishment of a successful, if temporary, herring fishery. This early herring fishery has been described in detail elsewhere (R. Smith 1986 ch. 7). In the 1820s it was believed that the industry was the basis for great economic advancement especially after the demise of the cod fishery, but by the early 1840s the fishing had collapsed. The belief within Shetland in the potential of the herring industry cannot be understated. There was massive investment in boats, (there were 500 at the fishery in the 1830s), in stores, land-fishing stations etc. At its height Shetland produced approximately 10 per cent of the total Scottish catch. The reasons for the failure of the fishery have mainly been presented as being due to natural causes: the destruction wrought by storms, decline of catches due to migrations of the herring etc. However, social causes are at least equally important. Most significant was that the herring fishery was organized around the needs of the *haaf* fishery. It was concentrated after the *haaf* had finished and was organized as an extension of the fishing tenure system. The result of this was an inferior product that could only be sold in the poorest of markets, the Irish and West Indian markets. The West Indian market disappeared after slave emancipation, and the Irish one declined rapidly in the early 1840s. In the context of these changing conditions the *haaf* remained dominant. The collapse of the herring industry brought down with it the Shetland Bank and the firm of Hay & Ogilvy who controlled most of the Islands' external trade. There had been a significant part of the fishery which had operated outwith the existing system. These were marginalized by the bad economic conditions of the late 1830s, and few were able to survive the collapse of the main pillars of the economy in 1842.

All these developments raise important issues as to how different forms of organization of production articulate. In particular they highlight the problem of non-capitalist labour relations existing within the wider capitalist world economy. In the case of the cod fishery its collapse was due to its weak economic base relying on state subsidy. The herring fishery was dominated by the *haaf* fishery and the fishing tenure system, which marginalized the fishery in terms of world markets. The whaling is in some ways more interesting; here was a clear-cut example of wage labour existing externally, though this was experienced within the context of the distinctive and unique culture of the whaling ship.

In 1842 the two pillars of the new economy, the Shetland Bank and the firm of Hay & Ogilvy, were declared bankrupt, so bringing to a head the crisis precipitated by the collapse of the herring fishery. This paralysed trade for several years, highlighting the poor state of the economy. In the context of this crisis the conservative elements in Shetland society came to the fore. As one contemporary (in 1841) put it:

> The eyes of most people are now open to the necessity of resuming the principles of the old system (New Statistical Account 1845 p. 161).

And that system was the one described in the Truck Commission. This meant a strengthening of the *haaf* as the dominant form of production, and there was an expansion of that fishery. More Shetlanders were employed in this than in any other form of production. The Zetland Method was once more supreme and a period of social and economic stagnation followed. This can be seen in many forms. There was an ending of the internal shift of population from the countryside to Lerwick (the percentage living there in 1831 was 9.4 per cent by 1871 it had risen to only 9.7 per cent). There was the growth of emigration for work (part of Shetland's position in the world economy as a supplier of labour). The sex ratio of males per 100 females fell from 86 in 1831 to 68 in 1871 (for the central parishes, other areas showed a similar decline), and for males of economically advice age (15–64 years) in 1871 it was 55.2 at which point only 48.3 per cent of all males were in this age group

(R. Smith 1986 pp. 352-3). Even at the height of the advances of the 1820s and 1830s the 'old system' had remained at the helm; its effects were described in 1837 in the following way:

> the system of fishing tenures... has therefore turned men, who might have otherwise have been tolerably liberal persons, into cunning, hard-hearted, grasping oppressors; and it has turned people, who might have been (like their neighbours the Norwegians) an independent, industrious, well-lodged, and well fed people, into an abject, indolent, and half-starved race of slaves. *(Shetland Journal 1837)*

If this was the state of the Shetland people in the 1830s how much worse was their condition to become?

## *The Establishment of Capitalist Social Relations*

A little over a decade after the Truck Commission another state body came to investigate matters in Shetland, the Napier Commission, and in that short period there had been remarkable changes in the social organization of the Islands: the Zetland method was well and truly in decline; the economy was expanding but now under free labour. There are three major reasons why the system was in decline: (1) the old ways were too far out of step with acceptable practices for the British state to continue to allow such a degree of local independence in such matters (this is related to the land question in Ireland and the Highlands of Scotland); (2) the position of land within the economy was changing, breaking down the old interdependence of tenant and laird; (3) most importantly the 'second coming' of the herring was under the control of Scottish curers, who organized the fishery according to the principles of free labour.

The first point relates to the criticism of the system in the Truck and Napier Commissions' reports. Most important was the Crofters Act (1886), which broke the direct link between owning land and controlling the labour of the tenant, with the result that the laird, factor or agent could no longer deal with the tenant with impunity. The 1880s and 1890s were marked by a massive number of claims from Shetland tenants for fair rents: by 1888 there had been 1209 applications from Shetland (only in Ross and Cromarty and in Sutherland were they higher); and by 1897 there had been 2607. The rental had been reduced from £11199 to £8012; and arrears of £9505 (out of £13425) had been cancelled (PP 1888 vol, LXXX p. 105. PP 1897 vol. LXXII p. 725).

Already by the 1840s there were signs that some landowners were looking for alternative uses of their land, usually as sheep farms, which required the division of the hill land. Divisions of land reached their peak in the 1860s and 1870s, although this covered only a minority of land in Shetland and was virtually halted by the Crofters Act. One of the main complaints to the Napier Commission was the removal of tenants' rights to use common land for the grazing of animals. This helped to break the lairds' side of the unwritten bargain with the tenants. We do not know enough about these estates at this time to say whether these changes were related to a more 'rational' organization to maximize economic returns, though there were certain individuals who did make this argument. The most important was John Walker, factor for the Cameron estate (he also argued for the introduction of free fishing). We do know that the landed families were increasingly orientated towards British society, and found their new careers in the military and legal professions. In this context their Shetland estates were seen as additional income which needed to be secured. It is no coincidence that it is at this point that many gave up the running of their estates to others; some of whom changed the organization of the estates while others operated the old system. Another influence was the poor economic conditions of the 1860s which saw large advances being made to the tenants; certainly some wanted to get out of this cycle of advances and debts that tied up their capital and wealth.

Above all other factors was the establishment of a herring fishery from the late 1870s onwards, under the control of Scottish curers who organized it under their system and as an extension of the wider Scottish herring fishery. This finally integrated Shetland into the mainstream of the British economy. As early as the Napier Commission the Shetlanders clearly understood that it was the coming of the Scots that was breaking down the old system. Local firms were too weak to prevent the Scottish penetration and were forced to follow the new organization. In 1884 out of the 80 curers 66 were from outwith Shetland, and at the peak of the fishing in 1905 out of the 1700 boats fishing off Shetland only 400 were locally owned.

*Conclusion*

Shetland presents us with a fascinating history that appears at first to be that of the creation of an insular isolated community, but soon reveals itself to be formed through the Islands' relationship with the external world. This relationship is not a clear-cut one in promoting social and economic development; it does not directly lead to the development of capitalism in the form of capitalist social relations of production. It was the very nature of Shetland's integration into the world economy that allowed the creation and imposition of a system of unfree labour which then hindered the indigenous development of capitalist labour relations from the late eighteenth century onwards. Before now the main historical explanation for the route of Shetland's history has emphasized trade over all other factors: the sociological insight that production relations are more important presents a more adequate explanation, although this cannot be understood in isolation but within the context of integration into the world economy. It is too easy to understand the history of the periphery of Britain as the inevitable outcome of overpopulation or poor resources, a fatalistic view that dominates the discussion on the Highlands as well as Shetland. Sociologists need to rewrite that history using the concept of the social organization of production from the perspective of the world economy.

REFERENCES
*Parliamentary Papers*
   (Third Report from the) Committee appointed to enquire into the State of the British Fisheries. July 1786 in House of Commons Sessional Papers of the Eighteenth Century, vol. 53, Geo. III, Fisheries 1785 and 1786.
   PP 1871, Report of the Commissioners Appointed to Inquire into the Truck System (and Evidence), vol. XXXVI).
   PP 1872, Second Report of the Commissioners Appointed to Inquire into the Truck System (and Evidence), vol. XXV.
   PP 1884, Evidence Taken by Her Majesty's Commissioners of Inquiry into the Conditions of the Crofters and Cottars, vol. XXXII.
   PP 1888 Report of the Crofters Commission, vol. LXXX.
   PP 1897, Report of the Crofters Commission, vol. LXXII.
*Newspapers*
   *The Orkney & Zetland Chronicle* (1825-6)
   *The Shetland Journal*
   *The Orkney & Shetland Journal*
   *The Orkney & Shetland Journal and Fisherman's Magazine* (1837-9)
*Books and Articles*
   Althusser, L., and Balibar, E. (1977), *Reading Capital*, London: New Left Books.
   Bettelheim, C. (1972), 'Theoretical Comments' in, Emmanuel, A., *Unequal Exchange*, London: New Left Books.
   Brenner, R. (1977), 'The Origins of Capitalist Development: A Critique of Neo-Smithian Marxism', *New Left Review* 104.
   Campbell, J. (1970), *A True and Exact Description of the Island of Shetland, containing an Account of its Situation, Trade, Produce and Inhabitants,* reprint of second ed. (1753), Edinburgh: Mercat Press.

Carter, I. (1974), 'The Highlands of Scotland as an Underdeveloped Region' in, Kadt and Williams (eds), *Sociology and Development*, London: Tavistock.

Frank, A.G. (1971a), *Sociology of Development and the Underdevelopment of Sociology*, London: Pluto Press.

Frank, A.G. (1971b), *Capitalism and Underdevelopment in Latin America*, Harmondsworth: Penguin.

Knox, S. (1985), *The Making of the Shetland Landscape*, Edinburgh: John Donald.

Laclau, E. (1971, 'Feudalism and Capitalism in Latin America' *New Left Review* 67.

Long, N. (1977), *An Introduction to the Sociology of Rural Development*, London: Tavistock.

Miles, R. (1987), *Capitalism and Unfree Labour*, London: Tavistock.

Munck, R. (1982), 'Imperialism and Dependence: Recent Debates and Old Dead-Ends' in, Chilcote (ed.), *Dependence and Marxism*, Boulder USA: Westview Press.

Shaw, W. (1978), *Marx's Theory of History*, London: Hutchison.

Smith, B. (1977), 'Shetland Archives and Sources of Shetland History', *History Workshop* vol. 1 no. 4.

Smith, B. (1979) '"Lairds" and "Improvement" in Shetland in the Seventeenth and Eighteenth Centuries"' in, Devine (ed.), *Lairds and Improvement in the Scotland of the Enlightenment*, Glasgow: Scottish Historical Conference.

Smith, H.D. (1974), 'Smuggling Days of long ago' *New Shetlander* nos. 107, 108, 109.

Smith, H.D. (1977), *The Making of Modern Shetland*, Lerwick: Shetland Times.

Smith, H.D. (1984), *Shetland Life and Trade: 1550–1914*, Edinburgh: John Donald.

Smith, R.J. (1986), 'Shetland in the World Economy: A Sociological History of the Eighteenth and Nineteenth Centuries (Ph.D. Edinburgh University).

Taylor, J. (1979), *From Modernization to Modes of Production*, London: MacMillan.

Wallerstein, I. (1974), *The Modern World System*, vol. 1, New York: Academic Press.

Wallerstein, I. (1980), *The Modern World System*, vol. 2, New York: Academic Press.

Wills, J. (1975), 'Of Laird and Tenant' (Ph.D. Edinburgh University.

Wills, J. (1984) 'The Zetland Method' in, Crawford (ed.), *Essays in Shetland History*, Lerwick: Shetland Times.

Wolpe, H. (1980), (ed.) *The Articulation of Modes of Production*, London: Routledge & Kegan Paul.

# 6

## Welfare, Government and the Working Class: Scotland, 1845–1894

IAN LEVITT

Over the past decade there has been a considerable and increasing interest in the way that nineteenth-century industrial Scotland development. Much has been written of industrialism and the promotion of a capitalist ethos. (Checkland 1984: Dickson 1982) Much too has also been written of the impact of this development on Scottish society and social life. (Smout 1986) The phenomenal growth of the towns, the tenement city and the mining areas are well documented; so too are political changes and the consequent growth of an enfranchised democracy. (Hutchinson 1986)

In recent years there has also been a renewed interest in welfare developments. Much has been written of the urban response to overcrowding and tenement life. (Gordon 1985) Similarly there has been a considerable interest in the role of philanthropy in meeting workers' needs. (Checkland 1980) But until now little has been said of the Scottish state's response to these issues and of its contribution to welfare policy. The role of the state, then is the basic theme of this chapter. In examining this subject, I acknowledge the thrust of recent writings, that Scotland's dominant ethos was a mixture of liberalism, capitalism and presbyterianism; and also, that as a consequence of this line of reasoning, the new institutions of the period, both public and private, tended to reflect a different coalition of values than had previously existed. I do not seek to dismiss this assertion outright, but rather to present evidence that can perhaps lead others to question it and undertake further investigation.

I have drawn on my recent work to focus the debate by looking closely at Scottish domestic government from the stance of those who ran it: who they were, what policies they elaborated and what attitude they held towards the working class. (Levitt 1988a, Levitt 1988b) The results of this study suggest that an element of a distinct social group, stemming from the old pre-industrial order, took precedence over the new in shaping a particular style of public policy. Whatever the other influences of the period, the formulation of this policy did have some considerable impact on workers' welfare. I therefore believe that Scottish sociology needs to look more closely at non-capitalist institutions and the way in which their values, beliefs and attitudes were transferred and incorporated into the new order.

Let the chapter begin by presenting a model: welfare management before the reform of the Poor Law in 1845 was largely based on the kirk session, that is the Church of Scotland (presbyterian) kirk-session. (Levitt and Smout, 1979) By and large those who controlled the Session were the local trades and middle-classes, respectable workers and prosperous, but not necessarily wealthy, local professionals, tenant farmers and the like. Invariably they were Liberals or Whigs, with a fair sense of democracy.

The 1845 reform removed control from this body to a parochial board with a sizeable property qualification (£20). It meant local Poor Law administration was in the hands of the large property owner. But the reform also brought in the Board of Supervision, a central-government department (answerable to the Home Secretary), to ensure that the intention of the Act was carried out: that reasonable allowances to the poor were provided. The Board was there both to maintain a consistent policy and to ensure that some reasonable local bureaucracy developed. Its role, ideas and policy, until its replacement by a Local Government Board in 1894, is therefore quite crucial to an understanding of nineteenth-century social policy.

Who then were the Board? The principal full-time officers were the chairman, secretary and the general superintendents of poor.[1] The function of the latter was to visit each parish in their territory once a year and comment on its administration. Occasionally they would also conduct special inquiries. In addition, from 1873, the Board was assisted by a part-time medical officer. Each had a varying responsibility for implementing national welfare policy and throughout the nineteenth century each could elaborate what they thought it should be. How were these officers selected? As with most government of the period, this was by crown patronage. In practice this meant that the appointment of the chairman and secretary was left to whichever party was in power, which apart from Walker's appointment as Secretary in 1852, meant Conservative governments. (Walker was, in fact, appointed during Lord Derby's coalition.) The selection of the general superintendents seems to have been left to the chairman, who made the appointments after some discussion with his secretary.

Who were the Board's officers? The first chairman was Sir John McNeill who was appointed when his brother, Duncan McNeill, was Conservative Lord Advocate. McNeill was the younger son of the laird of Colonsay, Oronsay and Gigha. After a medical degree at Edinburgh, McNeill entered the service of the East India Company as an assistant surgeon and quickly advanced to more senior positions on the North-West Frontier. In the 1830s he became British ambassador at Tehran, and although not entirely successful in thwarting Russian ambitions he returned to Britain with a considerably enhanced political reputation. Like his father and the rest of the family McNeill grew up a Presbyterian, but became converted to Episcopalianism. When in Edinburgh he attended St John's, the same Church as did the Alison brothers.

McNeill's first secretary was John Smythe. Smythe was the second son of Lord Methven, Senator to the College of Justice. The family estate at Methven Castle, Perthshire, covered about 1000 acres. It was said to be very profitable. Smythe was educated at Westminster School and Oxford. After a spell at the English Bar, he transferred to Scotland. He had been Secretary to the 1844 Scottish Poor Law Commission and was largely responsible for its drafting. Apart from being an Episcopalian, Smythe was also a keen Conservative.

When Smythe resigned in 1852 to manage the family estate, his place was taken by William Walker. Walker was the son of an East India Company General who had bought the Bowland estate, 2000 acres, near Galashiels on his retiral from active service. Walker was educated privately and at Oxford, and was subsequently called to the Scottish Bar. Nevertheless his principal interests remained developing his estate and the Scottish Episcopalian Church, which in the 1840s numbered only a few thousand and was virtually non-existent in the southern counties of Scotland. He became editor of the *Scottish Episcopalian Journal,* assisted the foundation of Trinity College, Glenalmond, a public school designed to 'wean' the sons of lairds away from their 'presbyterian tutors', and a number of other church schools. He was reportedly a keen huntsman.

Walker eventually replaced McNeill as chairman in 1868 and his place in turn was taken by John Skelton. Skelton was the son of a sheriff-substitute and was educated in Scotland and at Edinburgh University, graduating in moral philosophy and then in law. Skelton's principal interest, however, lay in literature, publishing regularly in *Blackwoods Magazine,* a Tory journal, and elsewhere. Although he was turned down for the chair of English Literature at Edinburgh in 1865, he began to write enthusiastically of Disraeli's new brand of Conservatism and was quickly rewarded during Disraeli's short premiership of 1868 with the Secretaryship. Although full-time at the Board (and after Walker the Chairman), Skelton continued to publish widely, especially on Scottish sixteenth and seventeenth century history. His best-known work was on Mary Stuart, causing quite a stir as he actively defended her position against what he termed the 'revolutionary' Presbyterians. Like Smythe and Walker, Skelton loved field sport, which he regularly pursued from his Hermitage Estate on the Braids.

Skelton's place as Secretary and later chairman was taken by Malcolm McNeill (in 1892), who had previously been an outdoor officer. McNeill was the nephew of Sir John and had been educated at Eton and Sandhurst. After service in the Seaforth Highlanders he retired with the rank of captain. Episcopalian by upbringing, he regarded himself as an 'ardent' unionist. When McNeill was an outdoor officer he was closely associated with Alex Campbell, the officer for the South Highlands. Campbell was born at Inverawe, Argyllshire and inherited an estate, some 7000 acres, at Lochgilphead. Educated abroad he was commissioned into the Dragoon Guards. After his retiral from the Army, Campbell was called to the Scottish Bar and then settled on his estate where he developed the local volunteer reserve. An Episcopalian, like Walker, he assisted the establishment of Trinity College. Campbell unsuccessfully contested Kilmarnock Burghs for the Conservatives in 1852.

By now the predominant composition of the Board's staff ought to be clear. How can it be summarized? If 'sons of' are included in the following categories, of the fourteen principal full-time staff between 1845 and 1894, the following results are obtained: Lairds, ten, other social groups four; Conservatives, eleven, Liberals, three; Episcopalians, nine, Presbyterians five; advocates and officers, eleven, other occupational groups, three. Indeed, ten of these officers shared at least three of the first named characteristics. Put another way, bar the part-time medical officer, there was not a single urban liberal Presbyterian, either working class or middle class amongst the Board's staff. There was certainly no industrialist. The type of Board created was simple: a Board of Highland Scots.

What did this mean in practice? What kind of perspective of welfare and their fellow Scots did these country officers have? How did they view the role of the state and the Board's own role? That they were predominantly Tory, having a status-orientated view of the world, can be seen through McNeill's own pronouncements. Speaking about contemporary industrial society to an audience at Edinburgh University, he commented:

> The minute division of labour in a highly civilised community reduced the individuals of whom it is composed to a

condition of helplessness... This restriction of man's daily occupation, to what may be truly described as the production of the fractional part of a unit, must have a tendency to narrow and cramp his intellect and prevent him from acquiring versatility of mind and variety of ideas... [and he added] It may be difficult to determine how far this effect of the division of labour ought to be considered as influential in producing that stolid ignorance and indifference to everything intellectual that marks a certain proportion of the population, especially in the large towns. (McNeill c.1856)

The only way forward for industrial Scotland was through moral education, where the working classes could learn, in the same way as farm servants had in the past, through imitation from their betters.

This kind of reasoning meant McNeill was not against a Poor Law or State involvement in welfare. In the new industrial world where there were few natural bonds between master and servant, it was impossible to prevent workers from becoming pauperized. As he told one Poor Law inquiry:

In a country where the relations of society are so complicated, where the occupations are so various, where the arrangements between man and man are a matter of bargain and contract, you cannot keep up the [old] feeling of independence. I do not know that a man who goes about from door to door begging for his food, is more independent than a man who comes to a parish and demands the relief he is entitled to. (Poor Law Committee, PP 1868–9 p. 81)

What that meant was that the 'burden' of supporting the poor had to be transferred from the vagaries of working class charity to property owners, to the 'rich' as he said on one occasion. (ibid. p. 80) These thoughts dominated his early years at the Board. A minute passed in 1848 after Govan had failed to provide adequate relief underlined this. It read, 'the due performance of these obligations [to provide relief] is one of the duties attached by law to the possession of property of a certain value. It is the legal responsibility of which no Parish can divest itself' (Board Minute 6, 4, 48).

Nevertheless McNeill was not in favour of any open-ended commitment to support the new working class. It was a matter of 'balance'. What he meant by that can be seen in his evidence to another Poor Law inquiry. A state system would cost more because:

You can never by any arrangement make a public management precisely as economical as a private management may be, you are to balance between the inconveniences and dangers of the two modes of proceeding. In the one case, if you narrow the circle too much, you may fail to provide the necessary funds, in the other case, if you extend it too much, you may destroy husbandry and economy. (Parochial Assessments Committee, PP 1850 p. 373)

McNeill was therefore a benevolent collectivist, one who believed that whilst only those legally entitled to relief ought to receive benefit, the actual process of administration should not 'oppress' the working class. The system had to be open, fair and just. This can be seen in both his and Smythe's attitude to three of the more socially marginal groups then eligible for assistance, the mother with illegitimate children, the Irish labourer and the vagrant.

Asked on one occasion whether the 1845 Poor Law Act had resulted in greater numbers wandering from parish to parish seeking the best relief, McNeill argued that there was little evidence for this (Poor Law Committee, PP 1868-9 p. 109). His policy, he said, on the contrary, produced a more stable community where individuals had less necessity to seek a casual way of life and become vagrants. Smythe, similarly, agreed. Unless the local police force was greatly increased and the law itself made more penal, whatever vagrancy that did exist could not be reduced (Poor Removal Committee, PP 1854 pp. 252-3). In fact, he said, if these ideas were pursued, it would do nothing more than increase the ratepayer costs (and hence defeat the object of the exercise).

Mothers with illegitimate children struck at the heart of contemporary morality. Not only were such women an indictment against the Presbyterian family ideal, but if their numbers did grow parishes would find themselves subsidizing what many felt was sin. At one Poor Law inquiry Smythe was specially asked whether the availability of parochial relief had actually increased their numbers, that fathers abandoned their cohabitees in the knowledge the parish would provide and that mothers realized extra children would always be supported. He replied that there was little to suggest a culture of dependence because, he said, 'I believe that many women have illegitimate children from a sort of expectation that fathers will marry them' (Poor Law Committee, PP 1868-9 p. 24). It was unlikely that the adoption of a stricter relief policy would alter behaviour.

The 1840s and 1850s had brought a renewed resurgence of Irish immigration into Scotland. With the Irish Poor Law operating a tight system of relief, many parishes in Scotland, particularly in the West, felt they had become a repository of Irish casual labour always on the verge of poverty. Many also thought their habits 'course and sensual', adversely affecting the 'morale' of the 'native working class'. (Poor Removal Committee, PP 1854 pp. 222–4) Between 1845 and 1854, some 6000 paupers were deported to Ireland.[2]

During one inquiry, Smythe was closely questioned on whether he accepted these views. Although he agreed that the Scottish Poor Law did offer considerably higher benefits than the Irish, Smythe refused to accept that migrants moved because they saw a more lenient system. (ibid. 262–4) Indeed when questioned on his 'conscience as a gentleman' he rejected claims that the 'great mass' of Irish in Scotland had deteriorated the morals of the indigenous working class.[3] In fact, Smythe argued, their migration had greatly assisted Scotland's economic development. Many employers found their labour 'excellent' and 'extremely useful'. He, like McNeill, saw little utility in subjecting them to special 'tests', like offering the poorhouse or by introducing an even stricter system of removal. That, he said, would have been unjust.

But McNeill's and Smythe's successors, although accepting much of what they had achieved, entered office during a different period. The 1860s were much more settled than the 1830s and 1840s. Indeed the depression of trade in the West of Scotland following the American Civil war resulted in remarkably little agitation for increased state assistance. McNeill knew he was insisting on a new system to cater for an urban-industrial society. Walker, Skelton and the others could reflect that McNeill's policy had worked. (Levitt 1986) There had been no outcry against the Poor Law in Scotland as there had been in England. But they also saw why not: rates had more than doubled and had been paid by those like themselves, the landed and large property owner. The rate contribution of the working class with their low house-rentals remained negligible.[4] So Walker's views were more cautious. Addressing one audience of the Edinburgh middle-classes he argued:

> It must be confessed that a Poor Law is but a clumsy and unphilosophical expedient to relieve the misery and destitution which, unhappily, result from the artificial condition of society in [industrial] countries... But, inasmuch as the Poor Law is a virtual announcement that all who can establish a claim under it shall be maintained without exertion, at public expense, the natural inclinations of mankind to indolence is directly appealed to, and encouraged. (Walker 1863–4, p. 269)

To Walker there had to be a much greater 'vigilance' against 'imposture': any attempt by the working class not to rely on their own effort, or obtain maintenance from their family. And so from the late 1860s the Board began to instil a new policy amongst parishes. The poorhouse, which had never resembled the English workhouse, was to undergo an administrative transformation and become far more discriminatory in offering assistance. Mothers with illegitimate children, the casual (and often Irish) labourer, the vagrant and those who the parish thought had 'comfortable' relations, were to be 'tested' with rigorous work routines, a leaner diet and much more spartan accommodation. What kind of attitude this created can be seen in two of McNeill's reports as outdoor officer to the Board. In the first, speaking about vagrants, his language appeared considerably stronger than the Board had previously used:

> Scotland, particularly in the southern counties, is annually overrun by tramps from beyond the Border; and the pest threatens to increase, through the influences of efforts, early attended with unlooked-for success, on the part of the northern counties of England, to rid themselves of their vagrant population. (Board of Supervision Report, PP. 1871 p. 55)

He, like Walker, felt a tough policy of offering the poorhouse and an alteration in police powers would reduce vagrancy.

In the second, commenting on the need for a greater work 'test' amongst casual labourers, McNeill argued that, 'probably no native of Great Britain is more plausible in presenting his application for relief than the "Galloway Irishman", and none is more ingenious in devising good reasons for increasing its amount'. (Board of Supervision Report, PP 1877-8, p. 12) They were all, as he later stressed 'ne'er-do-weels', those who refused to lead a moral life, improve themselves and save for retirement. (Commission on the Aged Poor, PP 1895 p. 492) Such sentiments were echoed by Skelton. Addressing one Parliamentary inquiry, he commented:

> The experience of the Scotch poorhouse is, that it has not the deterrent effect upon the Irish paupers that it ought to have. When the Scotch poorhouse is offered to a Scotch pauper, he does not accept it; but when an Irish pauper goes in, the great difficulty is to get him out. (Poor Removal Committee, PP 1879 p. 353)

The 'menace' of immigration could only be combated by a stricter poorhouse régime and by retaining the power of removal.

The other officers were equally adamant at the necessity for the new policy. After an attack by a local doctor on the harm the withdrawal of relief caused children of single mothers, Alex

Campbell was commissioned to undertake a special inquiry. He looked specifically at the effect on four north-eastern parishes and reported that whilst overall births had not declined, illegitimate ones had, albeit by a small margin (Board of Supervision Report, PP 1875–6 pp. 13–19). Despite the fact that children from the latter group remained far more likely to suffer an infant death, the Board's policy, he said, had worked; the mothers 'now looked after the fathers and obtained more assistance from them'. The Board agreed, breaking the culture of dependence meant the 'natural bonds' of family life were being restored. (ibid, p. ix) The children concerned now lived in a 'moral' environment.

The effect of this hardening attitude, not to dismantle a statutory system or to deny its necessity, but to shift the ground of eligibility – to sustain a new morality amongst the working class – was dramatic. By the 1880s the number of paupers dropped by over 30 per cent and the cost (in real terms) to the ratepayers by over 20 per cent.

This 'economic collectivism' had another and perhaps more important result, its impact on the Board's public health policy. Since 1867, it also had to superintend local authority efforts to implement the Public Health Act. (The local authority was the parochial board, unless a burgh already existed or the parish's more populous 'villages' formed themselves into police commissioners.)

The Board certainly faced new problems in implementing the Act. Many local authorities and indeed the local population remained, if not hostile, then bewildered as to why their water supply, their drainage and the care of the sick should be improved. As Walker explained to a Parliamentary Commission in 1870:

> I apprehend that the Act will not be fully carried out in consequence of so very much being left to the discretion of the local authority. We have observed indication that where there is a question of drainage or water supply, they are apt to be alarmed at the unpopularity of the measure. The bulk of the population are not aware of the advantages and they dread the expense, and in some cases within our knowledge even although the local authority had resolved that the water or the drainage was defective, they did venture to proceed without calling a public meeting in order to take their opinion as to whether they should proceed or not. (Sanitary Commission, PP 1871 p. 191)

Yet although the Board felt local authorities were slow to implement what the Act had intended, it faced two particular difficulties with its own policy and its view of welfare. First, the outdoor officers at their annual inspections throughout the 1870s and 1880s continued to press parishes to adopt the policy of 'economic collectivism'. This essentially labelled Poor Law expenditure as 'unremunerative', the ratepayers derived no personal benefit from their contribution to the Poor Rate. (Skelton 1894, p. vi) The Poor Law was simply a collective way of ensuring that basic working-class needs, which could not be provided by the family or by charity, would be met. But to the same parish at the same meeting, the outdoor officers argued that the rate for public-health purposes should be increased, for what the Board suggested was 'remunerative' public investment. It wanted the ratepayers to accept that monies spent on piped water, drains and hospitals was the only way to ensure working-class wellbeing and assist their moral development. Philanthropy or individual effort was not sufficient. The difficulty with this was that the Board had little faith in the more democratically elected police commissioners implementing the Act. Throughout his tenure as Chairman, Walker remained adamant that popular elections would retard sanitary improvement. (Sanitary Commission, PP 1871 p. 193; Housing Commission, PP 1885 p. 10) Those within a parish who appreciated sanitary science – the 'intelligent minority' – in fact, meant the large property owner. (Board of Supervision Report, PP 1870 p. 57) The diffusion of knowledge occurred by 'degrees' from this group to the middle class and on to the labouring poor. (Board of Supervision Report, 1881–2 p. 23) But, of course, it was the property-dominated parochial board that had objected to the increased cost of the New Poor Law, and in practice there was little to suggest they accepted the Board's logic of 'renumerative' public investment. Indeed the evidence suggests that not only were they equally ignorant of sanitary science, but they felt the working class ought to pay for whatever improvements the Board wanted. If poverty was the result of 'indolence' and 'dissipation' then so were working-class slum conditions. For instance at Mid Calder, the parochial board objected to employing a 'fatuous' pauper to clean the streets of 'the poorer classes'. (Levitt 1988a, p. 187) Despite their own houses having 'every convenience' it was up to the workers' themselves to undertake whatever scavenging was necessary. At Leadhills the parish could not see why a byre to every two miners' houses was not sufficient for their sanitary needs. (ibid., p. 200) An outbreak of cholera was unlikely.

The problem over the limits to acceptable 'public investment' can be seen through Walker's own statements. To one inquiry he argued:
> There are many questions regarding the poorer labouring classes in which their material interests are very strongly

concerned, but in which it would be unwise for the State to interfere. For instance, their house accommodation is often extremely bad, and the overcrowding that results from it is most unfortunate, and that affects health; but surely it would not be right or safe for the State to step in and say 'we will provide you with a better house', (Poor Law Committee, PP 1870 p. 266)

Intervention in housing meant securing a 'wholesome' water supply, constructing adequate drainage and preventing overcrowding.

This view reveals the second aspect to the Board's difficulties in tackling public health. It had a particular view of the working class, one that said they were unlikely to respond to whatever provision was provided. Walker freely admitted to the Royal Commission on Housing in 1885 that there was much overcrowding in the towns, but the scarcity of property to rent was not the only cause of the problem. He also argued that many workers did have the choice, but failed to appreciate the 'comforts of better dwellings'. They still preferred 'to pig it' together. (op. cit. p. 6)

It was a view shared right through the Board. W.A. Peterkin, one of the outdoor officers, to the same Commission was asked whether greater powers to introduce sanitary regulations might assist better conditions. He replied not, arguing, 'if you have a large community who have been accustomed for generations back to a particular set of habits and customs, it is impossible to eradicate those habits and customs by an Act of Parliament, or by giving a local authority any power whatever' (ibid., p. 97). His fellow officers were of similar opinion. After one inspection of slum property in Leith, George Falconar-Stewart remarked, 'assuming that new houses are erected, can it be proved that those who occupied the slum property will remove into better-class houses? I fear not. I find the rents paid by the tenants run from 1s to 2s a week, and they seem to grumble at having to pay even these small amounts'. (Levitt 1988a, p. 206).

This fatalism about working-class attitudes and behaviour had dire consequences. At Kirkintilloch, where the Board's own survey revealed between 15 and 20 per cent of the town living in 'damp, dingy holes', it refused to press the Burgh to implement any new improvement scheme, an action fully permitted under the 1890 Housing Act. The Board agreed with the Burgh that the immediate cost would have been too great. It also accepted that the householders should do more to keep their houses and 'their own persons clean'. (Levitt 1988a, p. 217)

What can be said about the administration of welfare in nineteenth-century Scotland? First, the government's executive, the Board of Supervision, was dominated by a particular social group. Second, although it initially held a Tory and paternalistic view of welfare, this changed to one of 'economic collectivism'. But this new view held a difficulty, on the one hand it said state welfare was about compelling the working class, through a residual Poor Law, to respond to the urban challenge. Those who had failed to secure regular work, or failed to save for retirement, or had illegitimate children, were simply 'ne'er-do-weels'. They required little sympathy. Indeed they should lose all their rights.[5] But on the other, it pressed for public-health measures designed to increase ratepayer expenditure. It was important to prevent the spread of disease. Yet if the working class was 'dissolute', and if, as one of their officers felt, squalor was 'hereditary', then it was not at all clear how far the ratepayer should tax himself for their sanitary health. (Board of Supervision Report, 1891-2 p. 7).[6] A 'wholesome' water supply, a more efficient system of nuisance removal and hospital provision might prevent the mass outbreak of infectious disease (and protect the middle class), but its impact on working-class 'habits' would remain minimal. They would still prefer to 'pig it' in overcrowded dwellings.

The Board, then, remained uncertain of the new industrial working class. Born into a country life, educated predominantly at English public schools and entering the established professions, its officials retained an element of the old Toryism: they looked at the working class as their ancestors had regarded their farm servants, hopeful that they would respond and imitate their betters, but pessimistic about the outcome. In the 1890s, instead of a social policy sustained by a desire to positively incorporate them into society, the Board's understanding of the way ordinary industrial Scotland was developing meant all it could offer was greater 'vigilance' on 'imposture' and even further restraint on behaviour. (Board of Supervision Reports, PP 1889-90 pp. 26-7; PP 1890-1 pp. 8-9; PP 1891-2 pp. 7-8). If the working class could not be trusted to seize the opportunity for self-improvement, then the state had a duty to compel them, by stricter inspection of their homes, by the use of labour colonies, and by tougher laws on vagrancy. The old values had certainly been incorporated into new welfare institutions, but by ignoring alternative explanations for urban overcrowding and family break-down, the Board could only retreat towards an ultimately narrow view of collectivism. State provision was not there to enhance – or protect, as Sir John McNeill had argued – it was there to control, direct and, if necessary, penalize. The alternative was a working class 'demoralized' by doles and lacking in the rudiments of any moral 'sense'. (Commission on the Aged Poor, PP 1895, pp. 492, 497)

The administration of nineteenth-century welfare in Scotland was dominated not by new forces, the new wealth, the industrial capitalists that ruthlessly exploited the natural and labour resources around them, but by an older set, one that looked back to an earlier, seemingly golden period. Scottish government meant the laird, who as was said of Skelton, sought the quietness of country life, but instead 'lamented the encroachment of Morningside suburbia' *(Scots Pictorial*, 1897, p. 434).

NOTES
1. Only the chairman was a full-time member of the Board. The part-time members included three sheriffs, two crown representatives, the solicitor-general and the Lord Provosts of Edinburgh and Glasgow.
2. Settlement, i.e. a right to relief from the parish, was either by place of birth or through five years continuous residence. Hence the recently migrated Irish or those that moved around seeking work were at risk in being deported.
3. McNeill, to the same inquiry, stated that although he could not accept such statements, he did accept that many emigrated to receive better relief.
4. An alternative method of raising a poor rate, by 'means and substance' (i.e. a local income tax) had, by the 1860s, largely been abandoned. Administratively it had proved to difficult to collect. Land-owners were also incensed by the fact that industrial property, which was increasing in value, attracted substantial rate deductions.
5. For instance: comment by McNeill on poorhouse inmates, 'every ounce of labour of which you are capable belongs to the public', and letter from McNeill on a mother's right of access, 'she is not entitled to prescribe to [a parish] how their duty is to be performed'. (Board of Supervision Report, PP 1875–6 p. 13: quoted in Levitt 1988b, p. 32).
6. He had previously stated that 'cleanliness' was 'somewhat foreign' to their 'nature' (Board of Supervision Report, PP 1887–8, p. 24).

REFERENCES

*Official Papers*

Board of Supervision Minutes, 1845–94, in Scottish Record Office, HH23.
PP 1871, Report of the Board of Supervision, 1870, vol. XXVII.
PP 1872, Report of the Board of Supervision, 1871. C. 462 vol. XXIX.
PP 1876, Report of the Board of Supervision, 1875–6. C. 1627 vol. XXXII.
PP 1878, Report of the Board of Supervision, 1877–8. C. 2166 vol. XXVIII.
PP 1882, Report of the Board of Supeervision, 1881–2. C. 3321 vol. XXX.

PP 1888, Report of the Board of Supervision, 1887-8. C. 5500 vol. L.
PP 1890, Report of the Board of Supervision, 1889-0. C. 6121 vol. XXIV.
PP 1891, Report of the Board of Supervision, 1890-1. C. 6442 vol. XXXX.
PP 1892, Report of the Board of Supervision, 1891-2. C. 6725 vol. XXXIX.
PP 1870, Report of the Select Committee on the Poor Law (Scotland) vol. XI.
PP 1895, Royal Commission on the Aged Poor, Evidence. C. 7684-1 vol. XIV.
PP 1884-5, Royal Commission on Housing, Scottish Evidence. C 4409-1 vol. XXXI.
PP 1871, Royal Sanitary Commission, Evidence. C. 281 vol. XXXV.
PP 1850, Select Committee of the House of Lords on the Laws relating to Parochial Assessments. 1850 vol. XVI.
PP 1868-9, Select Committee on the Poor Law (Scotland), Evidence. vol. IX.
PP 1854, Select Committee on Poor Removal, Evidence. vol. XXII.
PP 1878-9, Select Committee on Poor Removal, Evidence. vol. XII.

*Books and Articles*

Checkland, E.C. (1980), *Philanthropy in Victorian Scotland*, Edinburgh: John Donald.

Checkland, S., and E.C. (1984), *Industry and Ethos*, London: Arnold.

Dickson, A. (ed.) (1982), *Class and Capital in Scotland*, Edinburgh: John Donald.

Gordon, G. (ed.) (1985), *Perspectives of a Scottish City*. Aberdeen: Aberdeen University Press.

Hutchinson, I.G.C. (1986), *A Political History of Scotland, 1832-1924*, Edinburgh: John Donald.

Levitt I., and Smout, T.C. (1979), *The State of the Scottish Working Class in 1843*, Edinburgh: Scottish Academic Press.

Levitt I. (1986), 'Poor Law and Pauperism', in J. Langton and R.J. Morris, *Atlas of Industrialising Britain, 1780-1914*, London: Methuen.

Levitt, I. (ed.) (1988*a*), *Government and Social Conditions in Scotland, 1845-1919*, Edinburgh: Scottish History Society.

Levitt, I. (1988*b*), *Poverty and Welfare in Scotland, 1890-1948*, Edinburgh: Edinburgh University Press.

McNeill, Sir J., (*c*1856), *On the Working Classes*. Edinburgh: Edinburgh Philosophical Institute.

*Scots Pictorial* vol. 1 (1897), 'John Skelton'.

Skelton, J., *Report on Local Taxation in Scotland*. C. 7575 (PP 1894 vol. LXXIV).

Smout, T.C. (1986), *A History of the Scottish People, 1830-1950*, London: Collins.

Walker, W.S. (1863-4), 'The Effects of Poorhouses . . .', in *The Poor Law Magazine*.

# 7

## Patronage and Professionalism: The 'Forgotten Middle Class' 1760-1860

### A.A. MacLAREN

Harold Perkin, writing in *The Origins of Modern English Society, 1760-1880* first coined the term 'forgotten middle class' to describe the non-capitalist or professional middle class which he regarded as a crucial element 'playing a part out of all proportion to its numbers' within the class structure (1981, p. 252). Perkin argues that professional occupations such as university professors, clergymen, lawyers and medical practitioners constituted a separate and distinct class. Although these occupations were not entirely divorced from market forces they enjoyed incomes which were not the direct consequence of market bargaining but were related to the value placed on these occupations by society, partly as a result of their persuasive strategy. Of these professions

> the first ... was that of the clergy, whose income, significantly, was called a 'living': an income set aside by the laity ... to enable them to perform their office. The second and third were those of law and medicine, in which fees might seem to bear some relation in detail to piece-rates and in aggregate to profits. Yet fees, too, were not in theory fixed by competition, but by the value set by the profession and accepted to society, on services which the client could not judge and had therefore to take on trust (1981, 253-4).

In the tradition of Durkheim (1957) and following writers such as Carr-Saunders (1928) and Marshall (1964), Perkin maintains that the fundamentally altruistic nature of the professions and their cooperative rather than competitive spirit meant that

> their ideal society was a functional one based on expertise and selection by merit. For them, trained and qualified expertise rather than property, capital or labour, should be the chief determinant and justification of status and power in society (1981, p. 258).

Such had not always been the case. In the 'old society' there had been numerous cases of 'pettifogging attornies' and dishonesty and fee snatching. Perkin sees the real change as a consequence of the Industrial Revolution 'which emancipated the entrepreneur and the wage earner, [and] also the professional man' and marked the transition from dependence on the patronage of the rich and powerful, which had been the notable feature of such professional occupations in the eighteenth-century society (1979 p. 254). From the Industrial Revolution there emerged a learned and respectable professional man distinguished by high ethical standards of conduct which in turn were subjected to self-regulation and discipline within his profession. Above all, recruitment into the profession was by merit and authoritative scholarly examination. In short, the bonds of patronage derived from rich benefactors were finally broken and replaced by authentic professionalism based on merit.

The purpose of this chapter is to start to explore three fundamental propositions contained in Perkin's argument. These are first, that professionals constituted a separate and distinct class; second, that the Industrial Revolution broke the bonds of patronage in the manner described; thirdly, that the attitude of these 'new' professionals regarding the determinants of status and power differed significantly from their business associates. These three propositions will be examined on the basis of evidence relating to the emergence and development of four liberal professions in the city of Aberdeen over a hundred-year period (c. 1760–1860). Whether or not these professions have been 'forgotten' in Perkin's sense of the word, they certainly can be regarded as neglected as an area of research on Scottish society. At the same time therefore the purpose of this study is to offer a contribution to the understanding of the development of the professions and professionalism in Scotland. The four professions to be examined are university professors, clergymen, lawyers and medical practitioners. In fairness to Perkin it should be recalled that his three propositions are concerned with England, and no claim is made on his part regarding the circumstances prevailing in Scotland in the same period. It follows that, if the evidence tends to confirm the propositions, it might be assumed that a similar pattern prevailed in Scotland; on the other hand, if the evidence is contrary, this would not by itself be enough to discount these propositions regarding English society, where significant differences in class structure might be expected.

The first part of the chapter provides a very brief outline of the changing economic and social structure of the city from c.1760 to 1860; the second part gives an overview of the professions and goes on to examine them in two related but separate sections; finally some reflections are made on Perkin's three propositions.

## Economic and Social Change in Aberdeen 1760–1860

In line with other main Scottish cities in this period Aberdeen underwent a rapid transformation in its population and its economic and social structure. From a population of around 12000 in 1750 the city grew nearly six-fold to about 72000 in the 1850s.[1] However the rate of growth was not even and would seem to be related closely to the demand for labour in the local economy. Three broad although overlapping phases can be discerned; each of which possessed its own dominant economic and social characteristics whilst also containing the essential constituents of future growth.

In the fifty years after 1750 the population more than doubled and had reached 26000 by the turn of the century. This was a phase characterized by an overall stability in terms of both economy and society. The dominant industry was without doubt the stocking trade, which was conducted on a domestic form of production involving not just the city but also drawing on the rural hinterland where stocking manufacture also provided a vital supplementary income for the payment of agricultural rents. Within the city the stocking manufacturers formed a close kinship network bound by business partnerships and marital ties (Donnelly 1981, p. 30-1). However not all of these families were to survive the crisis brought on by the Napoleonic Wars. Those families that did survive successfully diversified into factory production of linen, woollens and cotton, to make textile manufacturing the most important single industry in the city by the beginning of the nineteenth century.

In the first thirty years of the nineteenth century, the rate of population growth reached remarkable proportions; in the three decades down to 1831 there was a decennial increase of 29.6, 25.7 and 29.5 per cent in each decade respectively. Whilst a proportion of this growth must be put down to natural increase – the population of Scotland showed an average decennial increase of about 13.5 per cent in these three decades – it is clear that most of the gains were made at the expense of the rural hinterland, which underwent a relative decline in the same period. The increase in population reflected the employment opportunities available in the city with the development of a dynamic industrial capitalism. Textiles remained the main source of employment but other industries such as shipbuilding, engineering, ropemaking, and paper and comb manufacturing contributed to the drawing power of the local economy. In these thirty years an industrial working class was created as a consequence of the successful entrepreneurial efforts of the families that had begun the industrialization process towards the end of the century, and throughout these years they maintained their dominance over all the economic institutions of the city.

In the third phase, between 1830 and 1860, the rate of population increase slowed notably. By the fifth decade in the nineteenth century, something approaching a rough equilibrium had been achieved between city and hinterland; the decennial increase 1851-61 in the city dropped to 5.5 per cent, which was marginally less than the increase for the rest of the county. In this phase economic growth fluctuated dramatically as the local economy became more and more exposed to wider capitalist crises. At the beginning of the phase textile manufacturing remained the main source of employment. By 1860 employment in textiles was no longer significant as a consequence of the closure of the main mills in the 1840s following a series of economic and financial disasters. The old ruling families who had held power in the city since the eighteenth century were bankrupted and demoralized. The survival and eventual recovery of the local economy have been explained in terms of its overall diversity.[2]

However, in at least one fundamental aspect of population Aberdeen differed radically from Dundee and other urban centres in Scotland. The population of the city was far more homogeneous than any other comparable urban centre. The 1851 census shows that out of a population of about 72000 less than 20000 were derived from outside the city or county. The influx of the Irish, which was a particular feature of the 1840s in other Scottish cities, was notably absent from Aberdeen.[3] Indeed the number of English residents slightly outnumbered the Irish. However, if this remarkable homogeneity of the Aberdeen city population was overall its most distinctive feature, it is clear also that the city between 1760 and 1860 underwent three demographic phases.

In these hundred years, then, the population of the city increased by six-fold from around 12000 in 1760 to about 72000 in 1860. Three broad phases can be identified: the period from 1760 to 1800 when the population doubled; the period from 1800 to 1830 when the growth averaged close to 30 per cent per decade; and the period from 1830 to 1860 when the population growth slowed, eventually falling away to a rate of growth broadly similar to that of the county. These three periods reflect extensive changes in the local economy which in turn had profound and far-reaching effects on the social structure. The effects of these changes on the four professions under review shall now be considered.

*The Professions: An Overview*

Whilst it is self-evident that the occupational nature of university professors, ministers of the church, lawyers and medical practitioners are remarkably different, it is possible to argue that these occupations bear a similarity to each other in a number of features. It could be maintained that these occupations all enjoy, perhaps to differing degrees, some measure of protection from full exposure to the market forces, which are a paramount feature in determining income in capitalist society. Thus, for example, a minister's stipend might bear a relationship with the overall wealth of the parish, which in turn would make one parish perhaps inherently more attractive than another. Generally, however, a stipend would be 'fixed' and not related to whether another person would be willing to undertake the work for less financial return than the incumbent. Broadly, these arrangements applied to all of the other three occupations, although, as we shall see, economic 'competition' was probably more evident in some cases than in others.

This relative freedom from market forces, it has been held, would allow these occupations to adopt a more generous attitude of co-operation among their own kind rather than the competition which prevailed between capitalists, and between capitalists and workers. This co-operation would take a number of forms but would certainly include some measure of internal discipline by means of institutional controls over practising members' professional ethics and behaviour. As we noted earlier, it has been argued by Perkin and others that factors such as these acted to demarcate a class which should be regarded as separate and distinct; a class liberated rather than created by the Industrial Revolution in the sense that it broke free the bonds of patronage and dependency and adopted a true professionalism based on merit.

In examining the four professions, it is helpful to follow Friedson (1970, p. 232), who argues that scientific knowledge should be distinguished in its pure and applied form. Thus professions can be classified broadly into two groups: scholarly (pure knowledge) and consulting (applied knowledge). In the first group can be placed university professors and ministers of the Church (hereafter referred to as ministers), both of whom arguably might claim to have access to pure knowledge. In the second group lawyers and medical practitioners (hereafter referred to as doctors) can be seen as consulting professions. It is recognized that this classification has certain drawbacks in that considerable overlaps might be expected to occur between professors who also practised as lawyers, doctors and ministers. Likewise in the nineteenth century many ministers might deny the distinction between scholarly and applied knowledge. However, as we shall see, the distinction remains a useful one.

## Scholarly Professions

Until 1860 the city possessed two universities which were quite separate in all aspects of administration, funding and the conferment of degrees. Both were ancient institutions. King's College was founded in 1495 and Marischal College in 1501. Broadly all chairs were replicated within each institution. Both universities stood on the present sites of the two colleges which meant that Marischal College was much more of a city university than King's, which lay in Old Aberdeen on the outskirts of the city. Although the professoriate at King's tended to sneer at Marischal, which had very run-down buildings, it is clear that by the beginning of the nineteenth century Marischal College was a much more progressive institution. Although as far as student numbers were concerned King's continued to hold some reputation in its Arts and Divinity classes, Law was weak, and Medicine had declined to the point of virtual non-existence. There is also some evidence to suggest that the content of the education may have been significantly different.[4] However, if certain differences can be detected between the two institutions, these are largely of a qualitative nature and the professoriate of both institutions can be treated as one regarding the process of professionalization.

Whilst not unexpectedly some changes occurred in the period from 1760 to 1860 regarding the professional status of university professors, what is remarkable is how little that change was. Anderson (1987 p.28) has pointed out how professors 'tended to see their chairs as freeholds' which carried certain rights to income 'rather than as professional men or as employees, either of the state or of the university'. The tendency was to regard their appointments as a form of sinecure to which was attached certain undefined property rights including among other things the possibility of choosing a successor. Professors were appointed for life, once they had taken up their appointment, little could be done to ensure that they carried out their duties satisfactorily. Professor Alexander Bannerman, who was appointed to the chair of medicine in 1792, thereafter gave one lecture in the next twenty-two years. On his death the chair passed to his son, who continued the same tradition (Rodger 1893, p. 70). Both practised as doctors and saw the chair as 'family' property. Indeed there are a number of examples of chairs being passed from father to son and brother to brothers.[5] In some cases a limited form of market control acted against such conventions in that the professor was entitled also to the fees of the students who enrolled in the class. However, where a class historically had long ceased to attract students, there was no effective inducement to recommence it. It was generally recognized at the time that the professors of medicine have never been in the practice of delivering lectures in that science, or on surgery, in either of the colleges; and, of course, no students have, at any time, attended them for the purpose of medical instruction (Kennedy 1818, p. 119-20).

It was not until the death of Bannerman in 1839 that King's College ceased to be 'hampered by an inactive professor of medicine' (Rait 1885, p. 225).

Whilst medicine suffered particularly badly in this respect at both universities, it is clear that it was not the only subject to be treated by its incumbents in this fashion. In 1824 the Senate under some pressure went as far as to suggest that those concerned with the provision of lectures in Divinity, Law and Medicine should perform their duties, but not one of those concerned found themselves able to comply with the Senate request either by lecturing themselves or by providing a substitute (Rait, p. 215-17). Indeed it was normal practice for a professor to nominate his successor by appointing a substitute who might well undertake the real work of the chair for many years for a small salary on the basis that he would eventually inherit the full appointment. Senate rarely saw the need to object to such a practice which was seen as a rational solution in the absence of funds for pensions. Nepotism of this sort was also defended as being a convenient means by which a professor's son or relative could be made 'familiar with the work and could have his qualities observed by his future colleagues' (Anderson 1987, p. 41). Such an arrangement stands much closer to a form of training apprenticeship which was the practice in medicine and law (see below), rather than any commitment or belief in selection by merit.

Professors were prepared to make a stand occasionally on a matter of principle regarding their appointment, but this was unusual and remarkable. An eminent and well-publicized case occurred in 1839 on the appointment of John Stuart Blackie to the chair of Latin in Marischal College. Blackie refused to sign the Confession of Faith 'except in his public professional capacity' and the Presbytery of Aberdeen maintained that he could not fill the chair under these conditions and another appointment was made in his place. The deposed Blackie then appealed to the Court of Session, which declared that the Presbytery had no rights in the matter and he was reinstated. This was the first challenge of the Test Act, which was amended in 1853 so that it no longer applied to lay chairs (Bulloch 1895, p. 184-5). On the whole however professors were reluctant to take such risks regarding their appointment. When the Disruption of the Established Church took place in

1843 even those professors most inclined to support the Evangelical cause forsook their previous position for fear of losing their appointment; the most notable example being Principal Daniel Dewar of Marischal College (MacLaren 1974, p. 221).

By and large pressure for change came from outside the profession itself and took the form of parliamentary commissions. The first of these was set up in 1826, but it was not until the colleges were finally joined by Act of Parliament in 1859 that the basis was laid for future reform of the profession.

It is difficult to detect any significant development away from patronage towards a general advancement in professional ethics. As Anderson (1987, p. 28) points out, university professors 'did not feel a need to elaborate a special ethical code or to adopt strategies for improving their social status which was already high'. Neither can the Senate be seen as a professional body seeking to impose a code of behaviour on its members; rather it reflected the interests of its constituent members, who regarded the defence of academic freedom in the same light as the maintenance of their academic property rights. Likewise it would be mistaken to see the process of industrialization in the city as having any immediate effects in terms of 'liberating' the profession. On the contrary the profession – if it can be so described – fought to prevent such an occurrence by resisting attempts to impose any new bureaucratic structures on the universities which might have led to changes in contractual arrangements.

It is when we turn to examine the other scholarly profession – ministers of the church – that the close links between them and the professoriate are evident. It was from the ministers that the divinity professors and indeed many of the arts professors were recruited. Divinity professors served as parish ministers before being appointed to their chairs. In a church with no bishops, the professoriate was the only permanent office above parish level. A typical pattern would be for 'ministers with academic tastes or ambitions . . . to settle in a country parish rather than a busy city one, so that they could attract attention to themselves by some work of Biblical commentary or ecclesiastical history' (Anderson 1987, p. 41).

However, in other important respects, ministers in this period suffered a conflict which led them to differ quite radically from university professors. The Disruption of the Church of Scotland in 1843 ostensibly took place over the fundamental issue of patronage in the Church, and the rights of patrons to 'intrude' their nominee upon the parish. Opposition to patronage in the Church of Scotland had a long history and had led to previous secessions in the eighteenth century. However the schism on this occasion was far more serious and about a third of the ministers left the Establishment to form the Free Church. The crisis developed over the ten-year period leading up to 1843 as the parties involved struggled for legislative dominance over the General Assembly of the Church. Although the crisis in the Church ran much deeper than the issue of patronage and was exacerbated by underlying social structural features (MacLaren, p. 1974), it would be true to say that as far as the professionalization of the ministry is concerned, the Disruption marked a distinct watershed in the process.

Whilst in 1760 a minister would be presented by a patron's recommendation with the acquiescence of the presbytery, by the middle of the nineteenth century clerical patronage had ceased largely to be of any real significance. By then kirk sessions and congregations chose and ordained ministers to serve in the respective churches; these ministers already having been educated at a university, tested and formally licensed by a presbytery as suitable candidates for the ministry. If this was certainly true of the Free churches in the city, it was by and large the case with regard to the Established churches, which were soon to follow their example. Although it is possible that Aberdeen may have differed in degree from other Scottish cities in this respect, since at the Disruption all fifteen ministers seceded (MacLaren 1988), the trend towards professionalism is clear enough and was likely to be replicated in other cities.

Presbyterian clergymen of the two major denominations – Church of Scotland and the Free Church – would appear to fit the model of professionalization in a manner very different from that of the professoriate. Formal patronage had been, or was being, eliminated by a combination of principle and necessity. Strict criteria were enforced regarding entry to the profession in terms of qualifications, competence and moral behaviour. A professional body (presbytery) ensured observance of the first two and maintenance of the latter. No minister could be presented to a charge, or leave to take up another, without a certificate from the presbytery as to his worth.

The main impetus in the process of 'liberating' the clergymen from the constraints of patronage can be related to the social-structural changes associated with the process of industrialization. These have been examined and analysed elsewhere (MacLaren 1983, 1988). However, whilst the clergymen were released from the former bonds of patronage, paradoxically they were now constrained by the same social forces which had been a decisive element in obtaining their release. There is little doubt that popular selection was accompanied by its own petty tyrannies. As far as the clergy were concerned liberation from the bonds of patronage was not necessarily accompanied by freedom of expression. Indeed, one of the consequences of the Disruption was to draw the clergy into a closer economic relationship with their new middle-class sponsors.

As far as the scholarly professions are concerned, a remarkable difference can be seen between the experience and attitudes of university professors and ministers of the church in these years. Whilst the latter broke away from the bonds of eighteenth-century patronage, the former continued to regard the rights of patronage as a form of heritable property to be retained as far as possible within their own possession. The effect of industrialization and social-structural change was very evident with regard to the professionalization of the clergy but resulted in little internal change with regard to university professors. Both professions were held in high esteem by society, and it followed that neither needed to consider advancement of their social status as a professional strategy. Although liberated to a considerable extent from the bonds of patronage, clergymen were much more tightly drawn into the bourgeois social structure than university professors, who were more independent of the need to respect market forces. However, the professoriate could scarcely be regarded as some form of moral vanguard seeking to advance the meritocratic society. On the contrary, if one can determine a uniform attitude it was one more easily seen as rooted in eighteenth-century privilege than emanating from ideas of nineteenth-century liberalism. We shall now examine the consulting professions.

*Consulting Professions*

It has already been noted that considerable overlaps occurred between the professions in so far as the professoriate was regarded by ministers of the church as an avenue of mobility for those with academic inclinations. This was also true to some extent of both lawyers and doctors. Generally, however, both these professions would not regard a university chair as a sufficient source of income by itself. Appointment to a chair was regarded as a status symbol and a useful additional source of income. This fact was recognized in the salaries attached to university chairs in that, in both law and medicine, the basic salary was considerably less than in other subjects (Royal Commission 1858, pp. 114–15, pp. 130–3).

Both law and medicine differed from the scholarly professions, however, in that acquirement of qualifications did not necessarily require any university attendance. Both professions employed a system of apprenticeship. Whilst broad comparisons might be made with the custom of appointing 'substitute' professors, supposedly to train them and to appraise their future worth, the form of apprenticeship practised by law and medicine tended to distinguish them effectively from their scholarly counterparts. It was customary for individuals to be apprenticed to a practising lawyer or doctor for a specified fee. Rodger (1895, p. 57) describes the process by which an indenture was arranged in the 1780s between Dr. William Chalmers, then professor of medicine at King's College, and the son of John Ross, weaver in the city. The agreement required his son to serve five years with strict penalties for absences 'in the capacity of house servant and apprentice'; 'to reveal none of the secrets of his business'; and to abstain from 'gaming, debauchery and bad company'. Such an arrangement was typical of both professions at the time, although it was not customary for those indentured to a lawyer to undertake household chores.

Indeed, the evidence clearly indicates that lawyers had progressed much further down the path of professionalism in the 1780s than their medical counterparts, whose learning retained a mystical near-magical aspect in the popular mind. The craft itself was ill-defined in terms of the distinction between surgical skills and medical knowledge. Many doctors acted as tradesmen in that they found a lucrative supplement to their income in the running of somewhat dubious but certainly profitable chemist shops for the supply of proprietary medicines. William Chalmers, mentioned above, acted as professor of medicine, practising doctor, and traded as a chemist. Throughout the hundred years under review, the absence of any effective body governing the profession made control over such activities very difficult. Nevertheless that is not to say that the profession, which remained profitable and attractive, did not wish to regulate itself and control such practices. Some of the problems of doing so are discussed below.

By and large, lawyers were much more clearly identified with the leading city families from whom many were recruited. The close-knit family and business relationships of the eighteenth-century city ensured in itself a professional standard, but as well as this a long-standing professional body – the Society of Advocates in Aberdeen, which drew members from throughout the north-east – exerted a degree of control over the behaviour of its members.[6] Whilst apprenticeship was a characteristic universal to all lawyers it is clear that attendance at Arts classes in either university increasingly became a normal and expected feature. Thus an examination of all lawyers admitted to the Society of Advocates between 1760 and 1799 reveals that of the 42 admitted

18 had not attended university. In the period from 1800 to 1829, of the 152 admitted, only 5 had not been at university; the last of the 5 being admitted in 1813. There was also in this latter period a remarkable increase in the numbers graduating as opposed to merely attending classes. (See Table 2) What is clear is that soon after the beginning of the nineteenth century a university education came to be regarded as an expected norm of a practising solicitor. In this aspect at least the legal profession was similar to that of members of the scholarly professions, although it is possible that the Aberdeen situation differed from elsewhere. Certainly this was not the case, till much later, in a large English city such as Birmingham.[7]

Table 2: **University Education of all lawyers admitted to the Society of Advocates in Aberdeen, 1760-1860**

|  | Graduates | Alumni | Total | Not Students |
|---|---|---|---|---|
| 1760-99 | 14 | 28 | 42 | 18 |
| 1800-29 | 70 | 82 | 152 | 5 |
| 1830-60 | 29 | 65 | 94 |  |
| **TOTAL** |  |  | **288** | **23** |

*Note:* The King's and Marischal College students have been combined. However, of the grand total of 288 students only 44 had attended King's College.

*Source:* These figures are derived from a head-count of all entries in, J.A.H. Henderson, *History of the Society of Advocates in Aberdeen,* Aberdeen, 1912.

Whether the wider development of university education and the considerable expansion in numbers of practising solicitors can be seen as a freeing from the bonds of patronage is difficult to assess effectively. Aberdeen solicitors had a long-standing reputation regarding their acquisitive natures. It was believed (in 1804) that they were 'so very sharp' that, had they been 'allowed to practise in London, they would in seven years have the fee simple of the whole of the county of Middlesex' (Henderson 1912, xii-xiii). At the same time not all solicitors saw the rapid social change taking place as commendable. William Kennedy[8] an eminent solicitor in the city, writing when the social divisions and other evils associated with industrialization were beginning to make themselves apparent, recalled the stability of the eighteenth century when the stocking trade had been conducted by many individuals to the benefit of the whole community. It was a trade which provided support for all by creating

> a never failing source of employment to the young and the aged of every description, to the deaf and the dumb, and

even those who were bedridden or disabled from every other kind of work (Kennedy 1818, p. 198–9).

Certainly, if the rapid industrialization between 1800 and 1830 caused new social problems, it also created a vast number of new economic opportunities for solicitors prepared to move into speculative enterprises. In a sense Kennedy represented the staid old ways of conducting business within the eighteenth century. When he died in 1836 (at 77 years) this period had long since passed. Many of the new legal men emerging were ambitious, aggressive and innovative in terms of business procedures. Few were bound by customary practices. One such man was Alexander Anderson[9] who in a fifty-year career became associated with numerous city financial institutions and investment companies. His reputation was fearsome and his period as Lord Provost in the city has been commemorated by the naming of Anderson Drive in his memory; a road aptly described recently as being like the man himself, viz. 'fast, wide, and dangerous to cross'.[10]

Whilst there is an element of methodological risk in viewing either of these men as necessarily typical of the legal profession, it is certainly the case that both were firmly rooted in the particular class structure of which they were a part. Neither Kennedy nor Anderson can be seen as representing separate class interests. If Anderson expressed any new professional identity freed from the bonds of patronage it took the form of successful money-making rather than any critique based on ideas of social justice and merit. Indeed fundamentally Anderson was simply a highly successful entrepreneur.

Not unexpectedly, when one turns to examine medical practitioners, remarkable differences are apparent in terms of the process of professional development. Although, like the lawyers, the medical practitioners maintained a system of formal apprenticeship as the cornerstone of professional training, admission to the profession could be obtained in a number of other ways. Indeed of the four professions under consideration, access to medicine was by far the most open. For example both Aberdeen universities operated a formal procedure of conferring medical degrees by recommendation rather than attendance. This was a similar pattern to that of St Andrews, but different from the Universities of Edinburgh and Glasgow, both of which produced well-trained graduates (Loudon 1986, p. 183). The normal requirement at Aberdeen was for a candidate to be recommended by a physician known to him and upon paying the requisite fee a degree would be conferred upon him. Even a cursory audit of the degree lists indicates that the majority of degrees conferred related to unknown candidates; many from England and some from abroad (Anderson 1893, p. 130-75, 1898, p.120-81).

Such a ready and useful means of raising money meant that at times scandalous errors were possible. In 1791 Marischal College took legal advice from the Solicitor-General regarding one of their medical graduates, who had been given a degree with little investigation or consideration as to his worth. As a consequence the Senate sought a means of 'degraduating' him for 'notorious and impudent quackery', but were informed that they had no power to expel because once a degree had been conferred, it became 'a matter of civil right or property which cannot be taken from him'. They were warned that 'it would be most prudent for them to submit to silence' and make the case 'a lesson of caution and circumspection to themselves for the future, in the bestowing of academical degrees' (Anderson 1898, p. 133-4). Minor scandals continued however. From as far away as Suffolk came the complaint that apothecaries 'after a few years in their shops' were in the habit of buying an Aberdeen or St. Andrews' MD and setting themselves up as physicians (Loudon 1986, p. 144).

In 1817 a series of new regulations were enacted at King's College regarding the conferment of medical degrees, which among other things required the recommendation of two physicians of eminence and 'an account of the classical, literary and scientific [sic] education of the candidate'. In 1825 a joint agreement was reached with Marischal College along the same lines. The net result of the tightening up of the regulations was that between 1826 and 1839 the total number of degrees conferred amounted to only 29 (Rait 1885, p. 210, 212-13) and partly as a consequence regulations were again relaxed.

For those unable to gain entry to the profession by means of an indentured apprenticeship qualifications could be obtained by other means. As a consequence of the Napoleonic Wars the armed forces found themselves desperately short of medical officers. In an attempt to alleviate the shortage the government sought to recruit 'young men of ability' from the universities. Placards were placed on the gates of King's and Marischal Colleges offering surgeons' commissions to Arts students 'who could pass some slight examination'. Others went abroad to practise as doctors 'with no more medical education than could be got from a little hospital practice and some medical books'. One eminent doctor began his career when 'at seventeen he went to Greenland with a sailing whaler as surgeon' (Rodger 1893, PP. 127, 104, 138). The East India Service attracted others. Patronage was a strong element in obtaining posts. Sir James McGregor, son of an

Aberdeen stocking merchant, rose to become Director of the British Army Medical Board. It was said of McGregor that 'he favoured Aberdonians before all'. Many of those recruited into the army and colonial service returned later to practise medicine in the city. Others saw Aberdeen as a stepping-stone to higher things and left to set up practices in Edinburgh and London: 'It was not that [the Aberdonian] valued culture little, but that he valued wealth more. Life was hard in his home, severe in its simplicity, and he who could learn to live in Aberdeen was safe to make his way anywhere' (Rodger 1895, PP. 203, 100).

What is remarkable about the medical profession as compared to the lawyers is the openness of recruitment. Such ease of access was clearly not conducive to the inculcation of a professional behavioural ethic, and, moreover, was likely to lead to economic competition for patients in what was believed by many to be an 'overcrowded profession' (Hamilton 1981, ch. 4 *passim;* Loudon 1986, pp. 208–23). Indeed it would seem that even those not able to pay fees and, therefore, least able to capitalize on the competitive situation, were able to do so. One Aberdeen doctor recorded that 'the sick poor are frequently tempted to apply to several medical men at the same time' and, still being dissatisfied, to seek the help 'of some ignorant empiric' (Henderson 1822, p. 17). Although by the 1820s some attempts are under way by the universities to restrict and control the conferment of degrees by specifying minimum qualifications, it was not until the 1860s that anything approaching effective controls are evident within the universities. Outside the universities – albeit with the support of certain members of the professoriate – there grew up a Medical Society which initially was no more than a students' debating chamber. Founded by a group of medical students in 1789, its early years were dominated by a struggle for survival in the face of a generally uninterested, and in some cases hostile profession. Entry to the society was regulated by a vote of all members and the need to maintain, or indeed obtain, respectability was a dominant theme. New entrants were sworn not to 'tell anybody who is not of the Society any of our proceedings so as to make sport of them or make the society or any of its members be thought of disrespectfully'.[11] Ultimately the Society survived and prospered under the patronage of a number of eminent doctors. Gradually it emerged as an institution which exercised a measure of control regarding entry into the medical profession but in this it lagged behind the older and broadly comparable Society of Advocates in the city.

*Conclusions*

Perhaps the first and most obvious conclusion which arises from the examination of university professors, ministers of the church, lawyers and doctors is the remarkable diversity which is evident between each of these occupations. Indeed the main difficulty is to achieve meaningful generalizations. Whilst it is possible to distinguish between scholarly and consulting professions, the distinction is not always clear, particularly with regard to recruitment into the ranks of university professors.

Moreover even after occupations have been allocated to either one of these categories, significantly different characteristics can be observed. Thus if professors and ministers can be grouped together in that they share the scholarly aspects of their respective professions in terms of recruitment, it is clear also that the differences between them are great. Whilst professors are intent on defending the rights and privileges of patronage in the universities and are remarkable for their lack of change in these hundred years, considerable steps have been taken in the eradication of patronage within the major Presbyterian churches. The behaviour of the clergy is also subject to strict regulation whilst university professors are under little or no bureaucratic control. Indeed, as we have seen, there is a strong case for the argument that the church may have been affected more than any of the other professions as a social consequence of industrialization. However, if freed from the overt bonds of patronage, many of the clergy were now subtly secured to the needs of their economic sponsors.

Regarding the consulting professions, similarities can be detected in the form of indentured apprenticeships practised by both lawyers and doctors. Thereafter comparisons become more difficult. In 1760 lawyers had gone much further down the path towards professionalism than any of the other occupations. Ethical behaviour was overseen by a professional institution, and by the beginning of the nineteenth century attendance at university was regarded as a concommitant feature of a lawyer's education. At no time can one detect lawyers being bound by any shackles of patronage; on the contrary the evidence suggests entrepreneurial involvement. Doctors were the least professional of the four occupations in terms of recruitment and were similar to the university professors regarding the lack of any effective institution concerned with the control of ethical standards. There is evidence that patronage, in terms of career advancement, was increasing rather than decreasing throughout the period.

Certainly as far as Perkin's three general propositions are concerned it is difficult to see how any of these professions could be regarded as constituting a separate class. Ministers, lawyers and doctors were embedded separately and in different ways within the developing capitalist middle class. University professors differed from the other three in this respect in that they, in a sense, represented something approaching a pre-capitalist conception of occupational property rights. One deviant profession can scarcely be seen as constituting a separate class.

Neither can the second proposition be substantiated that the Industrial Revolution broke the bonds of patronage in terms of these occupations. It can certainly be argued that social-structural change as a consequence of industrialization was of paramount importance in ending formal patronage in the church. Indeed the support of new and powerful elements within the bourgeoisie was a vital factor in achieving what was, in effect, the replacement of formal patronage by an informal variety. Industrialization certainly had important short- and long-term effects on these professions but in much broader terms than the narrow issue of patronage. Likewise the proposition that the newly emancipated professional men held social perspectives differing significantly from their business counterparts would be impossible to substantiate, certainly at the grass-roots level of each of their professions. One would expect from the evidence already assembled[12] that their viewpoints and attitudes would do more than reflect the great diversity of the professions they represented.

Whether Aberdeen can be regarded as typical, or as differing substantially from other Scottish cities, is uncertain. The most useful comparison in terms of size might be made with Dundee. However, unlike Aberdeen, this city was not endowed with a university, and the validity of such a comparison although interesting, would not be entirely satisfactory. It is possible that the absence of an easy access to a local university might lead to a greater emphasis on the apprenticeship system in both law and medicine. However, this does assume local recruitment into these professions and this may not have been the case. As far as the scholarly professions are concerned considerable geographical movement took place among professors and clergymen, but little evidence presently exists relating to consulting professions. One might suspect that lawyers and doctors, being more exposed to the vagaries of market forces, would respond more readily to economic opportunities available elsewhere. Such an assumption presupposes a model of economic man which may well be historically irrelevant. Certainly there is little or no evidence from the Aberdeen consulting professions to support an inward migration to the city of qualified lawyers, and with regard to doctors the initial impression would appear to be that those coming in to the city had prior Aberdeen connections in terms of family, education or apprenticeship. It is possible that the remarkable social homogeneity of the city's population may have acted as a formidable 'exclusive' feature to 'outsiders'. On the other hand many Aberdonians left the city to make their fortunes elsewhere. One is led to suppose that the professionals who remained were similar to, if perhaps less prosperous than, their Edinburgh or Glasgow counterparts.

### NOTES

1. The population figures in this section are derived from Mitchell and Deane (1962). For a more detailed account of city development see MacLaren (1974).
2. R.E.T. Tyson, 'The Economy of Nineteenth Century Aberdeen: An Overview'. Paper read at Centre for Scottish Studies, University of Aberdeen, October 1987.
3. The 1270 Irish were outnumbered by resident English. It is possible that even this number was inflated by the presence of railway navvies engaged in the construction of the railway, which reached the outskirts of the city in 1850. The small Irish presence might be explained by the city's relative isolation, combined with a sharp decline in job opportunities in the 1840s, coinciding as it did with the high-point in Irish emigration. *Census of Population* 1851; Watt (1903, p. 118-19). See also Saunders (1950, p. 130).
4. For example it is interesting to note that of the twenty-seven ministers ordained in Established and Free city churches between 1830 and 1860, sixteen had attended university in Aberdeen, eight at King's and eight at Marischal. All but one of those educated at King's remained in the Established Church; all those attended at Marischal were in the Free Church (see MacLaren 1974, p. 221-4).
5. An obvious example is that of the Gregory family who between 1725 and 1765 passed the chair of medicine at King's College from father to son, and then to brother (Rait 1885, p. 194).
6. The Society was an old one, founded in 1633 or earlier. 'Only those of good character, education or ability were admitted as members...' (Henderson 1912, ix-xii).
7. Reported by Andrew Rowley in discussion following his paper Professions, Class and Society: Solicitors in 19th century Birmingham', read at Annual Conference of British Sociological Association at the University of Edinburgh, 1988.
8. For an account of the life of William Kennedy, see Henderson (1912, p. 238).
9. For an account of Alexander Anderson and his many activities see Henderson (1912, 83-4) and Munro (1897, 84-6).
10. B. Balfour, 'No mean Aberdonians: Some Aberdeen entrepreneurs'. Paper read at Centre for Scottish Studies, University of Aberdeen, October 1987.

11. Rule 15 of the Regulations governing the Society. Despite the small number of founding members (12-14), the early years were marked by a considerable degree of internal squabbles and disagreements leading to 'desertions' and 'expulsions', often over non-payment of fees and fines. See Aberdeen Medico-Chirurgical Society Minute Book 1789-92.
12. A wider study is currently being undertaken by the author as part of the University of Aberdeen's Quincentennial Celebrations.

REFERENCES

Anderson, P.J. (1893), *Officers and Graduates of the University of King's College*, Aberdeen.

Anderson, P.J. (1898), *Fasti Academiae Mariscallanae Aberdonensis*, Aberdeen.

Anderson, R.D. (1987), 'Scottish University Professors 1800-1939: Profile of an Elite' in *Scottish Economic and Social History* 7.

Bulloch, J.M. (1895), *A History of the University of Aberdeen*, London.

Carr-Saunders, W. (1928), *Professions: Their Organisation and Place in Society*, London.

Donnelly, T. (1981), 'The Economic Activities of the Aberdeen Merchant Guild, 1750-1799', *Scottish Economic and Social History 1, no. 1*.

Durkheim, E. (1957), *Professional Ethics and Civic Morals*, London.

Freidson, E. (1970), *The Profession of Medicine*, London.

Hamilton, D. (1981), *The Healers: A History of Medicine in Scotland*, Edinburgh: Canongate.

Henderson, J.A.H. (1912), *History of the Society of Advocates in Aberdeen*, Aberdeen.

Henderson, W. (1822), *Observations on the Medical Attendance of the Poor in Their Own Homes*, Aberdeen.

Keith, A. (1936), *The North of Scotland Bank Limited*, Aberdeen.

Kennedy, W. (1818), *Annals of Aberdeen*, vol. 2, London.

Loudon, I. (1986), *Medical Care and the General Practitioner 1750-1850*, Oxford: Clarendon Press.

MacLaren, A.A. (1974), *Religion and Social Class: The Disruption Years in Aberdeen*, London: Routledge & Kegan Paul.

MacLaren, A.A. (1983), 'Class Formation and Class Fractions: The Aberdeen Bourgeoisie 1830-50' in, G. Gordon and B. Dicks, *Scottish Urban History*, Aberdeen University Press.

MacLaren, A.A. (1988), 'The Disruption of the Establishment: James Adam and the Aberdeen clergy' in, J. Smith and D. Stevenson, *Aberdeen in the Nineteenth Century: The Making of the Modern City*, Aberdeen University Press.

Marshall, T.H. (1964), *Class, Citizenship and Social Development*.

Mitchell, B.R., and Deane, P. (1962), *Abstract of British Historical Statistics*, London: Cambridge.

Munro, A.M. (1897), *Memorials of the Aldermen, Provosts and Lord Provosts of Aberdeen*, Aberdeen.

Perkin, H. (1981), *The Origins of Modern English Society 1789-1880*, London: Routledge & Kegan Paul.

Rait, R.S. (1885), *The Universities of Aberdeen: A History*, Edinburgh.

Rodger, E.H.G. (1893), *Aberdeen Doctors at Home and Abroad*, Edinburgh.

Royal Commission (1858), *Report on the State of the Universities of Aberdeen with a View to their Union,* Edinburgh.

Saunders, J.J. (1950), *Scottish Democracy 1815-1840,* Edinburgh: Oliver & Boyd.

Watt, W. (1903), 'Fifty years of progress in Aberdeen' in *Transactions of the Aberdeen Philosophical Society,* Aberdeen.

# 8

## The Domestication of 'Fallen' Women: The Glasgow Magdalene Institution, 1860-1890

LINDA MAHOOD

In Glasgow, as in other industrial cities in the mid-nineteenth century, interest groups were increasingly dissatisfied with the role of prisons and poorhouses in controlling young female misdemeanants, paupers and orphans. Reformers were critical of state institutions and the penal system for the part they played in 'hardening' young female offenders, particularly those charged with sexual misconduct. It was argued that bringing women charged with sexual offences before the court and subjecting them to prison sentences aided their corruption. Reformers did not object, however, to incarcerating 'fallen' women provided that they were not incarcerated with 'criminals'. Their solution was to establish non-statutory female penitentiaries, to entice these women into direct care early in their careers and supervise their reformation. This involved persuading a woman to commit herself 'voluntarily' to a long period of incarceration in a magdalene institution, where she would be subjected to moral education and industrial training, and taught to accept middle-class standards of femininity.

In *Visions of Social Control* (1985), Cohen uses the concept of 'destructuring' to describe the process whereby interest groups attempt to decrease the size, scope and intensity of the formal deviancy-control systems. Cohen identifies a paradox whereby as a result of destructuring in the 1970s, the entire criminal justice system expanded. There is evidence of a similar paradox at work in the female penitentiary movement as it developed throughout Britain in the mid-nineteenth century. The liberal and reformist programme designed to save women from the criminal justice system resulted in the expansion of the entire system, which began to include more women of a greater age-range and type of offence. The purpose of these penitentiaries was not to incarcerate professional 'prostitutes' or female felons, but part of the population not previously reached, namely those variously defined, as 'prostitutes', 'magdalenes' and 'fallen' women. The process therefore became more interventionist than it was at the beginning of the century, as a greater percentage of the female working class became potential clients. Instead of reducing the amount of stigmatization, labelling and the overcrowding of prisons, intervention came earlier, and was more intensive, as it swept in more forms of deviance, through extension to women not yet formally adjudicated.

Recent work on the history of sexuality and Victorian prostitution demonstrates that labels such as 'prostitute' cannot be regarded as a valid or ahistorical category. Foucault's work on sexuality traces the historical construction of sexualities (Foucault 1980). His argument can also be applied to the 'prostitute', which he does not directly examine. Contributions from feminists demonstrate that the 'prostitute' occupied a symbolic place in the sexual and class structure in the nineteenth century. For Walkowitz, the 'prostitute' was an object of class guilt and fear, and the 'symbol of economic exploitation' (Walkowitz 1980, p. 4). Hellerstein *et al.* (1980) argue that the symbol of the 'prostitute' was used to threaten women who defied established gender roles. Nead, on the other hand, explains that the image of the 'prostitute' as a 'wretched outcast' was an attempt to deflect the political threat of working-class women (Nead 1987, p. 68).

Studies of rescue work are less perceptive. They either argue that rescue work failed because philanthropists maintained an insufficient understanding of the causes of prostitution, or because the 'prostitutes' were intractable (Finnegan 1979). Other studies focus only on the significance of rescue work to the lives of middle-class women (Prochaska 1980), which helped them to carve out a place for themselves in public life (Walkowitz 1980, p. 131). This view of rescue work overlooks the fact that it was not an 'adversary to or alternative form of "patriarchal" state intervention, but a specific "political technology" in its own right' (Wood 1982, p. 75). Although these studies are more useful than the past tradition of portraying rescue work as an idiosyncratic pastime of Victorian gentlefolk, they overlook Donzelot's assertion that philanthropy was not an apolitical private intervention in social problems, but a 'deliberately depoliticizing strategy for establishing public services at sensitive points midway between private initiative and the state' (Donzelot 1979, p. 55). Wood, following Donzelot, maintains that in the guise of dispensing material aid and advice, philanthropy was also implicated in the execution of a 'familialist strategy' which functioned to 'depoliticize poor working class communities' (Wood 1982, p.75).

The purpose of this chapter is to examine the activities of the Glasgow Magdalene Institution, a non-statutory female penitentiary which opened in Glasgow in 1860. It will show that the Magdalene Institution constituted a 'technology of power'; a social-control apparatus designed for the surveillance, sexual and vocational control and moral reform of a segment of the female working-class population: chiefly, women whose dress, behaviour, appearance or vocation, rather than their criminal records, led to their being labelled as 'prostitutes'. As will be seen, these labels were censures applied to women who defied middle-class notions of feminine propriety (Sumner 1980). Attempts to define the 'prostitute' therefore, were not just technical, but deeply political.

*The Glasgow System for the Repression of Vice*

Evidence of a public discourse on the prostitution problem can be found in the stream of tracts and essays published throughout the nineteenth century. Public interest intensified, however, in the 1840s around the time that the Registrar General began to publish statistical inquiries into the living conditions of the nation's poor. These studies defined many of the traditional rural and urban working-class living arrangements as social problems and aroused a wave of social consciousness in many, who awakened to what they called 'the moral state of the nation'. The Scottish establishment had long claimed moral superiority over its European neighbours and was shocked by statistical exposés, especially those which reflected badly on the morality of Scottish women (Thomas 1861 p. 3).

Of these studies, prostitution became one of the most popular and frequently replicated. Between 1840 and 1890 Scottish moral reformers, notably, Wiliam Tait in Edinburgh, and Ralph Wardlaw and William Logan in Glasgow, and numerous evangelical clergy, physicians, professionals, local state representatives, and Owenite socialists contributed regularly to the discourse on the problem of prostitution. They were joined by local branches of the National Society for the Promotion of Social Sciences and the National Association for the Repeal of the Contagious Diseases Acts. In their analysis of the causes of prostitution these individuals and groups focused on the morality of working-class women. They were disturbed by the presence of large numbers of women, especially mill-girls in the streets, pubs and theatres, whom they described as 'unescorted', drunken and seducing men and leading them off to rooms or the Glasgow Green. On the behaviour of women at the Glasgow Fair, one observer remarked that he had never seen so many drunken women or heard such 'profane and filthy language in his life' *(G.M.I.* 1863). The argued that when the morals of the female were that low, it was logical that the morality of the male would follow. In order to elevate the moral tone of the working class, moral education and domestic training were prescribed for women. If moral reform was an attempt to remake working-class culture, as sociologists argue, then it appears that for contemporaries, the fastest path to reconstruction lay in controlling women.

In Glasgow part of the solution to containing disorders caused by women in the streets was the implementation of the 'Glasgow System', which was the system of police repression used to clean up street prostitution after 1870. The Glasgow System, can in part, be attributed to the zeal of the directors of the Glasgow Magdalene Institution, who marched into the Magistrates' Committee general meeting on 20 December 1869 and demanded that attention be paid to the 'great and growing' prevalence of 'prostitutes' in the streets (Mahood 1987; *Magistrates' Committee Book*, 1869; *Chief Constable's Book*, 1869). The Glasgow System was also promoted as an alternative to the Contagious Diseases Act (1864–1886), which was threatening extension to Scotland in the 1870s (McHugh 1980; Walkowitz 1980). It was composed of three institutional responses to the prostitution problem. These were regarded as encompassing 'repressive law, municipal vigilance, and organized benevolence' *(The Glasgow System 1881,* p. 4). The Lock hospital was a charity designed for indigent women with venereal diseases who were considered to be 'prostitutes', although only 496 out of 4147 patients gave it as their occupation (Patterson 1882, p. 408). The Magdalene Institution was also a charity. Its policy was to reclaim females who had been 'led astray' from the 'paths of virtue' and to 'dry up sources of prostitution' and repress the growth of the 'Great Social Vice' in Glasgow *(G.M.I. Annual Report* 1862). The final component of the system was the Police Act (1866), which provided the municipal police force and magistrates with extensive new powers to imprison or fine 'prostitutes' and brothel-keepers and to enter any establishment suspected of harbouring 'prostitutes'. This Act, however, like the preceding ones, remained a 'dead letter' until the appointment of Alexander McCall as Chief Constable in 1870.

The powers under the Glasgow Police Act (1866) which dealt with prostitution stated that 'every prostitute, or nightwalker loitering in any road or street, court, or common stair, or importuning passengers for the purpose of prostitution shall be liable to a fine of 40 shillings or 14 days imprisonment' *(Select Committee* 1881, p. 381). This legislation did not require that a complaint be filed against a woman by a private citizen, the testimony of a constable was enough for a conviction *(Select Committee* 1881, p. 372). The only 'test of a prostitute' was that she was 'known to be going about the streets by the police, following no other occupation, and earning her living in that way' *(Select Committee* 1881, p. 373). The problem with this 'test' was that it could be applied to any woman, including the unemployed and casual labourer found in the streets who could not give a satisfactory account of how she earned her living. The Chief Constable admitted that this legislation could be oppressive, but he dismissed the possibility of mistaken identity by claiming that there was no difficulty in finding out whether a woman was a 'prostitute' *(Select Committee* 1881, p. 382). He was confident in the abilities of constables who testified against these women. 'You may well know a prostitute as you would know a sweep', he explained: 'a man with a black face may not be a sweep, but at the same time you would say he was a sweep' *(Select Committee* 1881, p. 382).

The authorities did not stop with the suppression of prostitution *per se*. They were also concerned with reforming the women who were directly and indirectly affected, and to this end the Lock hospital and the Magdalene Institution were eager to assist the police. The Lock hospital performed the curative function and the Magdalene Institution played the reformatory role and they depended upon each other for the exchange of inmates. Before a woman was admitted to the Magdalene Institution she was expected to submit to a compulsory medical examination by the Institution's surgeon. If found to have venereal disease, she was sent to the Lock hospital to be treated. Following this she was sent back to the Magdalene Institution where she would be expected to stay for two years.

## The Glasgow Magdalene Institution

The history of the Glasgow Magdalene Institution and the changes in its policies and definition of target clientele allow us to identify three distinct phases in the Institution, which illustrate the process of the expansion of social control apparatuses in Glasgow. The Magdalene Asylum opened in Glasgow in 1815 as a refuge for the 'newly fallen' daughters of 'pious parents' (McGill 1819, p. 26). In 1840 it was converted into the House of Refuge for Females, which admitted girls under the age of sixteen who had been charged with minor criminal offences. By the late 1850s the directors concluded that this arrangement was no longer suitable. They argued that there was a clear difference between a 'magdalene' and a 'criminal', that the two categories should not be mixed and that the wrong populations were being admitted to the refuge while desirable clients were being kept out (Bryce 1859, p. 4). Their solution was to establish a new institution. The new Magdalene Institution opened in 1860, and by 1875 it could accommodate 180 women in its two houses. It was founded by a group of Glasgow merchants, bankers, industrialists and various professionals. Many of them were also members of the Association for the Promotion of Social Sciences. Their interest in the social sciences led them to compile detailed 'moral statistics' about the inmates. From the all-male board of directors were appointed various committees, the activities of two are of particular interest. The Repressive Committee was responsible for establishing an enlightened public sentiment on the question of public morality. Between 1860 and 1890 this included lobbies for amendments to, and strict enforcement of the Police Act, rallies against the Contagious Diseases Acts, campaigns against nude models in the art school, the banning of the 'demoralizing influences' of working-class theatres, public exhibitions and, most notably, the Glasgow Fair. The Reclamation Committee was responsible for the daily activities in the Institution which included the education, training, and placement of the inmates, who successfully completed their training.

To summarize, the Magdalene Asylum was initially intended to divert young women charged with sexual misconduct from the prisons and poorhouse system. The contradiction, however, was that they never intended to accept professional 'prostitutes'; they were only interested in the newly 'fallen'. In other words, their idea of a 'prostitute' was not a pre-existing woman who was readily identifiable by her criminal record. On the contrary, the directors developed their own definition of a 'prostitute'. The 'prostitute', like Foucault's homosexual, acquired a 'personage... a case history, and a childhood... ' (Foucault 1980, p. 43). But unlike homosexuality, prostitution was a vocation and a sexuality, and both were reformable. The 'prostitute' was a product of the discourse which the directors controlled. In the first case, she was a 'magdalene', an 'unhappy daughter' of the poor but honest working man, sentimentally modelled on popular perceptions of Mary Magdalene in the Bible (Bristow 1977, p. 67). In the second case, the House of Refuge was intended to divert young offenders from the adult courts. While the new Magdalene Institution was a second attempt to divert criminals and juvenile offenders away from 'magdalenes'. Clearly then, with each change in the internal management the directors redefined their clientele, and demanded the right to pick appropriate candidates for their programme, and in doing so they actually created the subjects who would benefit from their programme and diverted those who would be liabilities to other institutions.

As stated, the Magdalene Institution focused its attention on the young women who might respond positively to its programme for the least amount of cost (Rafter 1983, p. 293). The directors preferred women under twenty-four, who were not drunk, pregnant or 'diseased' at the time of admission, and who were judged to be of reasonable intelligence and willing to submit to discipline (Finnegan notes a similar policy in the York penitentiary). In other words, from among the women driven from the streets of Glasgow by the repressive régime of the city's police, only a fraction would have reasonably expected to find shelter in the Magdalene Institution. While it was hoped that they would come voluntarily, inmates were generally referred by various mission agencies, philanthropic citizens, the Lock hospital and increasingly the police. The directors described the inmates as having been brought up in poverty with little or no education. The family background of the inmates indicates that the majority were from the lower working class. Eighty-two per cent were in their late teens and were either orphans or from single-parent families. One quarter were sexually active before they reached sixteen, and one-half by the age of eighteen. The occupations given by inmates indicate that seventy-five per cent were low-ranking domestic servants or unskilled factory labourers who worked in trades which were poorly paid, frequently overstocked and vulnerable to seasonal unemployment. Inmates' employment patterns indicate that many either drifted from job to job and/or engaged in full or part-time prostitution until they were driven from the streets by the police, or until they contracted venereal disease and entered the Lock hospital and subsequently decided to enter the Magdalene Institution. These characteristics of the inmates should not be generalized to Glasgow's 'prostitute' population however. What the statistical information indicates more clearly is that the selection process operating in the Institution was a function of two premises: the directors' perception of the causes of prostitution, i.e. lack of education, early sexual experience, broken homes, and employment in the 'public' sphere; and their model of reform which required 'newly fallen' young women who would respond quickly to their programme.

*Moral Reform: The Domestication of 'Fallen' Women*

Recent studies (Brenzel 1980; Finnegan 1979; Rafter 1983; Walkowitz 1980) of statutory and non-statutory female penitentiaries have demonstrated that institutions like the Magdalene Institution developed a variety of techniques of social control to encourage moral reform: the incarceration of women for sexual misconduct;

infantilization; intensive moral education and industrial training; disruption of family ties; an informal parole system; emigration; and the transfer of 'problem' cases to state institutions where they could be held indefinitely.

The first step in the domestication process was the initial act of 'voluntary' incarceration, thereby separating inmates from unacceptable family members, friends and former support networks. The act of incarcerating women for sexual misconduct was used to protect them from being further corrupted or from becoming hardened 'prostitutes'. At the same time, it protected society from the spread of contagious diseases. The process of targeting women and not men for sexual behaviour supported the double standard by punishing only women.

The two moral reform mechanisms used by the Institution were moral education and industrial training. The first was accomplished through a régime of hard work and Bible reading. Each inmate received her own Bible as soon as she had learned to read. The significance of this, in the Institution's view, was that the scriptures would reveal the extent of the inmate's sin, defilement and guilt, and that she would learn to accept herself as a 'sinner'. Therefore, her punishment took the form of guilt and prayer as opposed to the régime of head shaving and solitary confinement used in Magdalene asylums earlier in the century (Bristow 1977; Checkland 1980). By individualizing punishment, the directors, could gloss over the consequences of class inequalities, poverty and hypocrisy which were responsible for her troubles (Finnegan 1979). Furthermore, through Bible stories, inmates were taught a morality centred on self-sacrifice and duty. Through the Christian chain of command which paralleled the Victorian social-class hierarchy and sanctioned female inferiority, self-abnegation and duty, she would learn her appropriate gender-role and social-class position.

Many of the letters sent to the matron suggest that the feelings of humility, subservience and loneliness dominated these women's perceptions of themselves and their situations, which was probably the reason that they were selected for display in the annual reports. It was interpreted as a sign of deep 'penitence' and true reformation.

> Dear Miss Nott, . . . my brother, telling [sic] me that his wife and himself freely forgive me, and if I do what is right that they will make me their sister, as I ought to be; so you see I have much to thank God for – the only friends of my own that I wanted to think of me are going to love me as a sister. And see the other friends that I have got. I want you to pray for me

every day, that I not get proud of my sinful self because my friends are so kind to me. I want to make everybody like me, but I want to be very humble *(G.M.I. Annual Report* 1877).

In addition to religious education, inmates were provided with a general secular education which ranged from reading and writing, to special classes in geography, financial management, music, singing, and weekly lectures on 'homely and interesting' subjects and Gospel Temperance meetings *(G.M.I. Annual Report* 1873, 1886). Education classes were intended to be a pleasant break from the other activities of the day, and it was considered important that inmates develop their minds. With the exception of the paid work in the laundry, what is striking about the evening curriculum and special events is the overall gentility and similarity to the manner in which middle-class women might spend their evenings. The emphasis on gentility reflects how closely penitentiaries associated middle-class manners and tastes with reform. It was not intended that inmates become learned or 'ladies', but rather that they appreciate the values associated with being a 'lady' (Rafter 1983, p. 296).

*Industrial Training: Proletarianization*

Education was supplemented with training in domestic service and laundry work so that inmates, having been taught the 'dignity of labour' would be able support themselves after they left the Institution. The majority of inmates had previous experience as domestic servants, but by their past employment records, they were considered unsatisfactory workers. The Institution intended to return inmates either to the labour force as competent and submissive domestics or as industrious factory labourers.

The process of training inmates for domestic service employs the social control mechanism of infantilization. From the moment women entered the Institution they were reduced to the status of children. They were supervised by a 'motherly' matron and 'fatherly' directors, and after they were released would either be sent back to their families or placed in service where they would continue to have a dependent status. Rafter argues that the very concept of an institution dedicated to the rescue and reform of women over eighteen, was rooted in the perception of women as child-like (Rafter 1983, p. 299). As stated, over one-half of the inmates were former servants, and if the directors saw the contradiction in sending women back into the very same situations that had got them into trouble in the first place, they soothed their consciences with the knowledge that the education inmates received would neutralize and fortify them against 'evil influences and temptations' *(G.M.I. Annual Report 1859).*

One quarter of the inmates had previous work experience in mills and factories. The directors obviously recognized that not all of the inmates would be suitable for domestic service. Considering the large number of orphans and the growing demand for female factory labour, they included industrial training in the Institution's laundry in their régime. Laundries were a common feature of penitentiaries because they helped to cut the cost of inmates' confinement. More important, laundry work served a symbolic function: through laundry work women daily performed a cleansing ritual. They enacted penance for their sins and purged themselves of their moral contagion (Bristow 1977, p. 66; Walkowitz 1980, p. 221). It is not surprising then, that the directors of the Glasgow Magdalene imbued it with great moral significance. Laundry work, they reported, '[is] . . . not only more healthful and more remunerative, but, in its moral tendencies, far superior to needlework . . . [which] is monotonous and less profitable' *(G.M.I. Annual Report* 1877). Throughout the 1870s and 1880s laundry work became an increasingly important part of the Institution's activities. The directors boasted that it not only paid for two-thirds of the cost of maintaining the home, but also played an indispensable part in training inmates for 'future usefulness':

> It would be no kindness to the inmates merely to give them the shelter of the Homes for a given period, and to keep them in semi-idleness, the condition of idleness having been the bane of many of them in the past. On the contrary, an endeavour is made to impress them with the dignity of labour, and to teach them self-respect and independence, thus raising them to a higher moral platform, to breathe a purer and nobler atmosphere *(G.M.I. Annual Report* 1879).

In order to pass this entrepreneurial spirit on to the inmates the directors introduced a profit-sharing system. Premiums varying from one shilling to 7s 6d were allocated to girls according to merit, conduct, industry and the class of promotion obtained. Thus, every inmate would be made to feel that the prosperity of the Institution, '[was] her prosperity in which she [had] a direct personal interest' *(G.M.I. Annual Report* 1879).

## A Fresh Start: Informal Probation and Community Surveillance

Moral education and industrial training was followed by an informal system of probation and community surveillance. The directors claimed that the two-year residency in the Institution provided inmates with a fresh start in life. They hoped that the education and industrial training plus the 'elevating' influences of the Ladies' Committee would provide inmates with the surrogate family so many lacked.

> When the girl ... is once more out in the world, the Homes have a new function to discharge for her help and benefit. To them she turns as indeed a home, and to the Matron as indeed a mother, without this tie maintenance of the cure would in many cases be followed by relapse. *(G.M.I. Annual Report* 1859).

'Cure' was announced when an inmate displayed a 'change of heart', which was believed to indicate her conversion to a new way of life. What the Magdalene Institution intended for their futures, and the social position to which they could properly aspire was, however, directly related to class. They believed that with the proper help and guidance it was possible for an inmate to rise to a respectable position within the working-class community. In cases where inmates took positions as servants in middle-class homes it was never intended that they should disguise their past. The opportunity to serve 'respectable' people was definitely implicit in what they meant by a 'fresh start'.

In order to ease the transition upon leaving the Institution, which the directors acknowledged was considerable after two years, they established an informal parole system. Inmates were expected to keep in touch with the Institution for at least six months, and were invited to come back to the home for advice or assistance in case of difficulty. Representatives of the Ladies' Committee made regular visits to girls in their new situations, and paid bonuses to ex-inmates who 'behaved' in their new employment for at least six months. It is clear then, that there was certainly some incentive to remain in contact with the Institution. A great deal of evidence suggests that former inmates returned to the Institution for advice and assistance in times of need. Former inmates who moved out of Glasgow wrote regularly to the Institution to inform the Matron of marriage, birth of children, career success, general well being and to collect their bonuses. The bonus, incidentally, was really just the balance of the money she had earned in the laundry.

Between 1860 and 1890, 16 per cent of the inmates were placed in domestic service. Considering the fact that the Ladies' Committee was frequently popping in, the ex-inmate's personal life would have been a source of common gossip throughout the household, where she may have been regarded with suspicion and hostility and victimized by members of the household, as the following letter implies:

> Dear Miss Nott, . . . I was glad to hear that some of the girls got situations, which I trust will be good ones . . . You say in your letter you hope I had a good cause for leaving my last place. I will explain to you someday the reason. I used to blame the girls for running away from their place . . . God helped me, and I was restrained from doing wrong . . . *(G.M.I. Annual Report* 1877).

It can be concluded, then, that in many cases a 'fresh start', at least in the sense of an anonymous past was impossible.

In addition to domestic service the Institution returned approximately 22 per cent of the inmates to their families if they were considered to be suitable. Inmates often assumed the position of unpaid servants in the homes of relatives. Household service and kinship obligations overlapped a great deal in the nineteenth century and it would not have been regarded as unusual to expect a young woman with no marriage prospects to spend her life looking after ageing relatives (Davidoff 1974, p. 411).

In cases where the family was unsuitable the Institution established strategies for the 'disruption of family ties' (Rafter 1983, p. 299) in order to ensure that inmates were not reunited with troublesome relatives. In some cases the directors arranged for inmates' emigration to the colonies, where they hoped that away from the corruption of the overcrowded cities they would have the opportunity to live respectably. Others were placed in 'respectable' employment in Britain far from their families. Without their own families it was hoped that inmates would continue to identify with their 'surrogate' family in the Institution, and were not exposed to contradictory value systems or tempted to return to their old ways. In the following case the writer was obviously aware of the contradiction, and wanted to ensure that the Matron knew that she was attempting to deal with it.

> Dear Miss Nott . . . my father was down seeing me on the Fast-day. When they came and told me I was quite surprised to seen [sic] him. He told me that the way [sic] that he did not write he was out of town working, and he was wishing he could come and see me. I am glad that he is not drinking any now . . . The master and them all was quite surprised to hear that he had come to seen me. I thought that I would just write and let you know that I had seen him *(G.M.I. Annual Report* 1878).

The Institution's efforts to become a surrogate family, and in the process to break down traditional working-class values and support networks, is a 'familialist strategy': an attempt to depoliticize poor working-class communities at the same time as it effected an increasing insinuation of non-familialist agencies into the family nexus (Wood 1982, p. 75).

## Domesticated Working-Class Women: Ideal Wives, Mothers, Workers

In relation to the question of marriage, the annual reports indicate that many inmates married in the years following those spent in the Institution. The Ladies' Committee regarded these marriages with some ambivalence. They were obviously uncertain of the suitability of 'fallen' women for marriage and motherhood. In one case, the Committee assured the subscribers that the man in question had 'been honestly dealt with ... Nothing [was] concealed from him that he ought to know' *(G.M.I. Annual Report* 1866). But on the whole, they appear to have accepted that inmates would marry and raise children. In fact they suggested that after receiving the 'benefits' of the Institution, former inmates made ideal wives for working-class men. The case of E.K., is typical of this attitude. They were 'pleased' to report that she 'lived comfortably with her husband, making a tidy wife and mother. She has frequently called at the Home since, and it is quite a pleasure to see how respectable she looks and how nicely she and her little son are dressed. Both herself and her husband are in full communion in the Church' *(G.M.I. Annual Report* 1864).

The Institution was aware that not all inmates would make suitable domestic servants or candidates for the marriage market, so they included industrial training in their régime. In the process they promised to turn out a skilled and well-disciplined industrial labour force. These 'success' stories clearly demonstrate what the directors had in mind for the inmates and the future of the working class.

> E.R., ... After remaining in the Home 15 months, and having been taught to operate on a sewing machine was sent out to a situation in a warehouse, where she earns about 12s per week. She attends Church regularly as well as a Sabbath evening class. Is residing with her parents, to whom she has been sent on leaving the Home. She puts a portion of her weekly savings in the savings bank *(G.M.I. Annual Report* 1865).

My Dear Miss Weir, I have commenced to wash and iron for myself, and I am doing very well. Any young woman can get from 25 to 30 shillings a-week. I have not regretted coming to this colony [Australia] I would advise any young woman to come out here; they would do so much better than at home... There is nothing but white clothes worn in the summer *(G.M.I. Annual Report* 1874).

## Act of Resistance: Defiance of the Moral Code

The statistics indicate that of the 4798 women admitted to the Magdalene Institution between 1860 and 1890, less than half were placed in situations more or less acceptable to the directors. The next 25 per cent were diverted to other institutions, such as hospitals, insane asylums and poorhouses, where in many cases they could be kept permanently. The remaining 37 per cent, however, were either dismissed or ran away before their full time was served. These cases were recorded as: untractable, disobedient and insubordinate (Mahood 1987, p. 183). The directors explained the high percentage by emphasizing that they had no power to detain anyone against her will *(G.M.I. Annual Report* 1880). And unless inmates had reached the stage of 'true sorrow for sin' no real reformation could be expected *(G.M.I. Annual Report* 1878). The high drop-out rate does not imply, however, that the Institution failed because the directors did not rescue enough inmates, or because they possessed a naïve analysis of the causes of the problem. Neither does it imply that a large percentage of the inmates could not cope or rebelled against irksome rules or that they were generally intractable, as Finnegan's study of the York penitentiary suggests. Although it is not articulated and therefore difficult to prove, indirect evidence suggests that rather than judging these inmates as 'failures', their refusals may be interpreted as acts of resistance to moral reform and surveillance. Resistance, in this case, meant the refusal to accept the Magdalene Institution's definition of the problem, because not all inmates saw themselves as subjects of the discourse: as 'magdalenes', 'fallen' women or 'sinners'. This highlights the process described by Foucault, who argues that wherever there is power there is opposition and resistance or the operation of an alternative discourse or subculture with its own definitions and norms for behaviour.

In the case of working-class women, historians have demonstrated that 'chastity' may not have had the same social meaning for working-class women, whose courtship and marriage customs differed from those of middle-class observers (Weeks 1981, p. 61). Walkowitz points out that many women who moved into occasional prostitution through economic necessity had previous sexual experience, and the distinction between occasional sex with a lover and clandestine prostitution for money, food or drinks may have remained fluid (Walkowitz and Walkowitz 1974, p. 193). In regions where pre-marital sex, pregnancy and prostitution were common, working-class communities accepted them as a fact of life (Smout 1980, p. 296). Generalizations about subjective attitudes toward sexuality are always difficult to make, but in this case it is possible that reformers defined certain women as 'prostitutes' who would not have defined their own behaviour as prostitution, and who would not have perceived themselves as potential clients of the Magdalene Institutions.

*Conclusion*

The moral reform activities of the Glasgow Magdalene Institution provide a unique opportunity to examine the process through which local state representatives and philanthropists established an apparatus designed for the social control and moral reform of women who defied middle-class standards of sexual and vocational propriety. The nineteenth-century public discourse on the prostitution 'problem' maintained a distinction between a 'magdalene' and a 'criminal', at least in the early stages of the career. These moral reformers argued that repressive punitive control was inadequate; they did not want to criminalize 'magdalenes' or to incarcerate them as a form of punishment. Rather, they wanted to 'save' them, hence justifying and supporting an institution or apparatus to catch women before they were 'hardened in vice'. The Glasgow Magdalene Institution was intended to catch young women and channel them into the appropriate régime of moral education and industrial training, and to save them from the courts and prisons, and thus prevent them from becoming inmates of state institutions. The consequence of this 'decarceration strategy' was that the system as a whole expanded, which meant that more females of a greater age-range were incarcerated than previously. New categories of women were drawn into the system, which began to include many who had previously escaped the notice of the authorities. In effect, by the late nineteenth century the process became more interventionist than it had been at the beginning of the century and a greater percentage of the female working-class population became potential clients. Instead of reducing the amount of stigmatization, labelling, and the overcrowding of prisons and poorhouses, intervention now came earlier, and was more intensive, because it swept in more forms of deviance, through extension to those not yet formally adjudicated.

Female penitentiaries served two social-control functions directly: sexual control and vocational control (Rafter 1983, p. 291). Their activities reflect the notion that a 'fallen' woman could regain her character, but this required intensive resocialization and moral education. Through moral education and industrial training the Magdalene Institution attempted to create an industrial labour force and competent domestic servants, which responded to the need for a pool of cheap female labour. It is necessary, however, to go beyond a simple economic explanation of their activities. The social-control mechanisms were also designed for the reform of inmates' sexual behaviour. This entailed the socialization of inmates to conform to the middle-class codes of class and gender. In this case, reformers hoped that inmates would embrace middle-class values such as family, cleanliness, chastity, domesticity and appropriate feminine gender roles (Brenzel 1980). Their desire to protect working-class girls was part of a larger programme to control their sexual and vocational behaviour, which reflects the desire to impose a middle-class social code on working-class women (Walkowitz 1980, p. 24). The activities of the Magdalene Institution, therefore, were not apolitical, but deliberate strategies for remaking working-class culture.

In order to assess the impact of the Magdalene Institution on the lives of former inmates it is necessary to admit that no simple cause and effect can be established. It appears, however, that a percentage went on to lead lives that met with the Institution's criteria for success: marrying, or remaining with relatives, or in domestic service. Others became temperate and industrious factory workers and self-employed tradeswomen. While others resisted the bourgeois moral code offered by the Institution either by ignoring it, refusing to enter, or leaving before the Institution classified them as 'reformed'. This challenges the idea that women are passive objects of social polices. In this research I have emphasized women's capacity for agency by focusing on indicators of women's choice either in the form of acceptance or resistance to the moral code offered by the Magdalene Institution. I have argued that once the social and historical construction of the category 'prostitute' is recognized, a naturalistic or empirical study of prostitution or 'prostitutes' becomes problematic. Moreover, attempts to define the 'prostitute' were not just technical, but political. Finally, if the discourse on the prostitution 'problem' in Glasgow in the mid-nineteenth century is conceptualized as the engineering of bourgeois hegemony in the area of sexuality, this has to be treated as a process rather than an automatic consequence of bourgeois economic domination. One must consider the problem of the engineering of consent, within the framework of agency, or the process whereby some working-class women may have accepted the definition of themselves as 'magdalenes' and chose to reform along bourgeois lines, whereas others resisted the bourgeois moral code, its sanctions on their behaviour, and its technologies of power.

## REFERENCES

I would like to thank Barbara Littlewood and Vic Satzewich for their invaluable assistance in the preparation of this paper.

*Abbreviations*

*G.M.I. Annual Reports:* Glasgow Magdalene Institution Report.
*Select Committee:* Reports of the Select Committee on the Contagious Diseases Acts, PP. 1881 (351), viii, 193; PP. 1882 (340), ix, 1.
*Chief Constables' Book:* City of Glasgow Police. Chief Constables Letter Book. Glasgow (E4/2.10) 1863-69.
*Magistrates' Committee Book:* Magistrates Committee Minute Book, Glasgow (1866-1876).

*Books and Articles*

Boyd, K.M. (1980), *Scottish Church Attitudes to Sex, Marriage and the Family: 1850-1914*, Edinburgh: John Donald.

Brenzel, B. (1980), 'Domestication as Reform: A Study of the Socialization of Wayward Girls, 1856-1905'. *Harvard Educational Review.* 50, May.

Bristow, E. (1977), *Vice and Vigilance: Purity Movements in Britain Since 1700*, London: Gill & MacMillan.

Bryce, J.D. (1859), *The Glasgow Magdalene Asylum, its Past and Present: With Relative Facts and Suggestions*, Glasgow: David Bryce.

Checkland, O. (1980), *Philanthropy in Victorian Scotland: Social Welfare and the Voluntary Principle*, Edinburgh: John Donald.

Cohen, S. (1985), *Visions of Social Control: Crime, Punishment and Classification*, Cambridge: Polity Press.

Davidoff, L. (1974), 'Mastered for Life: Servant and Wife in Victorian and Edwardian England', *Journal of Social History* 7.

Donzelot, J. (1979), *The Policing of Families*, (trans.) R. Hurley, London: Hutchinson Co.

Finnegan, F. (1979), *Poverty and Prostitution*, London: Cambridge University Press.

Foucault, M. (1980), *The History of Sexuality,* vol. 1, *An Introduction,* (trans.) R. Hurley, New York: Random House.

*The Glasgow System for the Repression of Vice,* (1881).

The Glasgow Magdalene Institution (1863), *Report Relative to the Glasgow Fair.*

Hellerstein, E., Hume, L., and Offen K. (1981), *Victorian Women: Documentary Account of Women's Lives,* London: Harvester.

Mahood, L. (1987). *'The Magdalene's Friend': The Control of Prostitutes in Glasgow 1840-1890,* M.Litt., University of Glasgow.

MacGill, S. (1819), *Discourses and Essays on Subjects of Public Interest,* Edinburgh.

McHugh, P. (1980), *Prostitution and Victorian Social Reform,* London: Croom Helm.

Nead, L. (1987), 'The Magdalene in Modern Times: The Mythology of the Fallen Woman in Pre-Raphaelite Painting', in, R. Betterton (ed.), *Looking at Images of Femininity in the Visual Arts and Media,* London: Pandora Press.

Patterson, A. (1882), 'Statistics of the Glasgow Lock Hospital Since its Foundations in 1805: With Remarks on the Contagious Diseases Acts, and on Syphilis', *The Glasgow Medical Journal* 6, December.

Prochaska, F.K. (1980), *Women and Philanthropy in Nineteenth Century England*, London: Oxford University Press.

Rafter, N. (1983), 'Chastizing the Unchaste: Social Control Functions of a Woman's Reformatory', in S. Cohen and A. Skull (eds), *Social Control and the State*, Oxford: Martin Robertson.

Smout, T.C. (1980), 'Aspects of Sexual Behaviour in Nineteenth Century Scotland', in P. Laslett, K. Oosterveen and R. Smith (eds.), *Bastardy and its Comparative History*, London.

Sumner, M. (1980), *Prostitution and Images of Women*, M.Sc., University of Wales.

Thomas, A. (1861). *On the Licentiousness of Scotland and the Remedial Measures Which Ought to be Adopted*. London: J. Nisbet.

Walkowitz, J., and Walkowitz D. (1974), '"We are not Beasts of the Field": Prostitution and the Poor in Plymouth and Southampton under the Contagious Diseases Acts', in M. Hartman and L. Banner (eds.), *Clio's Consciousness Raise*, London.

Walkowitz, J. (1980), *Prostitution and Victorian Society*, London: Cambridge University Press.

Weeks, J. (1981), *Sex, Politics, and Society: The Regulation of Sexuality Since 1800*, New York: Longman.

Wood, N. (1981), 'Prostitution and Feminism in Nineteenth-Century Britain', *M/F: a Feminist Journal* 7.

# 9

## Representing Scotland:
## Culture and Nationalism

DAVID McCRONE

Unlike many forms of nationalism, the cultural content of the Scottish variety is relatively weak. Compared to Welsh, Irish, Catalan, Breton or Quebec nationalism, it is less ready to call up the ancient ghosts of the nation, its symbols and motifs, in its quest for independence (Brand 1978; Webb 1978). There is, of course, less to call up, for the lack of linguistic, religious or similar cultural markers in Scotland forces nationalists to conjure up an alternative 'imagined community' (Anderson 1983). And in this regard, the modern model for an independent Scotland has been, at least since the 1960s, the Scandinavian countries rather than Ireland, for example. There is a reluctance among many Scottish Nationalists today to mobilize simply around the signs and motifs bequeathed from the Scottish past. This tendency within Scottish nationalism to look sideways rather than backwards has much to do with a wider characterization of this Scottish past. It is deemed to be dominated by negative motifs; it is deformed and distorted.

In this chapter I will examine the view that Scottish culture has been dominated by two 'mythic structures' of Tartanry and Kailyard (Craig 1982-3) to such an extent that they seem to offer only negative representations of Scotland, reflecting the political and cultural developments since the Union of 1707. I will argue that this view has been so predominant among Scottish intellectuals that their contribution to the development of neo-nationalism in Scotland has been negative and critical, that their very analysis represents a dominant discourse which itself has to be examined critically.

The most perceptive analysis of Scottish culture and nationalism is perhaps that of Tom Nairn, whose book *The Break-Up of Britain*, published first in 1977, provided the clearest critical account we have. Since then, no one can ignore Nairn's analysis of Scottish culture, while sceptics may still be waiting for Britain to 'break-up'. Nairn's view would seem to carry more weight after the 1987 general election than ten years before when he wrote the book. Nairn is a great denouncer in the tradition of John Knox and Hugh MacDiarmid, and his work makes fine polemic as well as analysis. MacDiarmid's own famous statement in 'A Drunk Man' fits the public face of Nairn well:

> I'll hae nae hauf-way hoose, but aye be whaur extremes meet, it's the only way I ken to dodge the curst conceit o' bein richt that damns the vast majority o' men...

And 'whaur extremes meet' is a good starting-point, for Nairn characterizes Scottish culture as being split, divided, deformed. This is a fairly familiar view of Scottish culture, epitomized in Walter Scott, that Scotland is divided between the 'heart' (representing the past, romance, 'civil society', if you like) and the 'head' (the present and future, reason, and, by dint of that, the British state). The 'Caledonian Antisyzygy' (Nairn 1977, p. 150) – this personality split between the Scottish heart and the British head – is perhaps the most common characterization of Scotland we have, and it is one which Nairn uses. Scotland, he says, suffers from 'sub-national deformation', or 'neurosis' (and psychiatric disorders are a Scottish speciality here). 'Cultural sub-nationalism' is a favourite phrase of Nairn's in representing Scotland (Nairn 1977, p. 156):

> 'It was cultural because of course it could not be political; on the other hand, this culture could not be straightforwardly nationalist either – a direct substitute for political action, like, for example, so much Polish literature of the 19th century. It would only be 'sub-nationalist' in the sense of venting its national content in various crooked [sic] ways – *neurotically,* so to speak, rather than directly.'

It is interesting, in passing, to note the source of this resonant phrase 'cultural sub-nationalism'. In a footnote (Nairn 1977, p. 156) he acknowledges that he borrows it from a third world context, in this case, eastern Nigeria. It seems that it refers to instances where the culture of a region develops into a nationalism proper. This seems an odd phrase for Nairn to borrow because it implies almost the opposite in Scotland: that a hitherto national culture became subverted into a sub-national variety, rather than the other way round, which seems to be the original allusion. Still, the meaning which Nairn has given it has stuck in a Scottish context.

This 'sub-nationalism' is, according to Nairn, a poor thing. While Scottish civil society survived in the bosom of the British state, the Scottish 'heart' was split from the British 'head'; the 'national', with its over-emphasis on the past, was separated from the 'practical', with its emphasis on the present and future. This

## Representing Scotland: Culture and Nationalism

came about because, by the late eighteenth and early nineteenth centuries, the intelligentsia was 'deprived of its historic nationalist role'. Says Nairn, 'there was no call for its usual services' (1977, p. 154) of leading the nation to the threshold of political independence. Intellectuals after the Union migrated, if not in body at least in spirit, to the bigger, more rounded culture of Anglo-Britain, leaving a stunted residue of intellectual life in Scotland (at least so it seems to Nairn). In this context, then, it is easy to explain the Scottish Enlightenment of the late eighteenth century, an otherwise awkward phenomenon to arise in a 'deformed' culture. In essence, says Nairn, it wasn't Scottish at all, or rather it represented the belated intellectual fruits of the Union. Operating on a much bigger stage before a larger and more sophisticated audience, it was

'strikingly non-nationalist – so detached from the People, so intellectual and universalising in its assumptions, so Olympian in its attitudes.' (Nairn 1977, p. 140)

Smith, Hume, the Mills, Robertson, Adam and other luminaries of the Enlightenment may have been Scots by birth and education, but they were universal men, and certainly 'British' in orientation.

The cultural void in Scotland was created largely by the migration of Scots intellectuals to the richer pastures of England. Macauley, Carlyle, Ruskin, Gladstone and many more were not even thought of as Scots at all. England, says Nairn, was a 'mature, all-round thought-world':

It was an organic or 'rooted' national-romantic culture in which literature – from Coleridge and Carlyle up to F.R. Leavis and E.P. Thompson – has consistently played a major role (1977 p. 156–7).

In contrast with this rich, southern feast of culture, Scotland's dish (quite literally) was 'cauld kail'. The Kailyard, or 'cabbage-patch' tradition flourished, with its petty obsessions and mean-minded parochial jealousies. In a splendidly splenetic characterization of the late-nineteenth century Kailyard tradition, Nairn writes:

Kailyardism was the definition of Scotland as wholly consisting of small towns full of small-town character's given to bucolic intrigue and wise sayings. At first the central figures were usually Ministers of the Kirk (as were most of the authors) but later on schoolteachers and doctors got into the act. Their housekeepers always have a shrewd insight into human nature. Offspring who leave for the big city frequently come to grief, and are glad to get home again (peching and hosting to hide their feelings) (1977, p. 158).

Kailyardism represented a popular literary style from about 1880 to 1914 (Campbell 1981; Carter 1976) described, as Nairn says, by the Penguin Guide to Literature, as consisting of 'minor writers who pursued Scottish country quaintness into whimsical middens'. The latter-day manifestations of this 'sub-cultural Scotchery' (Nairn 1977, p. 158) include 'Dr Finlay's Casebook', 'Sutherland's Law', 'Take the High Road' and above all, those *bêtes noires* of the Left, the Sunday Post, The People's Friend, their publisher, D.C. Thomson and all his works and pomps. Nairn argues that much of the Kailyard's output was produced by Scottish emigrés with rosy, romantic memories of the simple Scotland they had left behind for richer pickings in the south. Nairn's argument is that their pawky simplicities had a ready market in Scotland, and while kitsch was in no way unique to Scotland, it took on the character of a national popular tradition. At this point we may note in passing, the implication of what Nairn is saying. Scottish culture became overwhelmingly the Kailyard, and as a result, a proper 'mature, all-round thought-world' could not be Scottish (these, we might remind ourselves, are the words Nairn uses to describe English culture).

Welded on to this Kailyard tradition, in this characterization, is an older, altogether wilder tradition of 'Tartanry', what Nairn calls the 'Tartan Monster' (note the sub-Freudian motif of fear, nightmare, neurosis here: Scotland as a psychiatric condition, and not forgetting the 'real' monster in Loch Ness). Tartanry is never treated as seriously as the Kailyard by Scottish intellectuals; perhaps it is too unspeakable to be worthy of their analysis. Of course, it was not a literary movement, but a set of garish symbols appropriated by lowland Scotland at a safe distance from 1745, and turned into a music-hall joke (Harry Lauder represented the fusion of both Tartanry and Kailyard, with the jokes and mores from the latter, the wrapping from the former). The appropriation of Highland motifs by lowland Scotland has been described elsewhere (Chapman 1978; D. McCrone *et al.* 1982) but Tartanry has come to stand for tourist knick-knackery, visits to Wembley and the Edinburgh Tattoo. Oddly, no serious analysis of Tartanry, the set of symbols and images, has been carried out by Scottish intellectuals, although there are a number of studies of the history of tartan (the cloth) (Hesketh 1972; Stewart and Thompson 1980; Telfer-Dunbar 1962, 1981). Instead, it has been left to that archenemy of Scottish Home Rule, Hugh Trevor-Roper, a.k.a. Lord Dacre. In a knock-about piece in Hobsbawm and Ranger's collection *The Invention of Tradition,* Trevor-Roper attempts to demolish the authenticity of Tartan. Not only does it have no basis in history, it was invented, he claims, by *an Englishman* who did Highlanders a favour: Thus

'The kilt is a purely modern costume, first designed and first worn by an English Quaker industrialist, and that it was bestowed by him on the Highlanders in order not to preserve their traditional way of life but to ease their transformation: to bring them out of the heather and into the factory.' (1981, p. 22).

One only hopes the natives were properly grateful to the Quaker, Major Rawlinson, and to Trevor-Roper for showing them and us the error of their ways. It has to be said that Trevor-Roper's interpretation is thoroughly contentious, and Telfer-Dunbar, the major historian of tartan, dismisses this view (1981, pp. 69-70). Other parts of the tartan story are faily well known, and less contentious. The Proscription Act of 1747 forbad the wearing of tartan, and was not repealed until 1782. The kilt and tartan were appropriated by the British army in its colonial wars – quite literally stealing the enemy's clothes – and it set about with gusto inventing new tartans. Walter Scott, as impresario, persuaded George IV, a large man by all accounts and with a poor command of English, to visit Edinburgh in 1822, and worse, to wear a kilt set off fetchingly by pink tights. Despite, or perhaps because of, this, tartan became an instant fashion, and polite society clamoured to have their own. The weaving company William Wilson of Bannockburn duly obliged, and was not averse to allocating the same tartan to more than one clan label. The colonial market was booming, and slave owners in the West Indies and the southern States had found it a useful uniform for identifying their human property in a crowd. Queen Victoria's acquisition of Balmoral in 1848 gave the royal seal of approval to the tartan enterprise, and she and Albert had one of their very own designed. Behind all this was a considerable 'heritage' industry, bent (a good word for it) on authenticating the ancient designs for an anxious world eager to believe. The Sobieski Stuarts (the Allen brothers) claimed in 1842 to have discovered a sixteenth-century text of tartans *Vestiarium Scoticum* which was soon to be denounced as a forgery (Stewart and Thompson 1980), but which seemed to do nothing to dampen the desire to accept the authenticity of tartan.

This, in brief, is the tartan story. A form of dress and design which had some real but haphazard significance in the Highlands of Scotland was taken over by a lowland population anxious to claim some distinctive aspect of culture at a time when the economic, social and cultural identity was ebbing away in the late nineteenth century. It may have taken a High Tory English historian, master of Peterhouse, the home of neo-conservative ideologues, to put the critique together, but few left-wing/liberal Scottish intellectuals would dissent much from it. They would not have been, as they say, at all surprised.

What this critique does not do is explain why what Nairn calls the 'Tartan monster' survives to be a symbol of Scotland, whether at Wembley or at more douce occasions such as family weddings and university graduations. Nairn has little doubt:

> 'Tartanry will not wither away, if only because it possesses the force of its own vulgarity – immunity from doubt and higher culture'. (1977, p. 165)

This is rather an unsatisfactory explanation in many ways, because we are still left to wonder as to why it remains immune. Nairn argues that it results from the separation of 'high' and 'low' culture, and the fact that the latter remains unintellectualized for the reasons spelled out earlier. Scottish culture is schizophrenic; its low culture is a bastard product, partly indigenous and partly maintained by British Imperialist mechanisms (the Scottish soldier is the obvious example (Wood 1987)). This sense of separation, of fragmentation, runs throughout much intellectual analysis of Scotland. The historian, Chris Harvie (1975), for example, has argued that this Scottish schizophrenia has created a social distinction: between the 'red' Scots – those who leave in search of new opportunities, the outward-bound strain of 'Scot on the make', unspeakable or otherwise – and the 'black' Scots – those who stay to nourish the home culture, the Kailyard and Tartan Monsters. These are social, even psychological, types and little sociological evidence is proferred for their existence, but it is a typology which fits the conventional intellectual wisdom of Scotland. It is interesting that both Nairn and Harvie belong to the 'red' variety (nothing to do with politics, of course). It seems that only if you have lived in the 'wider' culture (the 'mature, all-round thought-world' of England perhaps), the 'real world', are you immune from the insidious psychological effects of Scottish culture. Indeed, at its extreme, this strain of criticism seems to imply that even to *think* about Scotland is proof of 'neurosis', thereby seeming to lock us into a pessimistic Catch 22. Indeed, to be 'normal' (not neurotic) you'd be advised not to think of Scotland at all. The language of this critique is certainly sub-Freud. It is replete with 'monsters', with 'neuroses', with 'split personalities'. And it was, after all, a Scotsman, Robert Louis Stevenson, who invented Dr. Jekyll and Mr. Hyde.

I have focused on Nairn's analysis of Scottish culture because it is the most comprehensive, and the one which has marked out the agenda for the debate subsequently. Let me now turn to its later manifestations, particularly those associated with the Scottish literary intelligentsia. The pages of the literary magazine *Cencrastus* provide a good hunting ground in this respect. Much of the discussion has focused around deconstructing the 'Scotch Myths' of Tartanry/Kailyard *(Bulletin of Scottish Politics* 1981). The exhibition mounted by Barbara and Murray Grigor at the 1981 Edinburgh Festival was a key event. This exhibition had gathered together representations of Scotland, from postcards to orange box labels from California to media representations of Scotland in film and television, and aimed to generate discussion of Scotland's 'deformed' culture. In 1982, the Edinburgh Film Festival held a showing of 'Scotch Reels', the film of the exhibition, as it were, together with a three-day discussion event around a collection of essays *(Scotch Reels, Scotland in Cinema and Television,* 1982), edited by Colin McArthur. The remit was clear. In McArthur's own words:

> Clearly the traditions of Kailyard and Tartanry have to be exposed and deconstructed, and more politically progressive representations constructed, circulated and discussed. (1981–2, p. 25)

Borrowing Althusser's idea of 'interpellation', McArthur argues that these Scotch Myths have had hegemony over Scots' perceptions of themselves to such an extent that they have a 'systemic' quality:

> Having had two centuries to develop, it [note that the two have become fused – author's comment] now constitutes a durable and hegemonic system, the representation of one part of which can dredge up into consciousness the system as a whole, and, of course, the complex articulation of attitudes to history, to nationhood and to political decisions in the here and now which it is *its objective function to serve* (my emphasis). (1981, p. 22)

This is powerful stuff. Two disparate cultural formations have combined into a hegemonic system which locks the Scots into a sense of their own inferiority in the face of a powerful Anglo-British culture. Much of the evidence is based on graphic representations in film, television and what its proponents call the 'sign media' generally. The semiotics of Scotland are presented by McArthur *et al.* as regressive in cultural terms, and in their political manifestations lock us into subordination and dependency. Tartanry/Kailyard maintains cultural hegemony over Scotland's sense of itself. In the words of McArthur,

> a limited number of discourses have been deployed in the cinema to construct Scotland and the Scots, and to give an

impression that no other constructions are possible (1982, p. 69).

There are, according to this analysis, other discourses which are healthier, and indigeneous to Scotland, 'Clydesidism' is one such which is spoken of with approval by some of the critics. It is 'extremely refreshing in the Scottish context', says McArthur, it is not a 'pernicious discourse'. He contrasts the comedy of Billy Connolly (good) with that of Harry Lauder (bad). What Clydesidism has in its favour is that it is constructed from 'real' images of working-class life, from the discourse of class, and from naturalism. Says John Caughie, the traditions are

> based in working-class experience which, since the twenties, have seemed to offer the only real and consistent basis for a *Scottish national culture* (my emphasis) (1982, p. 121).

And that is it. The search is for a national culture which will speak to people in their own terms, an integrated discourse which will connect with political and social realities in Scotland. The problem, however, with Clydesidism as a discourse is that it is resonant of socialist realism (heroic workers and all: 'Stakhanovite political iconography', says McArthur 1983, p. 3) and, as Cairns Craig (1983) has pointed out, it is itself becoming a 'historic discourse' even in its heartland of west central Scotland in the late twentieth century. Its language is redolent of early twentieth century Clydeside, with its appeal to the 'industrial masses'. It is fine, says Craig, to break out of the mental traps of the historic myths of Tartanry and Kailyard, to imagine a future, even a revolutionary future, through which to overcome the static quality of the dominant myths, but we risk embracing another myth based on a fast-disappearing working-class culture. Says Craig,

> What is worrying in the contemporary situation is the way that the death throes of industrial West–Central Scotland have become the touchstone of authenticity for our culture, (1983, p. 9).

and he continues,

> if we make the victims of that decline the carriers of our essential identity, we merely perpetuate the cultural alienation in which we negate the on-going struggle of our experience by freezing its real meaning in a particular defeat. (1983, p. 9)

This, to my mind, is a more fundamental criticism, and much more to the point. It seems to me that we search in vain for the 'true' image because none such exists, nor indeed should we be looking for it in the late twentieth century. To take McArthur's comment, and play it back on his own analysis:

a limited number of discourses have been deployed... to give an impression that no other constructions are possible. Not only are Tartanry and Kailyard such discourses, along with Clydesidism, but so is this radical discourse itself. And its problem is that it asks a particularly inappropriate question: What is (distinctive about) Scottish culture? My question is: why should there be an obsessive search to find one; why is the question even framed in this way; where does it come from?

The answer is that it derives from an older, essentially 'nationalist' assumption that all societies worthy of the name should have a distinctive culture. Despite the fairly critical stances taken against political nationalism by Scottish intellectuals, this perspective seems to echo its assumption that Scotland has (or had) a 'national' culture waiting to be discovered. This is essentially an idea traceable back to the eighteenth-century Enlightenment notion of sovereignty, embodied in the culture of a nation waiting to be brought to its political realization. This truth of European cultural nationalism seems today increasingly time-bound and anachronistic. Why, after all, should any country have a distinctive 'national' culture, when we know that many of these 'nations' were constructed with very little cultural straw? Gellner's rather terse dismissal 'nationalism is not the awakening of nations to self-consciousness; it invents nations where they do not exist' (Gellner 1983, p. 168) does seem rather sweeping, but has more than a kernel of truth to it. It is a convenient but distorted truth of nationalism that the nation is 'natural', that every nation deserves a state. Max Weber, for example, echoing Hegel, believed that a nation was 'a community of sentiment which would find its adequate expression only in a state of its own, and which thus normally strives to create one' (Betham 1974, p. 122). Gellner's perspective, on the other hand, is to argue that national sentiment of this sort is not a given, but is historically constructed and mobilized by social interests (most notably by national bourgeoisies in nineteenth-century Europe). We should not, in other words, take the existence of a prior 'national' culture as a given.

How does this perspective connect with the analysis put forward by critics of Tartanry/Kailyard? In some fundamental ways the critique of this 'mythic structure' as a discourse is not radical enough. It is premissed upon the previous existence or at least the future possibility of a rounded, mature national culture. As Cairns Craig points out, the problem of identity is precisely the one we should not be trying to solve, because

> the 'identity' we construct will be an essentialising, an idealising, a reduction to paradigmatic features, of Scotland

as *home,* a counterbalance to the 'home counties' as core of English/British culture. (1983, p. 8)

So, applying Tartanry/Kailyard as the essentials of our national culture, albeit negative ones, is to simplify and freeze them. This process will also predispose us to look for what we have lost, to reduce culture to a series of tragic failures – in which Scotland is not lacking – the 'Ally McLeod syndrome', with its devastating combination of 'if only' and 'we wuz robbed'. Once the issue is set up in this negative way, we can find any number of contradictory 'explanations' for the national condition. So it results from too little independence, or too much (insufficient incorporation into British civil society); it results from too little industrial capitalism (failure to have a thoroughgoing capitalist revolution), or too much; from too little Calvinism (the Catholic legacy) or too much. All seem plausible if we define the problem as a failure of a 'Scottish national culture' to develop. My point is that once we frame the problem in this way, we imply the uniqueness of the Scottish problem; we look inside for the explanation. The assumption that certain forms of kitsch are uniquely Scottish cannot be true in a comparative context. And Scotland did not invent the soap opera.

A considerable amount of effort has gone in to discovering the 'real' Scottish culture, especially in the pre-industrial past. Lying behind the deformed images is a sense of the 'golden age', pre-independence, when society and the state were one, when it was possible to argue that this Scottish culture, was a communal culture, reflected in the sturdy vernacular literature of the Makars, of Henryson, Dunbar, Barbour, then Ramsay, Fergusson, and above all, Burns. (David Craig 1961; and particularly, Kurt Wittig 1972). This search for a truly 'Scottish' culture is inevitably retrospective and romantic, a celebration of the past, the golden age, and helps to explain Scottish history's obsession with what has ended, as Marinell Ash's trenchant critique (1980) makes plain. This 'strange death' of Scottish history in the nineteenth century reflected real political and economic changes:

> The time that Scotland was ceasing to be distinctively and confidently herself was also the period when there grew an increasing emphasis on the emotional trappings of the Scottish past ... its symbols are bonnie Scotland of the bens and glens and misty shieling, the Jacobites, Mary Queen of Scots, tartan mania and the raising of historical statuary. (1980, p. 10a)

So the search into the past for a distinctive and un-neurotic Scottish culture is doomed to reproduce a new set of myths about what Scotland was like. Instead, I would argue that we have to look not simply into the future, but at what is going on in other societies. It seems that nation-states themselves are losing their political, economic and cultural integrity in a rapidly changing world (Beetham 1984). Scotland may be striving to attain something which is going out of fashion. Similarly, the quest for Scottish cultural independence from a culturally suffocating and homogeneous Anglo-British one ignores the fact that, as Cairns Craig has perceptively pointed out, the latter has fragmented. The post-1918 period saw the collapse, he argues, of the English cultural *imperium*, and subsequently 'English culture' could no longer be equated with 'the culture of England'. In most English-speaking countries, there was a burgeoning of indigenous literature: in Canada, Australia, South Africa, New Zealand, the United States and Ireland.

The Scottish literary renaissance of the 1920s expressed itself in the work of MacDiarmid, Grassic Gibbon, Linklater, MacColla, Muir and Bridie (Harvie 1981). These socio-cultural developments were rooted in a pluralistic cultural system in Scotland: in Gaelic (Sorley MacLean); in Scots (MacDiarmid, Gibbon etc.); even in standard English (Spark). These traditions have survived and prospered, and have ceased to be simply literary forms. Spoken language through radio and television has also contributed to a multi-varied culture which cannot in any serious way be reduced to the discourses of Tartanry and Kailyard. The point is that only rarely do they seek to address the Scottish condition as such. Who would care, for example, to categorize the award-winning BBC television series *Tutti Frutti* in simple terms?

These cultural developments are seeking to make sense of shared social, economic and political experiences: of urban living, of working or not working, of living in a capitalist society, a society in which our own ability to control even limited political power is severely constrained. The obsession with a unified Scottish national culture has its parallel in the assertion that, in order to explain Scotland's political divergence from England, its industrial and occupational structures must be different from those south of the border (Kendrick 1985). When this turns out not to be true, we worry about the fact that it is not, in case it denies Scotland's right to exist. Similarly, if we set out to look for what is distinctive in Scotland, we run the risk of focusing on the trivial and epiphenomenal, which will be found only in the past and in the museum.

My argument, then, is that the critique of Tartanry/Kailyard as the hegemonic discourse in Scottish culture arises from an essentially 'internalist' account of Scotland, that it ignores major cultural and social changes in the world generally. It arises because it sets out to address the issue of Scottish national culture, a hunting of a Scottish snark. The search for a distinct identity is likely to degenerate into a pessimistic conclusion that none is possible because we are prevented from seeing it by the power of the regressive Scotch Myths, rather than because in modern, pluralistic societies no single 'national' culture is to be found. In other words, the argument has been that we cannot find it precisely because the myths are hegemonic, when the real answer should be that the search itself is illegitimate.

*A Political Postscript*

It is an irony that in spite of the supposed deformation of Scottish culture that Scottish political behaviour has never been in post-war politics so divergent from its southern counterpart, a situation seemingly achieved with little help from 'Scottish national culture'. Here, it seems, is a political manifestation which is not tied to a specific cultural divergence. It is a form of 'neo-nationalism' in which neither Scottish culture nor even the Scottish National Party plays much of a part. Instead, it seems to be much more of a 'political' manifestation, a concern with the practicalities of decision-making and control. Perhaps this expression of political difference – a 'nationalism' if you want – has developed without the encumbrance of heavy cultural baggage. It is as if, having looked to see what was on offer, the Scots have decided to travel light. No icons need to be genuflected at, no correct representation needs to be observed in this journey into the future. If what we have is so thoroughly tainted and deformed, then we will leave it behind. It is almost a cultureless, post-industrial journey into the unknown. In this respect, it seems to conform to a kind of 'post-materialist' politics (Inglehart 1977), not in the sense that it is unconcerned with economic issues, but that it seems to have left behind the kind of nationalist/culturalist agenda bequeathed from nineteenth- and early twentieth-century politics.

While perhaps we journey more in hope than in expectation, we can be mindful of the more optimistive views of commentators like Neal Ascherson, who argues that it is the very chaotic and discontinuous character of the Scottish past – its unfinished quality – which gives it its energy:

Time is not generally used to enforce perspective, and instead there is a scrap-book of highly coloured, often bloody scenes or tableaux whose sequence or relation to one another is obscure. But there is a source of energy in this dislocation. As in Poland, what is more intense appears to be in some way nearer; its impact is not diminished by informed distancing. (Ascherson 1985)

The critiques of the 'heritage' industry by Patrick Wright (1985) and Robert Hewison (1987) have sensitized us to the reactionary quality of an obsession with history (or, to be more precise, the past). But perhaps the deterioration of history into mere 'heritage' with all its conservative and commercial implications is only possible when the past is seamless and complete, sweeping the present back onto older and more conservative agendas. Perhaps Ascherson is whistling in the dark. But his argument about an unfinished past, as in the case of Poland, is persuasive, and helps to unlock tradition from its reactionary fixings. And as Marx recognized,

and just when they seem engaged in revolutionising themselves and things, in creating something that has never existed, precisely in such periods of revolutionary crisis, they anxiously conjure up the spirits of the past to their service and borrow from them names, battle cries and costumes in order to prevent the new scene of world history in this time-honoured disguise and borrowed language (1959, p. 320).

Just so.

REFERENCES

Anderson, B. (1983), *Imagined Communities: Reflections on the Spread of Nationalism*, London: Verso Books.

Ascherson, N. (1985), 'Ancient Britons and the Republican Dream', John P. Mackintosh Memorial Lecture, reprinted in *Radical Scotland* 18.

Ash, M. (1980), *The Strange Death of Scottish History*, Edinburgh: Ramsay Head Press.

Brand, J. (1978), *The National Movement in Scotland*, London: Routledge & Kegan Paul.

Beetham, D. (1974), *Max Weber and the Theory of Modern Politics*, London: Allen & Unwin.

Beetham, D. (1984), 'The Future of the Nation State', in, G. McLennan (ed.), *The Idea of the Modern State*, Milton Keynes: Open University Press.

*Bulletin of Scottish Politics* (1981), 2.

Campbell, I. (1981), *Kailyard*, Edinburgh: Ramsay Head Press.

Carter, I. (1976), 'Kailyard: The Literature of Decline in 19th Century Scotland', in *Scottish Journal of Sociology*, 1.

Caughie, J. (1982), 'Scottish Television: What would it look like?', in C. McArthur (1982).

Chapman, M. (1978), *The Gaelic Vision of Scottish Culture,* London: Croom Helm.

Craig, C. (1982-3), 'Visitors from the Stars: Scottish Film Culture', *Cencrastus* 11.

Craig, D. (1961), *Scottish Literature and the Scottish People, 1680-1830,* London: Chatto and Windus.

Gellner, E. (1983), *Nations and Nationalism,* Oxford: Blackwell.

Harvie, C. (1975), 'The Devolution of the Intellectuals', *New Statesman* 90.

Harvie, C. (1981), *No Gods and Precious Few Heroes,* London: Edward Arnold.

Hesketh, C. (1972) *Tartans,* London: Octopus Books.

Hewison, R. *The Heritage Industry: Britain in a Climate of Decline,* London: Methuen.

Inglehart, R. (1977), *The Silent Revolution: Changing Values and Political Styles among Western Publics,* New Jersey: Princeton University Press.

Kendrick, S., Bechhofer, F., and McCrone, D. (1982), 'Is Scotland Different': Industrial and Occupational Change in Scotland and Britain', in, H. Newby *et al.* (eds.), *Restructuring Capital: Recession and Reorganisation in Industrial Society,* British Sociological Association, Explorations in Sociology 20, London: Macmillan.

McArthur, C. (1981-2), 'Breaking the Signs: Scotch Myths as cultural struggle', *Cencrastus* 7.

McArthur, C. (1982), *Scotch Reels: Scotland in Cinema and Television,* London: B.F.I. Publishing.

McArthur C., (1983), 'Scotch Reels and After', in *Cencrastus* 11.

McCrone, D., Kendrick, S., and Bechhofer, F. (1982), 'Egalitarianism and Social Inequality in Scotland', in D. Robbins (ed.), *Rethinking Social Inequality,* Farnborough: Gower Publications.

Marx, K. (1959), 'The Eighteenth Brumaire of Louis Bonapart', in L. Feuer (ed.), *Marx and Engels: Basic Writings in Politics and Philosophy,* New York: Doubleday.

Nairn, T. (1977), *The Break-up of Britain,* London: Verso Books.

Stewart, D.C., and Thompson, J.C. (1980), *Scotland's Forged Tartans: An Analytical Study of Vestiarium Scoticum,* Edinburgh: Paul Harris.

Telfer-Dunbar, J. (1962), *History of Highland Dress,* London: Batsford.

Telfer-Dunbar, J. (1981), *The Costume of Scotland:* London: Batsford.

Trevor-Roper, H. (1984), 'The Invention of Tradition: The Highland Tradition of Scotland', in E. Hobsbawm and T. Ranger (eds.), *The Invention of Tradition,* Cambridge University Press.

Webb, K. (1978), *The Growth of Nationalism in Britain,* Harmondsworth: Penguin.

Wittig, K. (1972), *The Scottish Tradition in Literature, Westport, Conn.:* Greenwood Press.

Wood, S. (1987), *The Scottish Soldier,* London: Archive Publications.

Wright, P. (1985), *On Living in an Old Country: The National Past in Contemporary Britain,* London: Verso Books.

# 10

## The Social Construction of Tradition: The Restoration Portraits and the Kings of Scotland

S. BRUCE AND S. YEARLEY

Weber's typology of kinds of authority and leadership has inspired and guided generations of researchers. Indeed, the primary identification of the three types (charismatic, traditional and legal-rational) has proved remarkably enduring. The terminology has been successfully employed in analyses of politics, religion and administration.

Where analysts have encountered difficulties is not with the principle of the types but with the methodological problem of identifying them in an unambiguous way. Thus, considerable attention has been given to the problem of how a putatively charismatic leader claims 'charisma' (Wallis 1982). If the charismatic authority is recognizable only because of its effects, then the term is dangerously close to being tautologous. Such authority is sometimes even regarded as a residual category; if someone appears to exercise authority without either a traditional or legal-rational warrant, then it must be charisma which is responsible. These difficulties with the notion of charisma are closely associated with another problem: charismatic authority may be recognized either by characteristics of the leader or by the fact that the person's followers ascribe charisma to their leader. Analysts, including Weber, seem to switch between the view that charisma is the property of the person and the view that it lies in people's response to the charismatic.

Ironically the legal-rational form of authority has also been questioned in recent sociological and philosophical writings. The apparent sufficiency of legal-rational rules to determine the correct behaviour or outcome has been undermined by, for example, Wittgenstein's analysis of the indefeasibility of rules and, along another route, by post-Kuhnian work in the sociology of science and medicine. In so far as scientific beliefs (particularly theories or paradigms) have come to be seen as possessing the character of social constructs, scientific expertise can no longer be routinely accepted without question; or, put it another way, opposition to any particular scientific statement cannot be ruled out as merely irrational. This assertion has been supported by such 'failures' of scientific authority as the Challenger disaster and continual leaks from nuclear-power-generating installations as well as by instances in which scientific expertise has proved inseparable from political and moral commitments: for example, in disputes over racial inequalities in intelligence. As the exercise of scientific authority has been seen to be underdetermined by the evidence, the conclusion has been reached that scientific expertise (the epitomy of rational authority) is at least to some extent socially constructed.

Between these developments affecting two of the forms of authority, tradition has been relatively neglected. Our aim in this chapter is to examine the use of traditional authority, illustrated through one case-study, and to review its status.

*Traditional Authority*

The meaning of traditional authority appears initially straightforward. A certain way of doing things is to be accepted, revered and adopted because that is how it has always been done:

> A system of imperative co-ordination will be called 'traditional' if legitimacy is claimed for it and believed in on the basis of the sanctity of the order and the attendant powers of control as they have been handed down from the past, 'have always existed' (Weber 1964, p. 341).

If traditional practices were sufficient to specify how people should behave then the tradition could be expected to stand as a straightforward template. But there are clear grounds for not expecting this to be the case in practice.

The first reason is that the environments in which societies, even very simple ones, exist are open. Past instances cannot be an exhaustive guide to future occurrences. A second reason is supplied by Weber himself. Weber notes that a person exercising traditional authority can legitimate commands in two ways:

> partly in terms of traditions which themselves directly determine the content of the command and the objects and extent of authority [and in] part, it is a matter of the chief's free personal decision, in that tradition leaves a certain sphere open for this (Weber 1964, p. 341).

Traditional chiefs are seldom autarchic and customarily have advisers. We can therefore anticipate a potential for conflict between the chief's personal decisions and certain interpretations of the commands which the tradition 'determines'.

1. The Gallery, Holyroodhouse Palace. *(By gracious permission of Her Majesty the Queen.)*

2. Caratacus, mythical as a king of Scotland. Note 'SPQR' on shield.
*(By gracious permission of Her Majesty the Queen.)*

3. Evenus I, one of the lesser mythical kings. *(By gracious permission of Her Majesty the Queen.)*

4. James V. *(By gracious permission of Her Majesty the Queen.)*

The third and most important consideration develops directly from this second point. Weber appears to entertain a highly realistic, almost essentialist, notion of traditions. But traditions are susceptible of various interpretations. One might attempt to argue this point in principle – perhaps, after translating the traditions into a rule-base, one might argue along Wittgensteinian lines that rules do not carry their own rules for use. Alternatively, one can point to the leading sources of traditional authority in the history of our society. All manner of competing Christian (and not just Christian) claims have been founded on the evidence available in the Bible. Even rule-like passages of the Word – such as the commandments – have been subject to a variety of interpretations. And it is not just in interpretation that one finds conflict. There may often be arguments about what actually occurred in the past. What this implies is that any particular version of a tradition could in principle be challenged and that the perceived unity of a tradition must be a social accomplishment. *Traditional authority is as much socially constructed as either its legal-rational or charismatic relatives.*

It is important to be clear about what we are claiming at this point. We are not saying simply that traditions are socially constructed. Unless one supposes that they really have been handed down by deities, traditions are evidently constructs in some sense. And there exist good case-studies documenting how contrivedly constructed some 'traditions' are: one need only think of the apparent tradition of Scottish tartan kilts which, it is claimed, was invented by an Englishman after the Union of 1707 and elaborated into the notion that each clan had its own tartan even later (Trevor-Roper 1983, pp. 21-3). What we are arguing is that even once established, the meaning and directive power of traditions is not straightforward or plain. Each use or invocation of a tradition is itself a social accomplishment. Thus, the 'traditionality' of actions which are said to comply with established traditions has to be managed and socially constructed. Ironically, it is the ease with which particular traditions can be debunked by showing them to be recent inventions projected onto the past which has directed attention away from the more subtle point about traditional action. The connection between a particular action and an established tradition is as open to social construction as is the link between a charismatic leader and the conduct of his or her followers or the link between legal rules and police conduct.

*Exercising Traditional Authority*

The exercise of traditional authority and thus its socially constructed character have received little attention from sociologists. This might be thought reasonable in the light of the disappearance of most traditional societies. But tradition is clearly still an important source of inspiration and legitimation. Radical writers have drawn our attention to the role of some traditions: to symbolic monarchies, for example, which express notions of national unity against the disunifying or antagonistic features of class (for example, Wright 1985). But this concern with the ideological and obfuscatory role of traditions have disinclined authors to examine the way in which traditions are constructed for particular legitimatory or rhetorical purposes. Their interest has been more in laying bare what they believe the myths conceal than in studying the construction and invocation of the traditions themselves. Although why people should want to present a particular view of the past is an interesting and important question, the answer is usually fairly obvious. The 'how they do it' question is more difficult and may produce answers which are little more than banalities but it is the problem we have chosen to examine. We are interested in the performance of 'being traditional'.

The case-study we present is concerned precisely with the use of tradition for legitimatory purposes. In Scotland's centuries-long struggle with England both sides engaged in military offence and in bargaining and hostage-taking. Both sides also devoted resources to legitimating their claims. The English promoted the 'Brut' mythology in which it was claimed that Britain had been founded by Brutus the Trojan who divided the kingdom between his three sons (Mason 1987). The eldest, Locrinus, inherited England. The second, Kamber, inherited Wales. The third son, Albanactus, inherited Scotland. Thus from the first Scotland had been subordinate to England. Furthermore, through the Middle Ages a succession of Scottish kings had paid homage to English rulers. This second claim could be answered by asserting that the Scottish kings only did homage for the lands they held in England. Answering the Brut myth required the construction of an ancient history for the Scots and from at least the twelfth century, Scottish historians laboured at the task. Where the English rested their claim on a Trojan, the Scots chose to go with the victors and traced themselves back to one Gathelus the Greek who married the eponymous Scota, daughter of Pharaoh. When God drowned Pharaoh's troops in the red Sea, Gathelus and Scota went to Spain. From there the Scoti went first to Ireland and then settled the west coast of Scotland.

With the formation of the petty kingdom of Dalriada in what is now Argyll, myth touches history. However it does so at rather a late date: in the fifth century AD (Dickinson and Duncan 1977, pp. 25-7). Through a gradual process of the accumulation of error (no doubt aided by a desire to believe the mistaken conclusion) the Latin regnal lists became so altered as to move the foundation of the Dalriadan Scoti kingdom back to 330 BC (the details of the errors are discussed in Bruce, forthcoming). Names of ancestors were borrowed from the well-known genealogy of the Scottish kings to fill in as early Scottish kings and non-Scottish historical figures were also enlisted to pad the history. The mythical history of Scotland reached its most sophisticated point of development in the history of Hector Boece, the first principal of Aberdeen University, who not only invented kings and events for their reigns but also had them deliver interminable 'orisouns'. In Boece's version we have not only Gathelus and Scota but thirty-nine completely fictional kings beginning with a spurious Fergus son of Feridaig and meeting history only at the authentic Fergus Mac Erc, the fortieth king.

Fanciful though this history now appears, it must be remembered that it was regarded as authentic by its advocates, was treated with considerable seriousness even by its detractors, and was frequently utilized in political argument. When Robert Bruce's chancery drafted a letter from the Scottish barons to the Pope opposing English claims to overlordship of Scotland (the famed 'Declaration of Arbroath'), the authors called on the history (Simpson 1977). When English and Scottish envoys met on the border at Kirk Yetholm in October 1401 to discuss Henry's demands that Robert III pay him homage, they argued history and claimed documentary warrants for their competing versions (Stones 1969). Scotland may have been a small kingdom, frequently dominated by its larger southern neighbour but its intellectuals were adamant that it would claim a more ancient and honourable history of independence.

At least by the time of the Stewarts the tradition of the mythical kings had been very actively elaborated; it was in active use in many spheres (for example, in representations to foreign powers); and it was articulated in many media: in the legends on coins, in genealogies, and in official portraiture. None the less, while succeeding generations deployed the 'same' tradition, the details invoked changed. To take just one example, George Buchanan, tutor to the infant James VI, used the mythical kings to argue for a conditional view of monarchy. He stressed the number of occasions on which a bad king was deposed and even murdered by 'the pepill' (as well he might, given his role as legitimator of the Scots Lords' revolt against Mary). In a wonderful feat of compressed propaganda, he had 'Pro Me Si Mereor in Me' inscribed on the reverse of the first silver coin of James' reign. The slogan is an abbreviated form of the request Trajan is supposed to have made to the Prefect of his Praetorian Guard when handing him his sword: '[Use this] for me or against me as I deserve'. (Stewart 1983, p. 454). While Buchanan drew on examples from the mythical kings to justify some notion of popular choice in the monarch's exercise of power, James on reaching his majority drew on the same material to argue for the absolute power of kings: the Scottish people only came into being because of the independent action of the leader in founding the kingdom. King first; then the kingdom.

*The Tradition of Kings and the De Wet Portraits*

We propose to focus on the last phase of the tradition of the Kings; a period which has been chosen because the 'data set' is on public view in Holyroodhouse Palace. The material consists of a series of portraits of the kings of Scotland painted between 1684 and 1686 by the Dutch decorative painter Jacob De Wet. Fortunately the contract for this work is still preserved and from it we can see that the artist was commissioned to paint all 110 kings up to and including the monarch of the day, Charles II. Charles died towards the end of the commission and the portrait of James VII (II of England) was added.

In many senses this was an obviously traditional representation of the monarch's lineage. The kings painted were all those cited in the established histories and the dates added to the figures reinforced the point about the antiquity of Scotland. Admittedly the faces of the kings, with the exception of the later Stewarts, could not be likenesses since no images of the models persisted nor, in some cases, could have existed. But the idea of painting a series of kings was not original. Edinburgh town council commissioned George Jamesone to paint likenesses of the Scottish kings for an arch which formed part of the decorations for the triumphal entry of Charles I to the city in 1633 (Thomson 1974, p. 99) and we have the word of Sir John Lauder of Fountainhall (1840) that De Wet based some of his portraits on the Jamesones.

At one level the portraits were a celebration of the tradition of monarchical rule, rejoicing at the restoration of a king after the civil war in England. In another sense, however, this depiction included an active interpretation of the tradition, which was evidenced in three features which we will identify and illustrate.

*Sequencing:* The paintings were arranged so that they ran in order of succession from the entrance, culminating in the Stewarts, who occupied the prime site in the room. In this way the very design of the room expressed the continuity and unbrokenness of the line. For the first thirty-nine kings, the claim of continuity was a smaller lie than the claim that they existed. In the case of the early genuine kings the neat sequence smoothed over many uncertainties of historical fact (although this was no more than the majority of regnal lists also did) and tidied up the reality. The order of the pictures offers only a simple image of succession and orderly descent. Thus, although Robert Bruce usurped the throne from John Balliol and John's son Edward tried to retake it from David Bruce, they are all presented in an orderly manner as if they had acquired the throne by Anglo-Norman primogeniture rules of succession.

The issue of succession has an additional significance. Even such early historians as Boece and Buchanan who anachronistically imposed the Anglo-Norman model on the early kings knew that until the House of Canmore in the thirteenth century, kingship, for what it was then worth, was assigned by *tannistry*. During the lifetime of the king, his successor would be selected by the lords from amongst the able-bodied males of the royal family. Thus kings were usually succeeded by their brothers, cousins and even uncles, but not immediately by their own sons. Although chiefship was thus limited to a small pool of contestants, the notion of kingship was very unlike the dynastic one in play at the time of the Stewarts. Yet since the pictures build stepwise to the case of the Stewart dyansty whose father-son continuity was marked in the succession of Jameses, the portraits project this model of inheritance back upon the tradition. The rise of the Stewarts to the throne was itself hardly defensible on the rules of primogeniture (they got there by marriage to the Bruces, whose claims were on the thin side) and the dynasty had struggled to survive. James I had been murdered by rebellious subjects as had James III. The intervening James II managed to control his rivals but was killed by one of his own bombards malfunctioning at the siege of Roxburgh. Mary was deposed, imprisoned and beheaded, as was Charles I. It was the inherited insecurity of that saga coupled with the precariousness of his own position which led James, Duke of Albany (later James VII) to bully the Scottish Parliament into passing an act of 1681 which asserted that:

> the Kings of this Realme deryving their Royall power from God almightie alone, doe succeid lineallie therto according to the known degrees of Proximitie in blood, which cannot be interrupted suspended or diverted by any Act or Statute whatsoevir. (*Acta Parliamentorum Caroli II,* 13 August 1681)

The continuity implied in the sequencing of the portraits was the pictorial expression of the same point. If the viewer accepted that the past had been 'like that', then the future was obvious. Contra the English Whigs who wanted to exclude him for his Catholicism, James was the next king.

*Highlighting:* A second major component in the contract was the specification of the sizes of the pictures. Of the original 110 (111 including James VII) eighteen were to be slightly larger than life size. The remainder were head and shoulders only. It seems likely that the decision to paint the later Stewarts full size (they were paying for it) was made first and that it was then felt that to have only the Stewarts life size would be a little too self-aggrandizing and that a few others should be given the same prominence. The shape of the Gallery suggested that seven others could be large and the ones chosen were (in putative chronological order):

Fergus I
Caractacus
Fergus II (MacErc)
Acajus
Kenneth MacAlpin
David I
Robert Bruce

Why were these chosen? The two Ferguses – one mythical, the other real – are the founders of the kingdom of Scotland. Fergus II, son of Erc, was the founder of the Dalriadan kingdom but he was relatively recent. In its developed Boecian form, the history claimed an earlier and fictional Fergus son of Feridaig as the founder and allowed the real Fergus to retain his status as a founding king by having the Scots being temporarily driven back to Ireland, whence they had come, and then returning to Argyll under the real Fergus. Both Ferguses are present as the dynasty's founding spirits. Kenneth MacAlpin united the Picts of the east with the Scots of Dalriada and thus laid the foundation for the expansion of the kingdom into something closer to the Scotland of Stewart times.

Two of the others represent martial prowess. In addition to helping the Stewarts to the throne, Robert Bruce's place was presumably earned by his decisive role in Scottish victories against the invading English. As a king he was characterized not only by personal valour and military ability but by success in defending and maintaining the kingdom. Furthermore, he succeeded where the House of Canmore had failed in persuading the Pope to recognize Scotland as a sovereign state and to permit Christian coronation. Unfortunately he died before he could benefit from papal recognition but his son was the first Scottish king to be crowned in the modern European style.

Caractacus was a real enough character although he was mythical as a king of Scotland. He was in fact a Brigantine leader who had enjoyed considerable success against the Romans. After eventual defeat he was taken to Rome where he so impressed the emperor that instead of being executed he was set free. He had been appropriated by Hector Boece as one of first thirty-nine kings because he exemplified military might and because his historical existence was well reported in such Latin writers as Tacitus. The same two virtues explain his attraction to the Stewarts. He is painted in battle dress carrying a Roman shield with 'SPQR' on it.

David exemplified the gentler virtue of Christianity. He founded Holyrood Abbey and gave considerable lands to fund monasteries and churches. He is painted with a large crucifix in his arms (and with a small tableau representing the legend of the founding of the Abbey in the background). As an aside it is interesting to note the relative autonomy of representations of the tradition. The tableau makes it abundantly clear that this is David, and the original De Wet contract told him to paint David full size. In 1746 there occurred an inadvertent testimony to the propaganda power of the portraits. Hawley's dragoons, stopping at the Palace on their retreat from their defeat by the Jacobites at Falkirk, took sabres to the paintings and severely damaged a large number. The part of the canvas with David's name on it was destroyed and in the subsequent restoration 'Davidus' was changed to 'Donadus' (not, as some guide books say, 'Donaldus'). What makes the confusion further understandable is that, in the Boecian history, the conversion of Scotland to Christianity was moved back (to predate that of England and thus deflect claims of the English Church to jurisdiction in Scotland) and attributed to a mythical Donaldus I. The restorers were faced with a king who clearly represented Christianity and whose name was badly damaged. Instead of identifying him correctly as David, they plumped for the mythical history and, in reconciling that to the remains of the name on the painting, produced 'Donadus I'. The point about the substitution (only one of the many renamings which occurred in that restoration) is that the same ideological purpose is served whether it is David (who really exemplified promoter of the Christian Church) or Donald (who mythically represented the same thing). Truth or fiction; either will do.

Apart from the Stewarts, this leaves Acajus. He is celebrated by Boece as being responsible for negotiating a military alliance with Emperor Charlemagne against the occupants of what is now England. (Boece appears to have taken the account of a treaty between Charlemagne and the Scoti of *Ireland* from Eginhard's *Life of Charlemagne,* and temporarily forgotten what in other parts of his history he demonstrated: that until the eleventh century Scoti meant Irish.) King Acajus therefore was the originator of the 'Auld Alliance'. Although the Stewarts were kings of England as well as Scotland, it was the English who had executed Charles I and France which had provided a home in exile. Although he could not have anticipated that he would himself soon be exiled to France, James, the Duke of Albany's relations with the French were clearly of great significance, and Acajus, as the claimed originator of that special relationship, would have been dear to James's cause.

The first impression created by the arrangement of the portraits in the Gallery is awe at the antiquity of the Scottish kingdom. There is simply an 'awe-ful' lot of monarchs. But the selection of a number to be painted life size cleverly elicits a more considered and complex response. As one looks around the room one is drawn to the majestic Stewarts and then back to the foundation of the kingdom with the eye alighting on a number of special kings. As our attention is drawn from the mass of small faces to the full-size figures, we see the Founders, the Warlord, the Diplomat, the Saint, the Unifier of Picts and Scots, and the Liberator. We see the embodiment of kingly and national virtues. And we see the Stewarts. The designer clearly expected us to make the connection: the Stewarts were the present exemplification of the virtues of the previous rulers.

*Gilding:* A third element in the commission is the gilding of the basic portraits with additional images. As one would expect the Stewarts are all accompanied by the regalia, the symbols of office. But crowns are also painted on some earlier kings who predated (or, in the case of the mythical ones, would have predated) the switch from Celtic inauguration to Anglo-Norman crowning. Acajus, for example, has a full crown rather like the genuine later crown although he pre-dates Bruce by 500 years. The anachronism has the effect of further linking together the succession of kings and reminds us of a similar device on a James VI lion noble coin. The circumscription read 'Post 5 et 100 Prosvos Invicta Manent Hec'. 'Hec' referred to the sword and sceptre being held by the lion and the circumscription effectively asserted that 105 Proavi (the correct term for ancestors remoter than a grandparent) had passed these on to James V and his grandson, James VI (Stewart 1983, p. 456).

The attire of the kings is also interesting; pre-Stewart they are dressed either in a hybrid Roman/Medieval armour or in ermine robes, both anachronisms which have the effect of making even the pre-Christian kings familiar and recognizable. The combined

## The Social Construction of Tradition

effect is to reinforce the single great anachronism of the commission: all these kings were like our kings.

### Royalism in the Portraits

What has been said so far indicates that the pictures draw on a traditional history of the kingship but that they reproduce it in a distinctive way. Details of the portraits can be tied to the interests of the Stewart dynasty as it approached the close of the seventeenth century, particularly the interests of James, Duke of Albany. For example, we have seen that a model of simple dynastic succession is implied in the pictures and that a vastly long dynastic lineage is presented. Moreover, the monarchs are accorded a decisive role in shaping the history of Scotland. It is King David, not missionaries, who is responsible for the promotion of Christianity. It is Acajus who is responsible for diplomatic successes. Robert Bruce defended the kingdom. This emphasis on the achievements of the kings themselves is perhaps most fully realized in the case of Caractacus's individualized success in earning the respect of the Roman Empire.

In earlier times the tradition had been chiefly invoked to establish that Scotland was an older kingdom than England. The exact rules of succession, the particular roles of kings – even their moral character – was subordinated to the sheer antiquity of the line. In its earliest underdeveloped form as merely a list of names and dates in a regnal list, the tradition could do little more than speak to age. As it was elaborated and stories attached to the names and dates, it became possible to use it for more elaborate ideological purposes. As was mentioned above, this all-embracing history allowed such subsequent commentators as Buchanan to focus on bad and ineffectual kings in support of limitations on monarchical power. But the Holyroodhouse portraits present a distinctively royalist instantiation of this tradition.

From what we know of the Edinburgh politics of the period and of the plans for the restoration and decoration of the Palace, we can be reasonably confident that James was behind the contract with De Wet. Although at one level the paintings merely represent the traditional history of the Scottish throne, the detailed form they take stands as an innovative and deliberate act of propaganda. In their style and arrangement, in the successions they imply, in the choice of monarchs to be emphasized and in the anachronistic details, the portraits exhibit a commitment to and an argument for royalism. Kingship is regular, 'natural' dynastic selection; Scotland has prospered under two millennia of uninterrupted monarchical rule; past kings have been personally responsible for the defence and improvement of the kingdom; and the Stewarts are the sole current representatives of that succession. The cause of history is served by the portraits, and the portraits serve to show that, whatever the Westminster Whigs think about it, history exclusively endorses James as the next king and ruler.

*Conclusion*

Although the tradition of Scottish kings – mythical and real – was well established and well documented by the time of the Holyroodhouse portraits, the invocation of that tradition allowed innovative and imaginative interpretative work to be done. James could invoke the tradition (De Wet was instructed to paint the 'regulation' number of kings) at the same time as reconstructing its detailed meaning to turn a national myth into a royalist myth. And it is very much in the details of the commission that the meaning lies: in the ordering, arrangement, size and incidental contents of the pictures.

To return to the question of how one enacts tradition, the creative work in the De Wet commission illustrates an important point which is apt to get lost in thinking about tradition mainly in comparison with the rational-legal authority which dominates modern societies. It is easy to suppose that traditions are self-evident and unchanging, that they have the taken-for-granted status of 'just how things were'. If they are interested in traditions at all, modern analysts often concentrate on demonstrating that 'in reality' this was not how things were, that traditions falsify the past. But our reading of the De Wet portraits of Scottish kings (and indeed of the other occasions in which the tradition of the mythical kings was invoked) indicates that an equally important issue concerns the way in which traditions are implemented on particular occasions.

A more useful appreciation of traditional authority is to be found by concentrating on what is deployed in persuasive work. What characterizes traditional authority is not its static nature, for traditions constantly change, with each re-working laying the foundation for the next deployment. Instead, its characteristic in its reliance on the past, both as a ratiocinative principle and as the source of data. Although the ratiocinative principle cannot change much without fundamentally altering the type of authority, the data deployed and their deployment are, indeed, must be, socially constructed. To paraphrase W.I. Thomas, just as we must actively define every present situation, so too every past which is called into the present must be defined.

## Acknowledgements

We should like to express our thanks for help in the study of the De Wet portraits to Colonel Wickes, the Superintendant of Holyroodhouse Palace; R.J. Snowden and A. Cummings of the Stenhouse Conservation Centre; Dr. Rosalind Marshall and Dr. Duncan Thomson of the Scottish National Portrait Gallery; Dr. M.R. Apted; and Iain MacIvor and Richard Fawcett of Historic Buildings and Monuments, Scottish Development Department. We would also like to thank Dr. Roger Mason of St. Andrews University and Dr. M.O. Anderson for their help in understanding the evolution of the history of the mythical kings. The Queen's University of Belfast provided funds for us to visit Holyroodhouse and to consult experts. Finally we would like to note that the De Wet portraits are Crown copyright and thank the Lord Chamberlain for permission to reproduce photographs of them.

## REFERENCES

Apted, M.R., and Hannabus, S. (1978) *Painters in Scotland 1301–1700*, Edinburgh: Scottish Record Society.

Bruce, S. (forthcoming), 'Mythical Kings: The Construction of a False Tradition'.

Dickinson, W.C., and Duncan, A.A.M. (1977), *Scotland from the Earliest Times to 1603*, Oxford: Oxford University Press.

Goody, J. (1986), *The Logic of Writing and the Organization of Society*, Cambridge: Cambridge University Press.

Lauder of Fountainhall, Sir John (1840), *Historical Observes of Memorable Occurants in Church and State*, Edinburgh: Bannatyne Club.

Mason, R.A. (1987) 'Scotching the Brut: Politics, History and National Myth in Sixteenth-Century Britain', *Scotland and England, 1286-1815*. Edinburgh: John Donald.

Maxwell, H. (1920), *Official Guide to the Abbey-Church, Palace and Environs of Holyroodhouse* Edinburgh: HMSO.

Simpson, I. (1977), 'The Declaration of Arbroath revisited', *Scottish Historical Review* 56, pp. 11–34.

Stewart, I. (1983), 'Coinage and Propaganda: An Interpretation of the Coin-Types of James VI', in, A. O'Connor and D.V. Clarke, *From the Stone Age to the 45: Studies presented to R.B.K. Stephenson*, Edinburgh: John Donald.

Stones, E.L.G. (1969), 'The Appeal to History in Anglo-Scottish Relations between 1291 and 1401', *Archives* 9, nos. 41-4, 11–21 and 80–3.

Thomson, D. (1974), *The Life and Art of George Jamesone*, Oxford: Clarendon Press.

Trevor-Roper, H. (1983), 'The Invention of Tradition: The Highland Tradition of Scotland', in E. Hobsbawm and T. Ranger (eds.), *The Invention of Tradition*, Cambridge: Cambridge University Press.

Wallis R. (1982), 'Charisma, Control and Commitment in a New Religious Movement', in *Millennialism and Charisma,* Belfast: The Queen's University of Belfast.

Weber, M. (1964), *The Theory of Social and Economic Organization,* London: Allen & Unwin.

Wright, P. (1985), *On Living in an Old Country,* London: Verso.

# 11

## Culture, Social Development and the Scottish Highland Gatherings

GRANT JARVIE

Sporting practices are something that most people in Western industrial capitalism tend to take for granted. Simon Pia has recently commented upon the surprising lack of serious discussion on Scottish sport given its popular location within Scottish culture (Pia 1987). Such a challenge lies precisely in acknowledging not only the voluntaristic pleasurable dimensions of sporting experience, but also that forms of sport themselves have emerged from the unique patterns, struggles and figurations which have contributed to the development of the Scottish social formation. Sporting culture, like all forms of culture, is itself created within the context of enabling and constraining structures. Sporting images, codes, relations of power and the ability to define the very nature of sporting practices in Scotland are things that not only work for or against particular sporting actors and players, but also operate through the differential capacity of different inter-dependent classes, genders and nations to define the rules which govern all forms of culture, including sporting forms.

The Scottish Highland Gatherings and Games as a particular cultural form consist of a number of complex traditions and practices which both mediate and are mediated by the unique pattern of figurational arrangements which have developed within Highland culture in particular and Scottish culture in general. The Highland Gatherings of today have not developed within a social vacuum and therefore are capable of encompassing some of the most basic questions that might be asked about Scottish cultural identity, dependency and social structure. What is the relationship between the Highland Gatherings and the prevailing social structure? What is the relationship between the Highland Gatherings and various specific figurations such as clans, landlords and emigrés? How have the Highland Gatherings been affected by the historical epoch in which they move? In what way do the modern Highland Gatherings differ from the traditional Highland Gatherings? Why did the Gatherings suddenly become popular after about 1840? What social forces have shaped this Highland tradition? In what way do the Highland Gatherings reflect Scottish cultural identity? Such questions are perhaps indicative of the potential richness that may be found in a historical sociological analysis which takes as its main focus the development of the Scottish Highland Gatherings. What theoretical concepts might provide meaningful points of departure for grounding such a discussion on this set of sporting practices?

*Historical Sociology and Sport*

Attempts to construct historical sociological models of sporting development have taken a number of different forms. The early ground clearing work of the late 1960s and early 1970s has itself developed into a multi-paradigmatic debate between similar and divergent epistemologies. At least three schools of thought have dominated discourse on British forms of sport. First writers who have been influenced by or have been actively involved in the work of the Birmingham University Centre for Contemporary Cultural Studies (CCCS) have undertaken work on sport to:

    1. delve into the broader conditions and social relations in which a dominant conception of sport is made or reproduced;

    2. examine how the struggles between different groups and classes have resulted in dominant, residual and emergent forms of sporting practices;

    3. demonstrate how a particular form of sport is consolidated, contested, maintained or reproduced in the context of the reproduction of society as a whole (Clarke and Critcher 1985; Critcher 1979; Horne, Jary and Tomlinson 1987; Whannel 1982).

Certainly, in considering any historical process, culture is a useful concept in that, through what Williams refers to as dominant, residual and emergent forms, it embodies, in part, the trajectory and experiences of group life through history (Williams 1977). Yet it is important not to lose sight of the fact that such dominant, residual and emergent forms of cultural production are themselves relatively dependent upon the people who personify such traditions. There is a very real danger of forgetting that this trajectory of group life involves a complex network of class, cultural, national and gender alliances and not just one all consuming dominant group. While the CCCS approach may be valued for its attention to historical context, its treatment of sport as culture and its avoidance of determinism and class reductionism, its relative neglect of the ways in which middle-class culture and indeed, the culture of the traditional aristocracy mediate popular cultural forms are problematic (Robbins 1987).

A second school of thought which has influenced work on British sport has been that of Marxist cultural analysis. In seeking to develop answers to unanswered questions and alternative codes for understanding the past and present the concepts of ideology and hegemony have gained a lot of credence in Marxist cultural analysis. Marxist cultural material on sport is distinguished from the cultural-studies tradition by the starting point of each discourse. On a number of occasions political economists have criticized the work of the CCCS for not paying adequate attention to the way in which culture itself mediates and is mediated by political economy (Gruneau 1988). It is perhaps more accurate to refer to the one discourse on sport as that of cultural Marxism and the other as a form of Marxist cultural analysis which starts out from the standpoint of political economy. As such work on sport within this tradition has been undertaken for some or all of the following reasons:

1. to determine if cultural production through sport is related to the maintenance of a class-based society;
2. to identify the dynamic of this relation; if there is one.
3. to generate strategies aimed at the amelioration of existing class relations (Gruneau 1983; Hargreaves 1982, 1986; Jarvie 1985).

In *Sport, Power and Culture* (1986), Hargreaves illustrates how sport in Britain cannot be dissociated from the context of class relations and specific hegemonic patterns. Almost all of Hargreaves' arguments are powerful, penetrating and greatly overstated. He writes from the stance of the thorough Marxist scholar rather than the polemical tradition of revolutionary neo-Marxism. Accordingly, his prime purpose is to demystify, strip bare and amplify the processes of domination and struggle in society and in particular the impinging of class relations and economic processes on cultural life, including sporting practices. Indeed Hargreaves has gone to some length to show how a Marxist cultural analysis of sport in Britain might proceed. None the less, there are some troublesome points of departure, in particular the lack of concern with the hegemony theory of sport about the notion of counter-hegemonic struggle as it was originally used by Antonio Gramsci (Gramsci 1971, pp. 1–20).

'Hegemonia', to Gramsci, referred to the process by which class or class fractions made concessions and alliances with other groups thus enabling them to adopt a leadership role and assert themselves as the embodiment of national interest. What was equally important to Gramsci, was the development of a counter-hegemonic struggle which would challenge and transform society. This counter-hegemonic struggle, for Gramsci, was rooted in the political, economic and cultural spheres. Yet, to return to Hargreaves, it is precisely this aspect of counter-hegemonic struggle so crucial in Gramsci's work which is relatively silent within the analysis of British sport presented by Hargreaves. Indeed the way in which sport might contribute to the 'war of position' is an aspect of the subject that is not adequately represented in many Marxist cultural scenarios on sport. While it is clear how the practices of the Gaelic Athletic Association or the South African Council on Sport might provide a basis for 'social antagonism' within the respective social formations, the concrete evidence to substantiate the extremely over-worked concepts of hegemony or counter-hegemonic struggle are in the last instance missing from many Marxist cultural accounts of sporting practice. Within the context of his discussion on American sport, MacAloon has recently argued that despite the grand claims of hegemony theorists that space has been won through sporting struggle from the dominant hegemony, at the level of ethnography it is certainly not apparent that blacks, hispanics, women, the poor or the athletically deprived children of the middle class have gained any power for their points of view through the institutional arrangements for sport within the United States of America (MacAloon 1988, p. 5). The problem lies not so much with the concept of hegemony but merely the balance between the theoretical claims and the ethnographical evidence.

Before considering a third and final discourse which has influenced historical sociological debates on British sport, I should like to mention briefly the work of one Canadian writer whose work has a direct theoretical link with the analysis of the Highland Gatherings presented in this chapter. In *Class, Sports and Social Development* (1983), Gruneau, having laid out his ground rules and strategy, proceeds to offer a case-study of Canadian sport that is located within the complex development of Canada as a dependent social formation. The whole notion of the structuring of play, games and sport within this unique context, argues Gruneau, must acknowledge at least two essential factors: first, the role of social class as a key factor in conflicts over various resources in Canadian society; and, second, the idea that class structures and patterns of social development are greatly influenced by the relations of domination and dependency between a metropole and a hinterland (Gruneau 1983, p. 94). The metropole, Gruneau goes on, has a greater capacity to define allocative rules and to appropriate certain resources, and this may lead to the underdevelopment or uneven development of certain features of the hinterland's organization.

Such notions of dependency and uneven development, I believe, provide the axial points of departure for grounding an analysis of Highland and Scottish development. One of the constant themes on the area has been community instability and in particular, the effect which a tenurial system of land control has had on past and present social structures. Although statutory groups with a specific Highland remit have been brought into being, many would argue that centralist control and landlord power still lie at the heart of many of the dependency problems experienced by the Highland social formation (Evans and Hendry 1985; Hunter 1979; McEwan 1981). Yet it is important to view dependency not as a condition but as a process, and therefore due attention should be paid to the historical developments and figurations which have given rise to any social formation or nation-state becoming dependent. Such an analysis should also encompass the notion that cultural forms, such as the Highland Gatherings, are also implicated in the process of dependency. By and large, dependency theorists have failed to pay attention to the many cultural aspects of dependency such as those involved in the selection of tradition and cultural identity.

A third and final discourse that has influenced writings on British sport has been that of figurational sociology (Dunning 1988; Dunning, Murphy and Williams 1988; Dunning and Sheard 1979; Elias and Dunning 1986; Rojek 1985). Like the Marxist cultural synthesis on sport, figurationalists have also been influenced by and have influenced theoretical controversies concerning the inadequacy of those sociological accounts that have been insensitive to historical or development concerns. Figurationalists have also raised questions about social structure and social transformation. Although problematically the texts differ, there are a number of similarities between the work of Gruneau in the early 1980s and the work of Dunning and Sheard in the late 1970s (Dunning and Sheard 1979; Gruneau 1983). Both texts are sensitive to questions about social patterns and social arrangements in society. The problems in both texts are approached from historical positions which in each instance are complemented by a penetrating sociological analysis. Sociologists working within the figurational framework have undertaken work on sport for at least three reasons:

1. to explore the implications of Elias's conceptual framework with regard to sporting development;
2. to reconstruct and explain the structures of long-term societal developments;

3. to map out the relative determining and yet flexible figurational dynamics at any particular stage in history.

It would be misleading and indeed incorrect to argue that the immanent dynamics of such figurations develop in a merely evolutionary sense. Consider Elias's discussion of a river with three essentially different currents running at different speeds (Elias 1983, p. 4). If the three currents are viewed in isolation, then they may seem unique; these currents develop at different rates and yet are still part of the river. Social figurations also develop at different rates and yet are still part of the social process of development. The concept of social transformation does not necessarily illustrate the complexity of historical development. Two crucial points need to be made. First, social processes can involve changes in different directions, for example, towards higher or lower levels of dependency or higher or lower levels of social differentiation, integration, domination and subordination. Second, while the concept of development entails a transformation towards higher or lower levels of social differentiation, such a process may or may not be reversed at any particular time. Critics of the figurational notion of development are ill-informed when they argue that implicit within this approach is a subtle dependence upon functionalism and evolutionism (Horne and Jary 1987, p. 100). Figurationalists have gone to some length to stress that while the Eliasian notion of development might entail evolutionary tendencies, it does not entail the inevitable process of change in any single direction.

A core concept within the figurational work on sport is the relational concept of power. In many ways, power is handled much more satisfactorily in this context than in discussions on power in cultural studies. The notion of power has proved to be a fruitful analytical concept for many social commentaries on sport and leisure. There is the partially economic theory of power found in both vulgar and sophisticated forms of Marxism. The basic assumption of this theory is that power, unequally distributed as a commodity or resource, is a factor in the production or reproduction of class domination through control of the means of production. Many neo-Marxist, and in particular Marxist-cultural, discussions of power have concentrated upon the process by which the main features of power in social life have been mobilized and reproduced (Nelson and Grossberg 1988). One of the major advantages that the figurational approach to power has over classical Marxist accounts is that the essence of power in social formations is seen to exist in all forms of human relationships, which in turn tend to become structured, through a process of negotiation and struggle, into forms, for example, of class domination and repression. The open-ended figurational analysis allows for social-class explanations of power relations but also for a multitude of other dynamic power relations at any particular instance or stage in the developmental process.

This introductory discussion on some of the core approaches and concerns of historical sociology has attempted to illustrate that such concerns have not been irrelevant to debates concerning the development of sport within industrial capitalist societies. All of these accounts of sporting development have some or all of the following characteristics. First, they ask questions about social structure or processes understood to be concretely situated in time or space. Second, they examine temporal processes and historical sequences in accounting for outcomes. Third, they attend to the interplay of meaningful actions and structured contexts in order to make sense of unintended as well as intended outcomes within any social transformation. Finally, they are all responsive to the controversies concerning the inadequacy of those sociological accounts that have been insensitive to historical concerns.

This introductory discussion has also drawn together a number of theoretical points of departure for the analysis of the Scottish Highland Gatherings and Games as a particular cultural form. Although the discussion is not new, there is a continuing debate in Scottish politics which urges historians, educationalists, sociologists and cultural critics to challenge the dominant cultural power, question its values and assumptions, enquire into the complex ways in which it mediates Scottish life and generate alternative codes for understanding Scottish culture. Work on sport within Scottish culture has been relatively underdeveloped although, some writers have indicated ways in which such work might develop (Jarvie 1986; Moorehouse 1986; Whitson 1983). Moorhouse, in particular, has questioned the extent to which cultural trajectories of British sport, such as soccer, organized around such concepts as class, class relations, hegemony and class resistance might in fact be over-simplified and, in some ways, inadequate when faced with Scottish sporting problems. I have argued here that any account of Highland sporting forms in particular and Scottish sporting forms in general can only be fully explained if it proceeds within a dependency framework which is complemented by the notions of 'figurations' and 'aspects' of cultural theory. Such concepts provide the theoretical grounding for the analysis of the Scottish Highland Gatherings that follows.

## The Development of the Scottish Highland Gatherings

In the first instance, it is important to make the point that many of the traditions and practices so central to today's modern Highland

Gatherings did in fact exist within the Highland social formation which existed before about 1750. At the heart of this social order lay the Highland clan figuration. Yet it is important to avoid somewhat romantic idealistic images of what was at times, a very violent, patriarchal and feudal way of life in which many Highlanders lived on the very edge of a materially impoverished existence. The following factors need to be mentioned briefly.

1. The social structure of the clan consisted essentially of a stratified set of social relations involving chiefs, chieftains, tacksmen, tenants and cottars, each with a greater or lesser degree of power.

2. A large sector of the clan economy was dependent upon cattle. Highland existence was at times violent with sporadic outbursts of cattle-raiding continuing well into the eighteenth century.

3. It was an essential feature of the system that the land was laid out to ensure the continued existence of the clan as a socially unified, effective, military organization. The land belonged to the clan and not to the chief.

4. The chief's power and status were not generally acquired through wealth, but through the clan's military status.

The Highland Clan way of life essentially gave expression to a way of life in which patriarchal, feudal bonds of kinship counted for much more than capital gains and profit.

It is against this harsh, materially impoverished, and sometimes violent way of life, that many of the antecedent forms of today's modern Highland Gatherings may be found. Many of these sporting practices were individual rather than collective in the sense that hill-racing, putting the stone and tossing the caber all existed as recreative practices in their own right rather than belonging to a specific Highland Gathering. Consider the following examples. First, Highland dancing and the playing of the pipes were important aspects of pre-1745 clan life. By at least the sixteenth century, many clan chiefs and many of the chieftains had their own hereditary pipers, with the most celebrated examples probably being the MacCrummens, hereditary pipers to the Macleods of Macleod, the Macarthurs, hereditary pipers to the MacDonalds Lords of the Isles, the Mackays, hereditary pipers to the clan Menzies (MacAoidh 1833). Second, the work both of Webster and of Colquhoun and Machell alludes to the fact that Highland chiefs often had stones at the entrance to their dwellings so that visitors could test their strength (Colquhoun and Machell 1927; Webster 1973). Isobel Grant indicates that the strength stones played a crucial part in Highland matrimonial ceremonies (Grant 1961). Third, reference might be made to the first minutes

of the Cowal Highland Gathering, where it is argued that
Highland Gatherings in Scotland go back many generations. This
ancient social tradition was a feature of Highland life in Scotland
and took place usually when the grain had been cut or stooked in
late August or early September (Yorke 1821). Fourth, reference
might be made to the traditional means whereby the clans were
called to council. The Gathering of the clans, in many instances
began with the dispatch of a fiery cross being carried round the
clan territory by a series of runners. The fiery cross was a signal for
the clan to gather, usually because some enemy had encroached
upon clan territory. The last instance of this practice was probably
the sending of the cross around Loch Tay by Lord Breadalbane in
1745.

As for the earliest point of origin, reference should probably be
made to the eleventh-century event which allegedly took place
upon the Braes of Mar. Today's Braemar Royal Highland
Gathering certainly asserts that its origin may be taken from an
eleventh-century incident in which Malcolm Ceannmore (1058-
93) summoned the clans to the Braes of Mar, whereupon a hill-
race to the summit of Craig Choinneach took place. Hill-races are
certainly one of the traditional sporting practices maintained at
today's Highland Gatherings. However, several qualifications
have to be made. While tradition and popular culture suggest that
this eleventh-century event might be the origin of the gatherings,
lack of original eleventh-century documentation precludes absolute
certainty. Furthermore, since the Highlanders did not arrive until
the fourteenth century, a question mark must be raised against the
assertion that the hill-race on Craig Choinneach was in fact a
Highland Gathering of the clans and not just a gathering at which
clansfolk were present. While the processes which eventually gave
rise to the social differentiation between Highlanders and
Lowlanders were certainly at work as early as the eleventh century,
there is little evidence to support the claim that the Highlanders of
the Highland Clan figuration achieved a distinct identity much
before the fourteenth century. All that can be said about the hill-
race up Craig Choinneach, and the gathering of the clans on the
Braes of Mar, is that today's Highland Gatherings have developed
out of a number of antecedent forms, some of which may date
back to at least the eleventh century.

Yet if a broad initial development phase may be identified as
occurring between the eleventh century or earlier until about 1750,
then a second phase of development lasted from about 1740 until
1850. At least three important factors affected the development of
the Highland Gatherings during this period. In the first instance,

the post-Culloden policies of the British state further accelerated a process of cultural marginalization and transformation. A number of writers have commented that the significance of Culloden was not so much that it was a catastrophic defeat for the Highland army, for there had been many such defeats in the past. What distinguished Culloden from previous defeats was the determined attempt by the British state to eradicate the social and political fabric of a traditional way of life. In the second instance, a number of Highland cultural practices, including sporting traditions, were transported with the emigrés to North America in particular. The Gathering of the Antigonish Highland Society was founded in 1816 and the Glengarry Highland Society Gathering in 1819. By 1867, Scottish Highland Gatherings and Games had been established in Boston, New York City, Philadelphia and New Jersey to name but a few (Donaldson 1986). Yet it is important not to divorce the development of these Highland Gatherings overseas from the general causes and conflicts which contributed to emigration from the Highlands during the eighteenth and nineteenth centuries. Third, in a determined attempt to retain selective aspects of Highland culture, such as dance and music, many Highland Friendly Societies such as Lonach, Braemar and Glenisla actively encouraged the development of a number of Highland Gatherings and Games.

It is certainly arguable that the collapse of a distinct Highland way of life after the failure of the '45 Rebellion gave rise to a process of cultural marginalization and subsequently, a process of cultural transformation. The Highlander was rendered safe for assimilation into the imagination of the Lowland Scot and the Scottish way of life in general. A culture was destroyed after Culloden, and yet, precisely because of this, its symbols became available not only to a nascent European Romantic movement, of which Walter Scott was a part, but also to Scottish cultural identity in general. Because of the obscurity of Highland history and because of the popular tide of feeling at the time towards the Highlanders, the literati had relatively few problems locating a sentimental Scottish nationalism north of the Highland line. What is of concern here is not so much the influence of writers such as Scott within the European context, but rather the legacy left to the Highlands after its culture had been marginalized and transformed. It was left with images of purple hills, monarchs of the glen, romantic heroes and kilts, tartans, claymores and other Highland symbols all being adopted as the real image of Scotland. Forgotten were the realities of the clearances, what the '45 Rebellion actually stood for and the experiences of famine, poverty and eviction (Hunter 1976; Hunter 1981; Prebble 1984).

The period between about 1740 and about 1850 was distinctively characterized by the British destruction of authentic Highland culture and its symbolic power. During this time the Highland Gatherings, like many other aspects of Highland culture, were influenced by the British state's post-Culloden policies. An initial phase of cultural marginalization was subsequently followed by the Highland Clearances and emigration, in particular to North America. The people who remained became increasingly dependent upon the actions of the Highland landlords, many of whom had been Highland chiefs within the old clan figuration. The process of emigration contributed to the emergence of Highland Gatherings and Societies overseas. Yet in Scotland, the paradoxical situation developed by the early nineteenth century in which many of the descendants of those landlords who had contributed to the demise of the Highland way of life became the guardians of its existence. Many of the graphic symbols which were adopted by the Highland and Friendly Societies became romanticized and, in part, divorced from their original social context. The romantic images produced by Walter Scott and other writers certainly contributed to a process of cultural transformation, which was to contribute not only to the emergence of the sporting landlord phenomenon, but also to processes of 'Balmoralization' and popularization of the Scottish Highland Gatherings. This period lasted from about 1840 to about 1920.

It cannot be argued that there was a direct mono-causal link between the financial difficulties of sheep farming and the development of the Highlands as a sporting playground during the Victorian period. However, the decline in the fortunes of sheep farming, the increasing wealth of the metropolitan sectors of capital, the influence of not only the traditional aristocracy but also the *nouveau riche,* the further entaglement of landownership with financial capital and an improved network of communication were certainly some of the key structural factors which contributed to the process whereby the Highlands became increasingly dependent upon the sporting landlords of the nineteenth century. The power of those at the apex of the Highland social structure to influence and implement political, economic and cultural changes, had an immense effect upon the way of life experienced by the small tenantry or crofting class.

With specific reference to the Highland Gatherings and Games, the power of the sporting landlords to control and influence the agenda led, in part, to the cultural production of these sporting practices in a somewhat romanticized form. Between about 1840 and 1920, the Highland Gathering became inextricably linked with images of Balmorality, loyalty and royalty. Highland dress again became a statutory mode of attire at the Games. Accessories that would have struck the old Highlanders as amazing were incorporated into the outfit. The patronage bestowed on the Braemar Royal Highland Gathering by Queen Victoria marked the beginning of this process of Balmoralization through which a bonding or social link was reproduced between the reigning monarchy, the Balmoral estate and the Braemar Royal Highland Gathering in particular although not exclusively. The process contributed greatly to the cultural production and reproduction of the Highland Gathering in a particular social form. However, it should not be forgotten that Queen Victoria and her husband were not only patrons to the Braemar Royal Highland Society, but also patrons to a number of Highland and Island Emigration societies, and, as such, were actively involved in the process of Highland depopulation. While the romantic storybook glens of the Lowlands and the South were being created, the real glens of the North were being emptied as Highland people were still being evicted from the land.

The Balmoralization process itself was inextricably linked with a broader process involving the popularization not only of the Highland Gathering, but also of the Highlands as a sporting playground for a certain leisure class. As wealth accumulated in the South and the area available to sport in England declined, the Highland sporting estates attracted a flow of capital against which the local sheep farming tenants could not compete, despite conflict, tension, resistance and struggle. What was particularly significant about the sporting landlord tradition was the emergence of individuals with economic and social power alongside the traditional aristocracy. The Highlands had become part of the cultural capital of the rich. Highland sport meant much more than social status in the sense that it was also a means of acquiring financial status. Only those with financial security and expendable resources could compete. In many cases there was a distinct interlocking between landownership and positions of power and influence not only within the local communities, but also within the committee structure of the Highland Gatherings and Games. The Earl of Mar, the Marquis of Huntly, the Earl of Airlie, the Duke of Atholl, Sir Charles of Forbes of Newe, the Farquharsons of Invercauld and the Duke of Argyll are all examples of titled landowners who held positions of influence within the social milieu of the Highland Gatherings and Games (Jarvie 1986).

Yet in stark contrast to the way of life experienced by the sporting landlord class, the crofters, and those who were primarily responsible for working the land, experienced poverty, famine and land congestion during the Victorian period. The future of the crofters, according to Hunter, during the 1840s was as bleak as it could be (Hunter 1976). Poverty, threat of eviction, overcrowding on the peripheral allotments of land and a yawning chasm between income produced and rent paid to the landlord were some of the crucial facts of life which structured crofting experiences. Such experiences of hardship and hunger were only exacerbated by the failure of staple products such as the potato crop upon which the crofters were relatively dependent. While losses were greatest amongst the inhabitatnts of the Western Isles, no area of the Highlands escaped the potato famine which emerged after about 1846 and continued through to the early 1950s. The Highland emigrés of previous years were soon to be joined by more of their compatriots who were forced to leave the land either through starvation or lack of income to pay the rent demanded by landlord and the subsequent eviction. It is against this historical background of contrasting experiences of landlord and crofters that the processes of Balmoralization and popularization occurred. While the passing of the Crofters Act of 1886 marked an important milestone in Highland social development, it fell well short of the crofters' demands for total liquidation of the power of the landlords.

Certainly since about 1910 to the present day, the modern Highland Gatherings have undergone a number of changes. The pressures and tensions of modernity are partially responsible for the contemporary expression of those groups of people who construct, control and negotiate the values, meanings and practices associated with today's Highland Gatherings and Games. It is important to understand that such a dominant expression has not merely evolved, but has developed out of a number of complex processes and mediations within and between a complex set of dynamic figurational arrangements. None the less, for all the complexity of their modern expression, it can be illustrated that a dominant interpretation of today's Highland Gatherings and Games is essentially different and yet constitutive of many of the traditions and practices from earlier epochs. Residual glimpses of earlier social arrangements and practices still partially penetrate the dominant interpretation of the modern Highland Gatherings and Games.

More specifically, in conjunction with increasing rationalization, bureaucratization and commodification, the emergence of the professional Highland Gatherings circuit helped to integrate further this Highland tradition into the market-place and legitimate the phenomenon as an area of open competition and commercial activity. The modern Highland Gatherings and Games continue to experience problems of cultural domination and contribute in no small way to the production of a romantic cultural identity. Expressions of these developments are numerous; the following are simply examples of some of the modern facets of today's Highland Gatherings and Games; advertising sponsorship and the expansion of a comprehensive consumer culture consisting of many of the kitsch symbols of cultural identity; the relative acceptance of uniform rules, regulations and records under the control of such incipient bureaucratization as the Scottish Games Association; and changing class relationships at the level of organizational control leading to a degree of democratization. The modern Highland Gatherings, argues Webster, provide the opportunity for the laird, crofter, shepherd and athletes in general to meet on equal terms and keep alive the great traditions of the past (Webster 1973). And yet the Highland Gatherings can hardly be regarded as a graphic symbol of meritocracy. It would be misleading and indeed incorrect to argue that such progress should be equated with meritocracy in any form. At the level of participation, competitors reflect a hierarchy of occupations with each person having a limited or expendable amount of resources at his or her behest. Furthermore, in terms of influence and control, even a modest perusal of the social composition of many of the Highland Gathering committees will reveal that the Duke of Argyll, the Earl of Huntly, the Duke of Fife, Sir Iain Colquhoun and many other titled landowners still exert a considerable degree of power in terms of patronage, influence and control of the present Highland Gatherings and Games.

Indeed it might be argued that the dominant interpretation of the Highland Gatherings includes not only a romantic cultural identity, but also an expression of a Highland way of life in which Highland chiefs, clansfolk, landlords and crofters all experience life in terms of harmonious social relations. There is a danger of basking in the crofting, clannish image of the past, the implication being that the political, social and economic climate has not changed and that the old tactics and demands used in the past would work today. There are many lessons to be learned from the past, but not if the lessons are divorced from the social reality and social context within which they were originally experienced. If history and social development is remembered, it would not be a romantic cultural identity which would be perpetuated through such cultural forms as the Highland Gatherings. Just as Highland culture has been capable of providing a basis of a romantic Scottish cultural identity, it is also capable of providing the basis of a counter-hegemonic struggle against the problems of modernity. What is required is not an identity based on a Highland fairytale, but one that engages social reality and understands the harsh realities of the clearances, the development of Scotland as a sporting playground and the problems of dependency and underdevelopment experienced within a modern social formation. If history is remembered, then no romantic satisfaction would be provided.

Furthermore, such developments have not been outwith the context of the broader problems of modernity experienced by Scottish and Highland social fractions. Industrial decline and renewal both within modern Scotland as a whole, and the Highlands in particular, has prompted the British state to become more closely embroiled within the social fabric of the Scottish way of life. The growing influence of a dominant metropolitan élite and the degree to which certain social-class fractions have the power to regulate and control traditional ways of life is certainly one of the contested problems of modernity experienced by the Highland social formation in particular. Despite the inception of the Highlands and Islands Development Board and the emergence of an offshore oil industry, the Highlands remain one of the most undeveloped, remote and sparsely populated regions within Britain. In essence, the power of those who own and control the land is as great as ever, and although statutory groups with a specific Highland remit have been brought into being, centralist control still lies at the heart of some of the contemporary problems facing the Highlands.

## Conclusions

Foreign accounts of Scottish culture have often proved to be misrepresentative. Inaccurate meanings have frequently been attributed to Scottish ways of life. While a number of Canadian, American and English sociologists and cultural critics have attempted to locate the formation of indigenous sporting forms within an analysis of their own nation and culture, similar accounts of Scottish sporting forms have not been forthcoming. In situating the development of the Scottish Highland Gatherings within the context of history and social development, the narrative as presented here has revolved around four inter-related phases of development. They are briefly stated in the following lists.

1. The initial phase of development lasted from at least the eleventh century until about 1750, during which many of the antecedent folk origins of today's Highland Gatherings emerged.

2. During the phase which followed, from about 1745 until about 1850, the Highland Gatherings were influenced by processes of cultural marginalization and transformation. Many of the cultural products of the Highlands including sporting tastes, were transported with the emigrés overseas.

3. In the third from about 1840 to about 1920, the Highland Gatherings were subject to processes of 'Balmoralization' and popularization. The power of the sporting landlords led, in part, to the cultural production of these sporting practices in a somewhat romanticized form.

4. A final phase of development emerged from about 1910 until the present day, during which the pressures and tensions of modernity, in part, gave rise to a modern expression of the Highland Gatherings.

Sport as a particular cultural form within Scottish society has been an important arena through which various groups actively rework their relationships and respond to changing social conditions as a whole. The crucial point is that the same resources have not been universally available in these negotiations and struggles. A dominant interpretation of the Highland Gatherings has resulted from the process by which some figurations have been empowered more than others to select and define the sets of social practices and arrangements within this cultural form. At least three notable measures of the power of different figurations to construct sporting practices might be mentioned: first, the capacity to structure sporting forms in preferred ways and institutionalize these preferences in sports rules and organizations; second, the capacity to establish selective traditions and rituals; third, the capacity to define the range of legitimate practices and meanings associated with the dominant interpretation of the Highland Gatherings. The resources which allow particular groups to do this are socially produced. They are constituted in and through the logic and patterning of formal and informal rules which underlie broader structures of economic, political and cultural life within Western industrial capitalism.

*Acknowledgements*

I would like to express my appreciation for the comments and support of Eric Dunning, Tony Mason, Carolyn Ison, Jane Douglas and David McCrone.

REFERENCES

Clarke, J. and Critcher, C. (1985), *The Devil Makes Work: Leisure in Capitalist Britain*, London: Macmillan.

Colquhoun, I. and Machell, H. (1927), *Highland Gatherings*, London: Heath Cranton.

Critcher, J. (1979), 'Football Since the War', in, J. Clark, C. Critcher and R. Johnson (eds.), *Working Class Culture*, London: Hutchinson.

Donaldson, E. (1986), *Scottish Highland Games in America*, Gretna: Pelican.

Dunning, E. (1988), 'Sport in the Civilizing Process: Aspects of the Figurational Approach to Sport and Leisure' in, C. Rojek (ed.), *Leisure for Leisure: Critical Essays*, London: Macmillan.

Dunning, E., and Sheard, K. (1979), *Barbarians, Gentlemen and Players*, Oxford: Martin Robertson.

Dunning, E., Murphy, P., and Williams, J. (1988), *The Roots of Football Hooliganism: An Historical and Sociological Study*, London: Routledge & Kegan Paul.

Elias, N. (1983), *The Court Society*, Oxford: Basil Blackwell.

Elias, N., and Dunning E. (1986), *The Quest for Excitement*, Oxford: Blackwell.

Evans, I., and Hendry, J. (1985), *The Land for the People*, Edinburgh: Scottish Socialist Society.

Gramsci, A. (1971), *Prison Notebooks*, New York: International Publishers.

Grant, I. (1961), *Highland Folkways*, London: Routledge & Kegan Paul.

Gruneau, R. (1983), *Class, Sports and Social Development*, Amherst: University of Massachusetts Press.

Gruneau, R. (1988), *The Politics of Popular Culture*, Ottawa: Garamond Press.

Hargreaves, J. (1982), *Sport, Culture and Ideology*, London: Routledge & Kegan Paul.

Hargreaves, J. (1986), *Sport, Power and Culture*, Cambridge: Polity Press.

Harvey, J., and Cantelon, H. (1988), *Not Just a Game*, Ottawa, University of Ottawa Press.

Horne, J., and Jary, D. (1987), 'The Figurational Sociology of Sport and Leisure of Elias and Dunning: An Exposition and Critique' in, J. Horne, D. Hary and A. Tomlinson (eds.).

Horne, J., Jary, D. and Tomlinson, A. (1987), *Sport, Leisure and Social Relations*, London: Routledge & Kegan Paul.

Hunter, J. (1976), *The Making of the Crofting Community*, Edinburgh, John Donald.

Hunter, J. (1979), 'The Crofter, the Laird and the Agrarian Socialist: The Highland Land Question in the 1970s' in H. Drucker and N. Drucker (eds.), *Scottish Government Yearbook*, Edinburgh: Harrison and Littlefield.

Hunter, J. (1981), 'The year of the Emigré in *Bulletin of Scottish Politics* 2, Spring.

Jarvie, G. (1985), *Class, Race and Sport in South Africa's Political Economy*, London: Routledge & Kegan Paul.

Jarvie, G. (1986), 'Highland Gatherings, Sport and Social Class', in *Sociology of Sport* 3, no. 4, December.

MacAloon, J. (1988), 'The Ethnographic Imperative in Comparative Olympic Research', University of Sussex.

MacAoidh, A. (1833), *Highland Bagpipe Music,* Aberdeen.

McEwan, J. (1981), *Who Owns Scotland?,* Edinburgh: EUSPB.

Moorhouse, H.F. (1986), 'Scotland v. England: Football and Popular Culture', in *The International Journal of the History of Sport* 4, no. 2, September.

Nelson, C., and Grossberg, L. (1988), *Marxism and the Interpretation of Culture,* London: Macmillan.

Pia, S. (1987), 'Scottish Football' in *Cencrastus* 27, Autumn.

Prebble, J. (1984), *The Highland Clearances,* Harmondsworth: Penguin.

Robbins, D. (1987), 'Sport Hegemony and the Middle Class Victorian Mountaineers' in *Theory, Culture and Society* 4, no. 4.

Rojek, C. (1985), *Capitalism and Leisure Theory,* London: Tavistock.

Webster, D. (1973), *Scottish Highland Games,* Edinburgh: Reprographia.

Whannel, G. (1982), *Blowing the Whistle: The Politics of Sport,* London: Pluto Press.

Whitson, D. (1983), 'Pressure on Regional Games in a Dominant Metropolitan Culture' in *Leisure Studies,* 2, no. 2, May.

Williams, R. (1977), *Marxism and Literature,* Oxford, Fontana.

Yorke, P. (1821), *Three Nights in Perthshire,* Glasgow.

# 12

## 'We're off to Wembley!'
## The History of a Scottish Event and
## the Sociology of Football Hooliganism

### H.F. MOORHOUSE

*Scotland v. England*

> There is one very interesting aspect of Scottish football, which becomes very prominent about the turn of the century, its association with border raids and forays and with violence generally. Often a football match was the prelude to a raid across the Border, for the same hot-headed young men were game for both, and the English authorities learnt to keep their eyes on the footballers.
>
> Marples, *A History of Football*, 1954

> *Not So Easy Tae Slew*
>
> In days of old
> Ere Scots were doled
> Each hard-up heilant sworder
> Kent unco'weel
> A yaird of steel
> Meant riches over the Border
> Today alack!
> We've lost the knack
> Or Sassenachs grow tougher!
>
> Reports on England v. Scotland, *Daily Record*, Glasgow, 14.4.1924

Graeme Souness: It's a minority. It's a shame you just can't pick those out.

Jimmy Hill: I always felt that about the England–Scotland game. Because you, er, Scots are always welcome in England, a lot of you live here, you know, and have done, and there's a great affection for the Scots and what a lovely weekend that match could be if they came down in peace when they did come. I think Londoners would give them a warm welcome and, as you say, share a glass of wine or a bottle of beer or something and make it a lovely sporting occasion.

> Discussion of Heysel Stadium disaster,
> National BBC1 TV, 29.5.1985

Scottish football fans travelling abroad have generally not engaged in the kind of activities which have gained English followers their reputation and English clubs a ban from European competitions. Scots pride themselves on this. The main exception has been when Scots have followed their teams to England. Marples's observation above about violence and football refers to the turn of the sixteenth into the seventeenth century, but combined with an additional element Marples mentions, alcohol, it could stand as a broad description of the behaviour of Scots travelling to club and international matches in England almost four hundred years later. At least, this is what English football, transport and state authorities came to think as they adopted a variety of measures to restrict the ability of the Scots supporters to attend the biennial International game. Attacks on railwaymen in 1973 provoked strikes in protest in 1975, which meant there was little public transport in London to carry Scots to and from Wembley. In 1977 Scottish fans invaded the pitch, tore up the turf and tore down the goalposts. In 1979 over 450 Scots were arrested over the Wembley weekend. In 1981 the Football Association tried to prevent Scots from obtaining tickets for the match. In 1983 the International was switched from the weekend to a mid-week date. Then, in 1985, at the behest of the Government, the venue was altered from London to Glasgow. In short, as Hill's televised comments reveal, to English eyes the Scots trip to Wembley had become an infamous 'instance' of football hooliganism, somehow equivalent to the riot of Liverpool fans which killed nearly 40 Juventus supporters at the European Cup Final of 1985.

Scots, in media or popular discussion, do not see things in the same way; far from it. For example, film of the pitch invasion of Wembley in 1977, which is routinely used on the British (i.e. English-based) media as an illustration of 'hooliganism' (and oddly, is used as the first illustration in the 'first post-punk book on soccer violence' (Redhead 1987)) is treated quite differently in Scotland. It formed part of the opening titles of a football highlights programme on Scottish Television for some years, while, in the weeks leading up to the last World Cup, both Scottish channels showed the invasion and a similar one of 1967 in features about football north of the Border, without a hint of censure *(Only a Game?* 1986; *Four In A Row* 1986). So what is condemned in one part of Britain is celebrated in another. Attempts at English condemnation and control are seen as unwarranted reactions to high spirits and exuberance, *or* as misguided 'challenges' to the superior ingenuity and determination of the Scottish supporters, *or* as downright hypocrisy given the depradations of English followers. The events in the Heysel Stadium and comments which equated England and Britain, raised quite a storm in Scotland for the slur they cast on Scottish fans.

I suggest, then, that this 'instance' of post-war soccer violence may pose problems of more general applicability to the study of hooliganism, not the least of which is that not all relevant authority, let alone ordinary people, agree that it is real violence. The attribution of violence is contested, rebutted, explained and interpreted in this 'instance', and I assume this may be true of a number of other examples used to illustrate soccer 'violence'. To portray just what is at issue here I will set out in this chapter to consider three questions:

1. Did the behaviour of the Scots fans alter in the 1970s and 1980s?

2. How were English attempts at control viewed in Scotland?

3. How adequate are attempts to relate violence and popular culture?

*Did the Behaviour of the Scots Fans Alter?*

Scots have always travelled to the away game against England in large numbers, but it was in the inter-war years that the mass movement to Wembley became institutionalized as an event of some significance in Scottish popular culture and adopted forms it maintains to the present (Moorhouse 1987). Every two years tens of thousands of supporters, turned out in tartan and topped off by tam o' shanters, left Scotland by train and bus on Friday evening and arrived in London on Saturday morning. Excursionists spent the morning sight-seeing. Many went to the match (or matches: fans with no international tickets went to other London games to cheer on any Scots in view) while some went shopping. Afterwards, the West End became the focus for drinking, dancing and theatre going. At around midnight the trippers returned to the stations for more singing and dancing and the long journey north. A good deal of alcohol was consumed. Still, at this time there were very few arrests, four in 1936, and in 1928 for example, when the match coincided with the Boat Race, the police in London were on the lookout for student rags (that older form of 'violence' of another social class) rather than bellicose Scots *(Daily Mail* and *Evening Standard* 31.3.1928).

Table 1: **Passenger Groups on Special Wembley Trains**

| Dundee to London Marylebone 1949 | | Edinburgh to Kings Cross 1953 | |
|---|---|---|---|
| Leaving Dundee 6.12 pm Leaving London 10.15 pm | | Leaving Edinburgh 7.50 pm Leaving London 12.45 am | |
| Inverkeithing FC | 16 | Royal Signals WC | 21 |
| Mr J. Thomson | 6 | Blandfield WC | 10 |
| James Low | 20 | Miller & Co. Ltd. WC | 20 |
| Northern Recreational Club | 35 | Brown Bros. WC | 20 |
| M'Ara Social Club | 40 | J. & G. Stewart Ltd. | 20 |
| Slaughterhouse Party | 15 | Wm. Thyne WC | 10 |
| Glenesk Party | 50 | Bruce Peebles & Co. | 30 |
| Mackay Bros. | 6 | Peter Nimmo & Co. WC | 10 |
| South Mills | 40 | Gayle Muir Motor Co. | 10 |
| Princes St. WC | 16 | W.M. Duncan Ltd. WC | 11 |
| Tartan WC | 24 | Victoria WC | 30 |
| Mays | 53 | Munro & Miller WC | 11 |
| Raith Rovers Supporters Club | 113 | Eskmills Social Club | 10 |
| | | Morrison & Gibb WC | 40 |
| Messrs. Machan, Servan Parr and Cycles Parties | 17 | St. Margarets Loco. WC | 15 |
| | | Hibs. Supporters Assn. | 117 |
| Mackay Bros. | 6 | Hearts Supporters (Queensferry) | 27 |
| TOTAL | 457 | Nelson & Son WC | 10 |
| | | T. & A. Constable WC | 10 |
| | | Eyemouth FC WC | 51 |
| | | Duns Supporters Club | 22 |
| | | Chirnside United Supporters | 25 |
| | | Advertised | 84 |
| | | TOTAL | 614 |

*Note:* WC = Wembley Club

*Source:* British Rail (Scottish Region), 'Relief, Excusion and Special Train Arrangements' (1949), p. 285; 'Programme of Special Trains' (1953), p. 268. Documents held in Scottish Records Office.

The Wembley weekend became like a little Scottish festival in London, with ceremonies at the Cenotaph, concerts by the Orpheus Choir, amateur teams meeting in competition and so on. By the 1930s the trip had become well organized within the economy of working-class Scots through an enormous number of shilling-a-week Wembley Clubs in which savings were accumulated for the trip south.

The table, derived from existing records (which are not too helpful) provides some evidence about the range of such clubs, and the great variety of popular institutions on which they were based: supporters' clubs, work places, local areas, pubs, social clubs, church groups, ex-servicemen's clubs, masonic lodges etc. (see also Moorhouse 1987). Clearly such clubs structured the huge crowd of excursionists and may have exerted their own pressures 'not to go too far'. From the 1930s the Scots could not obtain enough tickets to meet demand, even though the four British Associations agreed in 1946 that the Scottish FA should get 30 per cent of all Wembley tickets, and 'scandals' about the distribution of tickets were scarce, became a staple of the popular press. So it should be clear that many features of the trip were well established in the 'traditional
era' of British soccer.

This point becomes the more significant when it is realized that there have been any number of incidents that could have been construed as 'violent', as in Manchester in 1926, when among other things:

> A brewer's dray unloading at a hotel in the centre of the city was raided. From it a crowd of young bonnetted bloods rolled a barrel of beer and would have broached it. But good humour and common sense prevailed and thus a tragedy was averted *(Manchester Evening News* 17.4.1926).

And what about the 'ugly scenes' at Wembley in 1930, when thousands, with and without tickets, were locked outside and rushed the stadium:

> some even went so far as to remove earth and concrete from under the railings, and, in this way, caused a breach through which they could pass ... Fortunately, however, the timely intervention of foot and mounted police reduced the danger of thousands flocking into the already crowded enclosure *(Daily Record* 7.4.1930).

Then there have been any number of pitch invasions by widely varying numbers of supporters. In 1949 the journalist Bob Ferrier, at his first Wembley, felt the Scots in the crowd sensing victory: 'When it came, no barriers built could restrain them. They were over the dog track, over the speedway track, over the touchline, over, in a flood, the Scottish team' *(Daily Record* 11.4.1949). While in London that night:

> Thousands of deliriously happy fans bedecked in tartan scarves and tam o' shanters, with rattles, bells, bagpipes, thronged London last night celebrating Scotland's win over England in the international championship. It was London's most vivid and colourful celebration and Piccadilly Circus,

Coventry Street, and Trafalgar Square were solid with people. The Circus had to be closed to traffic. A police guard was put around Eros in case some too enthusiastic Scots climbed the statue. Hundreds of visitors went driving. They blew horns, waved flags, sat on the roofs and windows of the buses. Diners from restaurants in evening dress, gathered at the balconies to watch as groups of Scots sang national airs... One miniature army of Scots carried swords fashioned out of sticks as it marched along Regent Street. *(Sunday Express* 10.4.1949 and see *Sunday Mail* 10.4.1949).

Such events seemed to have passed with little or no official condemnation, and even the invasion of the Wembley pitch in 1967, when strips of turf were pulled up, exhibited in the bars of central London and carried back to Scotland, created little furore, it was not even mentioned in some Scottish papers and the English authorities and media did not dwell on it to any extent. How would an event like this be interpreted today?

> One party of about two hundred 'invaders' solemnly formed fours outside Euston Station and marched to the ground to the skirl of pipes, conducted by a bandmaster who used a whiskey bottle as a 'baton' *(Daily Record* 11.4.1932).

The biennial movement of Scots was, it would seem, accepted and enjoyed for some decades, for its eccentricity, as one of the threads in the rich tapestry of London life, as 'brightening up' the metropolis with a dash of provincial charm:

> Wi' many Och ayes! Hoots, mon! and wild throwing about o' saxpences (tied to bits of string) the 'invaders' roamed through the 'Big City' on sight-seeing tours after the match and filled the streets wi' a gay whir-r-l o' colour wi' their tartans and tammies. They invaded all the places of entertainment and went about in parties singing at the tops of their voices *(Daily Mirror* 11.4.1938).

Scots were able to call on this 'tradition' in the 1970s and 1980s, when what appeared to be rather similar actions came to be defined, by the English authorities, as quite reprehensible.

In fact, the 'violence' of the Scots fans is relatively hard to define. In the categories of Dunning *et al.* (1986) it rarely involves fighting with rival fans. Pitch invasions are not designed to fight or to stop games but to celebrate victory, all part of that fervour and identification with their team (pitch invaders of 1967 and 1977 became internationalists in their turn) which, so it is held in Scotland, the English football authorities envy, resent and try to stifle. It is, apparently, like 'horseplay' and rowdiness which in certain circumstances is accepted as normal, or is tolerated, but in other circumstances is defined as deviant. So a more fundamental issue is, I think, posed by this particular 'instance' of soccer 'violence': to what extent are we dealing with something new and strange in behaviour and attitude, and to what extent is it a matter of changed perceptions of what is 'allowable' and 'suitable' by the media and other control authorities, thus sparking self-fulfilling 'panics'? Broadly speaking, opinion in England tends to the former explanation, Scots to the latter.

It is worth clearing away some possibilities here. To begin with, there was no big increase in the numbers 'marching' on London, from the 1930s to the 1980s, estimates of '40000', '50000', 'over half the crowd' etc. are standard. Nor is any sudden injection of alcohol a likely cause of 'violence'. Newspaper stories of the trip to Wembley pre- and immediately post-war are replete with allusions to 'mysterious brown paper packages' containing 'sustenance' or 'refreshments' for the trip and the like, but we can go back much further than this. A report of the international in Blackburn in 1891 not only refers to numerous examples of what would be termed hooliganism today with riotous singing, impromptu football matches, 'the crash of glass and the smash of door panels', disruption of the morning market, and so on, but also to the visitors:

> double work with the crooked elbow. Long before dinnertime drunken men were staggering about the streets in all directions and the accommodation offered by the police cells was tested to the bursting point. At the railway station still more singular scenes occurred. As each of the trip trains arrived the porters had to clear out armsful of whisky bottles very few of which were quite empty ... As the trains disgorged their contents it was apparent that many of the passengers were too far gone to walk alone, but the railway people hardly liked the unanimous manner in which the unsteady ones took possession of all the seats and recesses on the platform and settled themselves for 'forty winks'. When the platforms became inconveniently crowded in this manner the order was given to 'move on' and with much difficulty and a good deal of noise the station was at last cleared. But Blackburn streets in the early morning, and with the rain pouring down, does not offer an inviting prospect to the shivering ones, and so it happened that scores of householders found drunken men asleep in their doorways and passages when they came down to breakfast. *(Northern Daily Telegraph* 6.4.1891).

After the game many Scots were let out of the cells to catch their trains back home. Moreover, the Scots have *always* crossed the border surrounded by an 'ideology' which, probably more than any other travelling support, speaks of battles, raids, armies, troops, invasions, hordes, sacks, and the like. This is true of the chants and banners of the fans, but also of media reports in Scotland *and* England. The *Daily Record* poem, quoted at the start, is but one example of all manner of violent imagery which, at least since the 1920s, has set the trip to Wembley in a specific (if mythical) historical context of 'war' and 'revenge'. The *Daily Record* poster for the 1930 Wembley trip, carried south by some of the 30000 Scots, showed a kilted Highlander of fearsome aspect, claymore in one hand, bottle in other, football at feet, declaiming: 'Here's tae us, wha's like us, deil the yin.'

If these aspects seem to have remained the same, it is possible to suggest some things that *may* have changed. With post-war 'affluence', the Wembley trip seems to have extended over a longer period. Whereas, as the railway records above indicate, it was once a matter of a rush from work on a Friday, a long journey, and a few hours in the capital, from the 1960s it became, for some, a matter of a few days, a true 'weekend' with quite a lot of support moving down on the Thursday even the Wednesday before the game. Scottish newspapers in the 1960s, maintaining the prevalent military metaphor, began speaking of 'advance guards' 'reconnoitring' for the 'main forces' (see, for example, 'Invasion Report from the Wembley Battle Front', *Glasgow Herald* 22.5.1971). Many travelled by road, with double the normal traffic crossing the border in 1963 *(Glasgow Herald* 6.4.1963) which perhaps lessened the inner structuring of the crowd by larger, group-based, train parties, and many travelled by air (4000 in 1979) which may have had the same effect and certainly increased the fans' contacts with the bewildered English middle class (see the report 'Chaos as Ally's Army Takes Over Heathrow', *Glasgow Herald* 6.6.1977, in details remarkably close to the Blackburn report of 1891). So perhaps, while actual numbers remained the same, the 'day out' of the traditional working class suffered a sea change into a longer, and, for the London authorities, more taxing jaunt. Along with this, but even harder to prove, it may be that the age composition of the Scots altered too, becoming younger. Comparison of film of the crowds on the Wembley pitch in 1967 and 1977, reveals that there were about the same number of people on the pitch but suggests that they were younger at the later date (those who actually climbed and cracked the goalposts were very young). The 1967 invaders have ties and suits. Given a high collar or two they resemble their ancestors photographed in the Edwardian era *(Evening Standard* 5.4.1913). Their clansmen of a decade later are much more casually attired. But the casual dress of the 1977 crowd suggests another factor, for many are wearing the Scottish team's strip and shirts. This was the 'Tartan Army', whose very name (though in use from the 1930s) derived from a group of political deviants intent on taking on the English with bombs rather than boots. The English victory in the World Cup probably had influence, and some Scottish observers do date a change in attitude from 1966 (see 'Walking Backwards to Wembley', *Sunday Standard*, 17.5.1981) but, given the significance of football in Scotland as a way of displaying separateness and distinctiveness, it is perhaps the case that the renewed interest in a *political* nationalism in the 1970s, with many causes, but certainly fuelled by the (apparent) promise of North Sea oil, made more assertive an always strong *cultural* quasi-nationalism. Certainly, the Scottish National Party began to use or try to use football motifs to argue its case. (It was refused use of film of the 1977 victory by the Scottish FA.)

Whatever the reality, whatever the causes, English authority, indeed English entrepreneurs, with over half the pubs of the West End closed on Wembley Saturday and Soho boarded up, took a variety of actions to curtail the trip to Wembley. In 1985 with the match switched to Hampden, one defiant group of Scots still went to Wembley, camping outside the ground and watching the game on television, but the English authorities were determined to break the Scottish tradition. In 1986 the Wembley game was played mid-week in a half-full stadium.

*How were English Attempts at Control Viewed in Scotland?*

At the outset it must be said that there was Scottish condemnation of the Scots fans. In 1978 the Annual Report of the Scottish FA made its first reference to supporters' behaviour, condemning the invasion of the pitch. The message was repeated in 1980 about activities away from the stadium in 1979: a minority of hooligans were spoiling the Wembley tradition:

> It is a fact that many of those who choose to attend Scotland's biennial match at Wembley are quite incapable of conducting themselves in a civilized manner. Drunkenness and violence are the order of the day and things have deteriorated to such an extent that the future of the fixture is in serious jeopardy.

and similar statements were made in later years (SFA 1978; 1980; 1982). The Scottish media carried pieces which castigated the supporters for their activities, and a certain nostalgia for 'the good old days' permeates some reports.

Overall, however, the Scottish response was much more equivocal, both to English attempts to define what the Scots did as 'hooliganism' and to the barriers they tried to erect to limit Scottish access to Wembley. Even the Council of the Scottish FA rejected plans agreed by its full-time officials and those of the English FA to prevent tickets being allocated to or sold in the 'away' country. Such 'bans' then had to be 'forced' on Scotland (Minutes 1979). The Scottish media was much more ambiguous. So, for example, the *Sunday Mail,* on the day after the 1977 pitch invasion, did publish a centre-page feature and a front-page story deprecating the action, but journalists on other pages could begin exultant pieces: 'Wembley was taken at precisely 4.42 pm in a bloodless coup by the greatest supporters in world football' or, under the headline 'The Lion Has Roared': 'Contrary to stories filtering back from the front, the twin towers of Wembley are still standing. This is because Scottish fans could not reach up ... ' *(Sunday Mail* 29.5.1977).

Even 'quality' papers became more assertively nationalistic in the 1970s, reflecting and reinforcing the Scottish mood. There is a sheer glee in a lot of the reporting in the *Scotsman* and *Glasgow Herald* along the lines that 'we're making our presence felt' 'they're genuinely fearful'. A host of examples could be given but 'Stepping into a New Ballgame' *(Scotsman* 24.5.1975) and 'The Long Walk to Wembley is only the Shortest Distance Between Two Pints' *(Glasgow Herald* 24.5.1975) give the flavour.

Then, as English efforts to deter fans increased in the 1980s the Scottish media found various ways to contest the labelling of the Wembley trip and to ridicule the control strategies adopted by the English. I perceive five inter-related propositions that ran (and run) through the media discourse. The first is that, even when the attribution of 'hooliganism' was allowed it was located as the work of a very small minority of the support. The vast bulk of the Scots were simply 'enjoying themselves', engaging in behaviour that was boisterous, outlandish but essentially good humoured (and wasn't this the people's game?). They might *look* tough, and could be uncouth, but 'there was no harm in them'. Moreover, any harm they did do was to property, not people, and the sums required to rectify this were miniscule in terms of the money Scots poured into gate receipts or into the economy of London, often at prices specially inflated for their benefit. The attitude to drink was itself equivocal, sometimes over-indulgence was seen as the cause of regrettable incidents, but then 'a good bevvy' had always been a part of the excursion, and reporters, even the same ones, could write happily of the number of pints put away and of their hangovers.

Second, many of the 'bans' and strikes were seen as silly. Either they would create, through frustration, what they nominally set out to prevent, or they would be swept aside by the superior enthusiasm, cunning and contacts of the Scottish followers. The Secretary of the English FA who claimed only 3000 Scots would get into Wembley in 1981 was likened to King Canute. The Scottish banners that filled the stadium and mocked his 'ban' were lovingly reproduced on television and in the Scottish papers.

Third, much of the trouble was seen to be the fault of the English, ill-prepared for Scottish fervour. Poor stewarding and lack of fences were seen as conducive to the 1977 pitch invasion even by the Tory shadow Scottish sports minister: 'Scotland had a splendid victory, it is slightly understandable what happened. While damage like this cannot be accepted, Wembley should have been better prepared' (Hector Munro in the *Scotsman* 6.6.1977). Moreover, if Scots were to be banned from London what did this say for the abilities of the London police and transport authorities if Glasgow could cope quite easily with crowds as large? Gradually, one of the villains of the situation was identified as the London media, with its week-long 'tartan terrorist' stories preceding match day, making Londoners lose their nerve in quite an unjustified way, thus causing the boarding up of shops and windows, the closing of hostelries, and the unwelcoming atmosphere that would annoy anyone. An editorial in the *Scotsman* in 1977 entitled 'The Aftermath' argued that the pitch invasion had spoiled the victory and could not be condoned, but then came up with six justifications, one of which was the near racism of the London media, including the *Guardian!* It ended: 'Scots may have behaved like bulls in a china shop but they had been baited' *(Scotsman* 7.6.1977). One can see, then, one section of the press blaming another for its role in creating a moral panic. In any case, Scots could locate this as just one of any number of slights they can list at any moment, just as the 'irony' of 'West Indian' bus conductors in London refusing the fans' Scottish banknotes revealed how they were made to feel unwelcome 'in their own country'.

Finally, the Wembley 'violence' was put in 'proper perspective' by reference to the 'real' hooliganism of English fans. The rampages of the London papers was seen to rise in proportion to the activities of the English hooligans. In any case, London any weekend, at grounds or on the tube was a violent city (like the Glasgow of old): why pick on the Scots? In 1981 the *Scotsman* could begin a front-page story 'Nae Bother at A' at Wembley' by cataloguing all the scenes of disgusting violence in London that month, *none* of which had to do with the Scots *(Scotman* 25.5.1981). The London police were called in witness that the number of arrests was usually no worse than at the English Cup Final (always an irksome event to Scots as this was the Wembley occasion the English got excited about). This interpretation, that Scots were being used as the scapegoats for English soccer violence, reached a peak in 1985, for two reasons. Scottish clubs and fans were afraid that they might suffer from European bans on the English, and the State had provoked a decision to switch the match-venue after rioting by English fans at English grounds. For some years the Scottish media had pointed out that London, its police and transport workers, were willing to put up every weekend with trips by the notorious fans of Leeds or Manchester United, as well as the cockney fighting crews, but baulked at shepherding some jolly Jocks, but now the double standard was truly apparent. The Secretary of the Scottish FA called the switch: 'A slur on the Scottish fans, but we decided, rightly or wrongly, to make the best of a bad job' *(Sunday Mail* 21.4.1985) and this was the general view. While some tried to argue that it was because of Scotland's success in the 'war' against hooliganism that the match was transferred, the overwhelming reaction was that the Scots were having to pay for what the English did. Again and again it was pointed out that Scots fans travelled the world, to all those World Cups the English could not qualify for. They were welcomed, liked and peaceful everywhere else, why couldn't they get a game in 'their own country'? The Scottish National Party produced one of its football-related posters: a huge Thatcher in English strip loomed over a Scots player at the toss-up, 'Heads I win, tails you lose', she said. The message in the background said 'Get off the sidelines Scotland'. Scots were asked to muse again on just what is to be meant by 'violence' around soccer.

Since then the Scottish authorities have adopted a holier-than-thou approach. The Scots note every 'outbreak' of English hooliganism, counterposing them to the 'trouble-free' state of Scottish soccer. As the Secretary of the Scottish FA put it recently, vigilance is necessary but: 'We do not have the skin-headed, leather-jacketed, neo-Fascist that one reads about elsewhere and we have to be thankful for that' *(Scotsman* 23.2.1987).

*How Adequate are Attempts to Relate Violence and Popular Culture?*
I have sketched some of the history of one 'instance' of post-war hooliganism to point to some of the complexities involved in the study of soccer violence, complexities that can get buried in the rush to advise policy-makers or lost in airy references to 'class backgrounds' or 'aggressive masculinity'.

The first analytic point I want to draw from the evidence above is to question, yet again, the primacy given to class in explanations of soccer violence. In fact, no very profound class analyses have been used in current accounts, but the reiteration of the basic importance of 'class', 'class relations' and 'class resistance' is quite marked. Scottish football, internally and externally, points to the importance of Weberian status groupings, based on common lifestyles and feelings of communality, rather than economically based classes as a basis for antagonism. It is true that there is a 'class' element in the Scottish 'sacks' of London but it is a mystified and mystifying one. Attention to the formation and maintenance of status groups, more thought as to what is actually meant by 'regionalism' or 'local community', might be a way forward in the analysis of soccer violence and in the cultural significance of football more generally. Scrutiny of Scotland deals a blow to accounts of the 'meanings' of football which dwell on class.

But the Scottish case is troubling to other attempts to explain violence around football. The latest book on football hooliganism, by Dunning *et al.* of Leicester University (1988) scarcely mentions Scotland, which is odd if only because Glasgow was far and away the leading British city for huge crowds for at least the first sixty years of the game's emergence as a spectator sport. This neglect of Scotland is, however, quite understandable, since, as I tried to point out in an article which those Leicester authors ignore (Moorhouse 1984) the various trajectories of violence around football in Scotland simply do not fit their model. In this recent text, Scottish history is rifled briefly for a couple of colourful pages on the 'sectarian' football hooliganism of the inter-war years, which, since it involves organized gangs, is said to be close to the modern English form, while the authors remain oblivious to the fact that the features they claim as the 'sociogenesis' of modern football hooliganism can hardly have applied in the 1920s and 1930s on Clydeside. Overall, while we are told:

> historical analysis is crucial in order to provide a comparative frame of reference which can highlight what, if anything, the distinctive features of the contemporary problem really are.
> (p. 2)

The obvious, but disturbing, opportunities for detailed comparisons with Scotland are ignored. The only England versus Scotland game that gets a mention is the one in 1890, and there is no mention of the fixture in an 'After Heysel' postscript, even though the first act in Margaret Thatcher's campaign against 'hooligans' was to keep the Scots out of London. It may be, however, that Dunning *et al.* do not regard the Wembley trip as football hooliganism in any sense. They divide hooliganism into three categories: swearing and horseplay, pitch invasions to halt a match, and large-scale fracas including fighting with the police. Their book concentrates on the third of these – their 'modern form' – and, of course, this is not what the Scots have been engaged in. However, what Scots have done has come to be *defined* as violent, dangerous, hooliganism and so on, and has provoked action by the state. This points to a quite unresolved strain in the Leicester account. There is a tension in this text between a moral panic, labelling, kind of analysis of the development of modern football hooliganism and the declaration by these authors that they want to dig through this to get at some 'roots'. These roots are held to be 'aggressive masculinity' and the structural characteristics which 'generate' 'it'. The authors argue:

> The sociological problem is to explain why they should behave like this. What is it in the experiences of these fans that makes them want to fight? Why do they fight in groups and choose to fight in public?... Who, precisely, are these groups and why do they tend to behave in ways that regularly bring them into conflict with the authorities and 'respectable' people? (p. 12)

It is not at all clear why this is 'the' as opposed to 'a' sociological problem about violence around football but, even in its own search for roots the book is none too convincing.

The authors want to locate modern hooliganism in a 'rough' section of the working class drawn to football, from the mid-1950s as a moral panic about 'football violence' caused grounds to be advertised as places where masculinity could be displayed and excitement sought. Unfortunately, it is not clear from the authors' evidence that there has been much of an increase in *actual* violence around football (they tend to trip, at the end of the book, over '*reported* violence' and 'violence'). The little evidence that is provided about actual 'hooligans' seems to reveal the 'respectable' committing violence as much as the 'roughs'. It is by no means shown that some rougher element has become a larger component in the football crowd in the last decades; this remains one of any number of assertions about the 'changing nature of the crowd' (and, indeed, working-class occupations) which have to be made to confirm the 'theory'. The 'generating milieux' of roughness seem, when you get down to it, to produce very few actual 'hooligans'. West Ham's Intercity Firm mustering 400 at most from all London's East End. And, crucially (echoing the faults of most 'class' analysis of football), it is never made clear how the 'roughs' are to be defined independently of 'aggressive masculinity'. In fact, all the grubbing for 'roots' produces a Chinese boxed set of tautologies. How do we know that they are rough? Because they fight. Why do they fight? Because they are rough. How do we know 'aggressive masculinity' is crucial to hooliganism? Because they fight. Why do they fight? Because of 'aggressive masculinity'. And so on, and so on.

What can be drawn from the evidence in the Leicester group's book, as opposed to the heavy varnish of 'the civilizing process' they try to paint on top of it, is that somewhere, at sometime, some group has always engaged in some kind of 'violent behaviour' around football and that what is really sociologically significant is why this is sometimes used as the basis of a moral panic which then helps produce what it sets out to control. This is certainly what my research suggests has happened to the trip to Wembley. The history of this trip, just like a considered analysis of the 'sectarian' hooliganism around Rangers and Celtic, poses considerable problems for the Leicester analysis. For example, they date the rise in the moral panic around violence and football as beginning in the mid-1950s and reaching a high watermark around the 1966 World Cup. They point to a *Times* third leader of 1958 which mentions the boarding up of Eros on certain match days and take this as an indication of increasing official concern with football hooliganism including that connected with the Scots. But a lot more arguments are needed to explain why *The Times* in 1967 did not mention the Scots pitch invasion and turf removal, not even in the match report, whereas in 1977, an apparently similar act produced two references on page 1, a page 3 story on fences for hooligans plus pictures of fans on the pitch and the disgruntled groundsman, a reference on page 10 by the planning correspondent, and condemnation in the page 12 match report. Why did the *Sunday Express* in 1967 scarcely mention the invasion, while in 1977 it had a page 1 story, 'Scots Rip Up Wembley', and a back-page one, 'Wrecked! England and Wembley too!' (16.4.1967, 5.6.1977)? Why in 1967 the football correspondent of the *Daily Express* could write, under a headline 'Great Scots':

> I could have stood and cheered as their ecstatic fans kissed the Wembley turf which had borne their heroes, pocketed tufts of grass and danced massive reels (17.4.1967).

While in 1977 among other condemnations, the same paper carried a news story, 'Tartan Rip-Off', which began:

> The famous Wembley pitch had the look of an allotment yesterday as groundsman Don Gallacher surveyed his devastated domain. Back over the border had gone the

Tartan hordes who got so drunk with victory that they dug up the pitch with daggers (6.6.1977).

Similarly the *Daily Mirror* had minor references in 1967 to the pitch invasion, and quoted a Wembley spokesman on the need for a lap of honour in future, as 'supporters had to find some way of letting off steam' (17.4.1967), while in 1977 it not only had a *Mirror* 'comment', 'Clod Off, Mac', and a spread across pages 2 and 3: 'Shame of the Scots', but also led its front page with the headline 'Jock the Ripper' over a picture of the archetypal laddie: brawny, hairy, kilted, arms aloft over the tartan tammy, waving a huge strip of English pitch in wild delight. This story, though, served to reveal just a few of the ambiguities surrounding all the attributions here, as it transpired that this 'Jock' was a thirty-eight-year-old with a cockney accent, who had left Scotland at the age of four, lived in Essex and was now being roundly chastised by his English wife and mother-in-law (6.6.1977, 9.6.1977). All these, and many other examples, throw doubt upon the rhythm of the moral panic that the Leicester group seek to lay down.

Then too, the trip to Wembley, however it has been perceived, points to continuity and tradition in behaviour rather than any 'new' group engaging in 'new' behaviour. As with Rangers and Celtic, even if young people or rough people *are* more involved than they used to be, and this is by no means certain, then it seems to present no 'break with the past' but the continuation of a tradition which, as I have tried to sketch, extends back almost the length of the fixtures of the oldest international match in the world. In this example too, one theoretical puzzle the Leicester authors need to try to explain is why, given a high value on the norms of masculinity, heavy drinking and pre-existing social antagonisms, the mass trips to England have not been a lot *more* violent. Lives have been lost on the way to Wembley, but only Scots lives and rarely in fighting.

In fact, my research suggests that an event of some importance in Scottish popular culture, and one with long historical roots, was reinterpreted in the light of English concerns about 'crime on the streets' and 'the violent society'. From 1975 onwards the English newspapers began to report the statements of various figures in authority, union officials, football officers, MPs, who declared the behaviour of the Scots – which, as I have tried to show, does not seem to have altered that much over almost a hundred years – to be crude, nasty, dangerous and violent.

This is yet another error in the Leicester account which for all its claims to grasp some societal sweep, actually severs soccer from what is happening in the rest of society about violence as much as any other phenomenon. For there is a sharp change in the tone of the national press about the Scots, as the reader can perceive in some of the material already quoted. In part this reflects the switch of certain papers to a more tabloid style. The *Daily Mirror's* headline of 1977, 'Jock the Ripper', can be compared to the one in the edition following the 1967 pitch invasion, 'Brown Makes it up with UN Team' above a story about the Foreign Secretary and Aden. Also apparent is the general attempt to 'talk up' sport, to present football and its events in a more stark and dramatic way. However, the underlying thrust behind the change in tone and definitions seems to be a much more generalized panic about the development of a 'violent society' in England. The way the Scots trip came to be spoken about reflects that crisis in hegemony, the push towards 'a disciplined society' which perceptive students were pointing to in the late 1970s (Hall *et al.* 1978), in which all manner of disparate actions are all 'understood' as symptoms of some common, deeper, social sickness. Consideration of this would cause Dunning *et al.* to enter into some sustained discussion of the activities and interests of the powerful in society (rather than the powerless) but this is unlikely both as a result of the limitations of their model of social change and because their kind of sociology has now become one of the roots of the moral panic growing up around football and 'violence'.

This new labelling of the Scots is noticeable in the language used and in the way that Scottish fans were juxtaposed, often on the same page, with 'young thugs', 'anarchy in the classrooms', the 'crime wave' etc., for example *Daily Mail* 30.3.1985) and in the rather fevered attempts to attribute 'violence' to the Scots. In 1977 the *Daily Mirror* fulminated about 'Corks deliberately ground into the grass' (6.6.1977), while in 1985, in the same paper, the football correspondent argued:

> London is well rid of the lunatics who pollute the fountains parade the streets, poison public transport and overpopulate the pubs *(Daily Mirror* 30.3.1985).

These charges, limited as they are by a predilection for ps, reveal little that is too dastardly except getting in the way of what had, anyway, become a more scuttling city, and one with half an economic eye focused on some sanitized 'tourist industry'. Again and again, in the late 1970s and 1980s things the Scots had always done became called in evidence against them: 'Taking over the West End', 'beseiging Piccadilly', 'cavorting in the fountains', 'holding up rush hour traffic', 'astonishing tourists' and so on were now presented not as endearing naîvety but as symptoms of lawlessness. The frequent complaints of 'uncivilized behaviour', 'bad manners' and 'drunkenness' did not allow for the effects of the media's labelling process; nor did they take any account of general changes in 'standards of behaviour' common to most of the population. Almost everyone had become 'less civilised', had worse manners, drank more. The *Mail* saw nothing amiss in complaining about 'alcoholic thousands invading London' next to a picture of the Liverpool manager being presented with the 'Bells Whisky Manager of the Year Award' *(Daily Mail* 26.5.1979). The Scots, it seemed, had simply become one unwanted nuisance to the harried Londoner, to be condemned in a kind of rhetorical hyperbole that prefigured Hill's crassness on the night of the Heysel disaster:

> In recent years the appalling behaviour of the Scottish supporters at Wembley has done more to harm the image of the game than any other match, incident or individual *(Evening Standard,* 22.5.1982).

Those whom the *Birmingham Mail* of 1922 had defined as 'lively adventurers from the North' had now become much more sinister, part of a whole Demon stalking London. Something much more than dislike of the Scots seems to inform the extraordinary article entitled 'Ian Wooldridge Saving London for the Nation' in the *Daily Mail* in 1979, which included:

> When instinct advises you to slip three sharp coins between the knuckles of a bunched fist against the possibility of being waylaid by some manifestation of racial passion during the short walk from the car park to the entrance at Wembley, sport is not worth attending. *(Daily Mail* 28.5.1979).

Who is the 'hooligan' here? Who is displaying aggressive masculinity?

## *The End of Wembley?*

In 1988, for the first time since 1981, the international was played in London on a Saturday. In England, the match was set in a prevailing context of 'crowd trouble' and, especially, the 'test' of fans which English participation in the forthcoming European Nations Cup tournament would entail, with the hope that the ban on English clubs participating in Europe might be lifted. In Scotland there were clear signs that the appeal of Wembley was waning with match tickets readily available and empty football specials.

At the game fights broke out in a crowd of less than full capacity. These were referred to in rather muted fashion in the sports sections of the main television news bulletins on Saturday night. However, what these incidents 'meant' was quickly redefined. A

Tory MP calling, among other things, for on-the-spot birchings, a sealing of the Border on international match days, and a year-long dye on the foreheads of hooligans, suggested:
> These pigs from Scotland should have no human rights. They should be treated like the evil animals they are in the same way they dish it out to others. They should not be let loose on decent people *(Scotsman* 23.5.1988).

Pressed on a Scottish TV programme he instanced two examples of the behaviour which called forth such language. Some Scots fans had been abusive in front of ladies on a tube station and, when reprimanded, one had urinated in front of them. On another London station the waiting-room had been used as a urinal. A Labour MP, the Chairman of the all-party House of Commons Football Committee, declared:
> I would clearly want to know more facts but, on the face of it, it looks like some kind of revenge by the Scots knowing that it is important for us, the English, to have a clean sheet to ensure our return to Europe. *(Scotsman* 23.5.1988).

The national media picked up such views and, by Sunday, the 'crowd trouble' had become a major news item on television, with stories of over 200 arrests, interviews with the Minister of Sport intent on blaming the FA for poor crowd control, indications that the FA was considering holding the fixture in mid-week in future to avoid trouble and so on. Reports continued in the vein, 'meanwhile the Tartan army is on its way home' with talk of damage caused to trains on the way down, pictures of reeling Scots at London termini, police searching for alcohol and supporters downing their drink before boarding the trains.

All this caused quite a reaction in Scotland where the main cause of fighting in the crowd was believed to be England's neo-fascist support looking for trouble. The *Daily Record's* headline on the following Tuesday was: 'Forget it: Wembley Isn't Worth All This', while pages 2 and 3 contained analysis under the headline 'Ban This Shame Game'. An editorial began:
> Enough is enough. Although we hate having to say it, Scotland should not play England at Wembley again *(Daily Record* 24.5.1988).

Some journalists did point to the loutishness of 'a lunatic fringe' of Scots supporters, though, again, what they pointed to – swearing, drunkenness and pushing past people in London's West End – requires stretching to be defined as 'violence'. On other pages, other journalists pointed out that the crowd had not been segregated and that the number of arrests in and around Wembley was less than that for the previous week's English Cup Final which had provoked no such furore.

In Scottish newspapers and on Scottish television, the Secretary of the Scottish FA left no doubt as to official annoyance about the way this Wembley trip had been framed in television bulletins:

> We are quite determined that we are not going to stand by and have the reputation of Scottish football supporters maligned in the fashion that it has been maligned this weekend by the London dominated media.

He also indicated that the Sports Minister and English FA were not the only parties who could decide on the fixture's future:

> Certainly we will be discussing the future of this fixture at the first opportunity. We haven't been given the chance or the courtesy of doing that yet. Everyone else has pontificated upon it for us. Clearly if the fixture is going to put the reputation of the nation of Scotland, not the football team of Scotland, but our nation at risk, we will have to consider its future very seriously *(Reporting Scotland* 23.5.1988).

In short, in 1988 as before, Scottish officials and media tended to reject the labels attached to the Wembley trip by English control agencies, which stemmed from English preoccupations, and this is also a matter which should provoke thought among the Leicester group and all others who seem quite content to equate 'violence' in society with a fist in the face.

Scots contest the attribution of 'violence' and justify their activities by locating them in a specific history. By that I do not mean football history, though that is important in signifying certain wider relations between groups (Moorhouse 1986*b*), but a political history and an economic history, and what these say about 'violent' relations between groupings. In Scotland and elsewhere (Shaw 1985) football alludes to other kinds of violence, often the historical or present violence done to people's lives by the central state, apparently outwith the ability of ordinary people to alter. Thus most Scots can understand the weight of neglect and disdain by England that might drive football fans to seek and enjoy symbolic victories against the old enemy. In 1977 one young Scot was fined £100 for ripping up the Wembley pitch but all Scots could appreciate his motives:

> The turf was from the spot where Kenny Dalglish scored the winning goal. It was a piece about six inches square and I was going to take it home and put in on a jar on my mantlepiece and just watch it grow and remember the match *(Daily Record, Glasgow Herald, Scotsman* 7.6.1977)

Set against the burdens and slights of the centuries, against de-industrialization, bad housing, high unemployment, and poll taxes, how can this really be called 'violence'?

# REFERENCES

*Books and Articles*

Dunning, E., Murphy, P., and Williams, J. (1986), 'Spectator Violence at Football Matches: Towards a Sociological Explanation', *British Journal of Sociology* 37, pp. 221-44.

Dunning, E., Murphy P., and Williams, J. (1988), *The Roots of Football Hooliganism* Routledge & Kegan Paul.

Hall, S., Critcher, C., Jefferson, T., Clarke, J. and Roberts, B. (1978), *Policing the Crisis,* London, Hutchinson.

Marples, M. (1954), *A History of Football,* London: Secker & Warburg, p. 61.

Moorhouse, H.F. (1984), 'Professional Football and Working Class Culture: English Theories and Scottish Evidence', *Sociological Review* 32, pp. 285-315.

Moorhouse, H.F. (1986a), 'Repressed Nationalism and Professional Football: Scotland versus England', in, J. Mangan and R. Small (eds.), *Sport, Culture, Society,* London, E. & F.N. Spon, pp. 52-9.

Moorhouse, H.F. (1986b), 'It's Goals That Count?' Football Finance and Football Subcultures', *Sociology of Sport Journal* 3, pp. 245-60.

Moorhouse, H.F. (1987), 'Scotland Against England: Football and Popular Culture', *International Journal of the History of Sport* 4, pp. 189-202.

Redhead, S. (1987), *Sing When You're Winning,* London, Pluto.

Scottish Football Association Annual Reports, (1978) 8; (1980) 8; (1982) 7.

Scottish Football Association Ltd., (1979) Minutes of Committees, 142-443.

Shaw, D. (1985), 'The Politics of "Futbol": Spanish Football Under Franco', *History Today* 35, pp. 38-42.

*Newspapers and Television*

*Birmingham Mail* (8.4.1922)
*Daily Mail* (various dates).
*Daily Mirror* (various dates).
*Daily Express* (various dates).
*Daily Record* (various dates).
*Evening Standard* (various dates).
Four in a Row, broadcast on STV, May 1986.
*Glasgow Herald* (various dates).
*Manchester Evening News* (1926).
*Northern Daily Telegraph* (1891).
Only a Game? 5: The Team, broadcast on BBC (Scotland), May 1986.
*Scotsman* (various dates).
*Sunday Express* (1949).
*Sunday Mail* (various dates).
*Sunday Standard* (1981).
Reporting Scotland broadcast on BBC (Scotland) (1988).
*The Times.*

# Index

Aberdeen
    economic and social change, 124, 125-6, 131-2, 134
    professionals in, 9, 123-40
Acajus, 182, 183-4, 185
age, and voting patterns, 87
alcohol, and violence, 208, 213, 216, 224
Alexayev, V., 40
alienation, 20, 23, 168
Althusser, Louis, 83, 93, 167
Ancram, Michael, 57
Anderson, Alexander, 135
Anderson, Arthur, 101
Anderson, B., 161
Anderson, P.J., 136
Anderson, R.D., 128-30
articulation, of modes of production, 92-3, 103
Ascherson, Neal, 2, 11, 172-3
Ash, Marinell, 170
authority
    charismatic, 175, 177
    legal-rational, 175-6, 177, 186
    traditional, 175, 176-80, 186

Balfour, B., 135
Balliol, Edward, 181
Balliol, John, 181
Balmoralization, 199-201, 204
Bannerman, Alexander, 128-9
Barbour, John, 46
Bettelheim, C. 93
Birmingham University, Centre for Contemporary Cultural Studies 190-1
birth-rate, 76
Blackie, John Stuart, 129
Boece, Hector, 179, 181, 182-3
Braemar Royal Highland Gathering, 197, 200
Breadalbane, Lord, 197
Breuilly, John, 31, 33-4, 37, 38-9, 44, 46-7
Brewer, John, 7-8, 13-27
Bridie, James, 172
Briggs, Asa, 25

Bromley, Y., 40, 46
Bruce, David, 181
Bruce, Robert, 179, 181, 182, 185
Bruce, Steve, 10, 175-86
Brut mythology, 178
Buchanan, George, 179-80, 181, 185
Buchanan-Smith, Alick, 68
Burns, Robert, 48, 170

Campbell, Alex, 112, 117
Campbell, J., 97
capitalism, 109, 125
    client, 55-6, 61, 69, 74
    and nationality, 46-51
    and Shetland Islands, 92, 99, 101-2, 104-6
Caractacus, 182, 185
Carr-Saunders, W., 123
Carter, Ian, 91, 92
Caughie, John, 168
Ceannmore, Malcolm, 197
Chalmers, William, 133
change, economic, and electoral divergence 53, 57-8, 62-5
    *see also*
    economism
change, social
    Aberdeen, 124, 125-6, 131-2, 134
    eighteenth-century, 14-18, 24-7
    and electoral divergence, 8, 53, 73-7, 80, 88-9
    and football violence, 223
    and nationality, 43
    Shetland Islands, 96, 99, 100-4
charisma, *see* authority
Charles I, 181, 184
Charles II, 180
Church of Scotland, 59, 65, 110
    Disruption, 129-32
clan, 10, 44, 196-9
class
    and analysis of sport, 10, 190-1, 192, 195, 202
    conflict, 23, 31, 40-1, 51

and football violence, 218-24
and nationality, 40-3, 4-9
Clearances, 48, 198, 199-200, 203
Clydesidism, 168-9
cod fishery, 95-7, 102-3
Cohen, S., 143
collectivism, economic, 114, 117-18, 120
Colquhoun, I. & Machell, H. 196
Comte, Auguste, 15
Connolly, Billy, 168
consensus politics, 80, 84
Conservative Constitutional Forum, 68
Conservative Party, 50, 57-8, 62-9
    decline in Scottish support, 51, 53, 57, 73, 86-8
    nineteenth century, 110-12, 120
consumption sectors approach, 79
Contagious Diseases Acts (1864-1886), 146, 148
control, social, 9, 47, 143-5, 147-50, 157, 157-8
    and football violence, 209, 213, 215-18, 226
core-periphery relations, 54, 58, 71, 91-2, 93
Craig, Cairns, 168, 169-71
crofters, and Highland sport, 201
Crofters Act (1886), 104-5, 201
Culloden, effects of, 198
culture
    national, 10: *see also* nationalism, cultural
    popular, and football violence, 218-24
    and sport, 10, 189, 190-1, 193, 195, 198-9, 204

Dalriada, 178-9, 182
David I, 182-3, 185
De Wit, Jacob, portraits, 10, 180-5, 186
Declaration of Arbroath, 179
defence policies, 67
dependency theory, 54-5, 58, 71
    and sport, 193, 194, 195, 203
development, social, 193-4
devolution, 65, 67, 68
Dewar, Daniel, 130
Dickson, T., 8, 44, 53-69, 71, 74
Dickson, T., McLachland, H., Prior, P. & Swales, K. 63, 74
Dimitrov, 41
Disraeli, Benjamin, 111
Disruption of the Church of Scotland, 129-32

doctors, professionalism, 132-3, 135-7, 138-9
Donaldus I, 183
Donzelot, J., 144
Dundas, Henry, 59
Dundee, professionalism, 139
Dunleavy, P. & Husbands, C., 77
Dunning, E. & Sheard, K., 193
Dunning, E. *et al.*, 212, 219-23, 226
Durkheim, Emile, 17-18, 123

economics, classical, 8, 21
economism, 53, 54-7, 69, 71-2, 74, 77
education system, 59
egalitarianism, 3
Elias, N., 6, 193-4
élites, Shetland Islands, 97, 100-1
    Scottish, 37, 45, 203
emigration, 154, 198-9, 201
English, attitudes to, 61, 64, 67, 213-15, 216-18, 225-6
Enlightenment, Scottish, 8, 13, 59, 163
Episcopalian Church, 111-12
equality, and nationality, 41, 43
ethnicity, 39-40, 42
evolutionism, 92, 194
expenditure, government, 60-1, 63, 66, 76

Falconar-Stewart, George, 119
familialism, 154-5
femininity, middle-class standards, 9, 143, 145, 151, 157-8
Fergus I, 182
Fergus II (MacErc), 179, 182
Ferguson, Adam, 7-8, 14-16
    on division of labour, 18, 19-22, 23, 25-6
Ferrier, Bob, 211
feudalism, opposition to, 44-6, 47
Finnegan, F., 149, 156
fishing, *haaf* fishing, 95-7, 100-1, 102-3
fishing tenure system, Shetland, 94-7, 98, 100, 102-4
Foley, V., 27n.
football, 10, 61, 207-26
    behaviour of fans, 209-15, 222
    pitch invasions, 208-9, 211-12, 214-16, 217, 220-3
Foster, John, 8, 31-51
Foucault, M., 9, 26, 144, 149, 156
Frank, A.G., 92-3
Free Church of Scotland, 131
Friedson, E., 127
functionalism, structural, 6, 93

# Index

Gaelic, literature, 172
Gathelus and Scota myth, 178-9
Gellner, Ernest, on nationality, 31-3, 34, 36, 38-9, 44, 46, 169
General Election 1987, 53, 57-8, 61-5, 73, 162
Gibbon, Grassic, 172
Giddens, A., 13
Glasgow, prostitution, 9, 143-58
Glasgow Magdalene Institution, 144-58
Glasgow System, 146
Goldthorpe, J.H., 76
Gouldner, A. 13
Gramsci, Antonio, 191-2
Grant, Isobel, 196
Gregory family, 140n.
Grigor, Barbara and Murray, 167
Gruneau, R., 192-3

half-catch system, 102
Hamilton, 137
Hamowy, R., 27n.
Hargreaves, J., 191-2
Harris, James, 17
Harvie, Chris, 166
Harvie, Christopher, 2
Hay, James, 97, 101
Hay, William, 101
health, public, 117-20
    expenditure, 60-1
Heath, A., Jowell, R. & Curtice, J., 77
Heath, Edward, 64
Hechter, Michael, 2
hegemony theory, 191-2, 195
Hellerstein, E. *et al.* 144
Henderson, J.A.H., 134, 140n.
Herder, J.G., 20
herring fishery, 97, 101, 102-3, 104-5
Hewison, Robert, 173
Highland Gatherings, 10, 189-90, 193, 195
    development, 195-203, 204
    and Highland sport, 199-200, 203
Highlands, depopulation, 25, 203
Hill, Jimmy, 207-8, 224
hill-racing, 196, 197
history
    conjectural, 7-8, 13, 14-17, 18-19, 21, 22-3, 26-7
    philosophical, 15
    and sociology, 7-10, 18-19
Hobsbawm, E., 38
hooliganism, football, 208-26
Hopfl, H.M., 21

Housing Act (1890), 119
housing, public, 60-1, 76, 79, 119
humanism, civic, 8, 22-3, 26
Hume, David, 8, 21, 46, 163
Hunter, J., 201
Hutcheson, Francis, 25

identity, British, 46-9, 87-8, 163, 167
identity, cultural, 189-90, 193, 198, 202-3
identity, national, 10, 31-5, 37-41, 44-9, 51, 58, 61, 63-5, 82-9, 168-72
    and tartan, 165-6
ideology, national, 34, 38-9, 41-2, 45
illegitimacy, 114, 116-17
individualism, and nationality, 32-3
industrialism
    and capitalism, 109
    and end of patronage, 124, 127, 130, 131-2, 134-5, 138-9
    and nationality, 32-4, 37
industry
    decline, 59-60, 62-4, 72, 203
    eighteenth-century, 24-5
    new development, 60
infantilization, 151
intelligentsia, and nationalism, 163, 167
intervention, state, 144, 157
Irish, in Scotland, 114-15, 116, 126, 140n.

James I, 181
James II, 181
James III, 181
James VI, 179-80
James VII (and II of England), 180, 181-2, 184, 185-6
Jamesone, George, 180
Jarvie, Grant, 10, 189-204
Johnston, Tom, 50

Kailyardism, 161, 163-4, 167-70, 172-3
Keating, M.J. & Bleiman, D. 81
Kendrick, S., Bechhofer, F. & McCrone, D., 8, 54-6, 57, 71-2
Kendrick, Steve, 8, 71-89
Kennedy, William, 129, 134-5
Keynesianism, 51, 80
Kindleberger, C.P., 25
King's College, Aberdeen, 128-9, 136

labour
    free, 97, 101, 104
    unfree, 91-7, 98-9, 101, 106

labour, division of, 8, 14, 16, 19-22, 23, 25-6, 43
  eighteenth century, 17-19, 46
  and nationality, 32-5
  nineteenth century, 112-13
Labour Party, 35, 50-1, 57, 62, 68-9, 73, 81
  decline in support, 83, 87
land tenure, 193, 196, 203, 45
  *see also* fishing tenure
landlord, and sport, 193, 199-201, 204
Lauder, Harry, 164, 168
Lauder, Sir John, 180
Lawson, Iain, 68
Lawson, Nigel, 57-8, 60, 66
lawyers, professionalism, 132-5, *134*, 138-9
leadership, *see* authority
legal system, 20-1, 47, 59
legitimacy, 38, 176, 178
Lenin, V.I., 41
Levitt, Ian, 9, 109-21
Liberal/SDP Alliance, 58, 62
liberalism, 109
Linklater, Eric, 172
literature, Scottish, 172
Lock hospital, 146-7, 149
Locke, John, 17
Logan, William, 145

MacAloon, J. 192
MacAlpin, Kenneth, 182
McArthur, Colin, 167-9
Macarthur pipers, 196
McCall, Alexander, 146
MacColla, 172
McCrone, David, 10,161-73
MacCrummen pipers, 196
MacDiarmid, Hugh, 162, 172
McGregor, Sir James, 136-7
Mackay, John, 57
Mackay pipers, 196
MacLaren, Allan, 9, 123-40
McNeill, Duncan, 111
McNeill, Sir John, 111, 112, 113-14, 120, 121n.
Mahood, Linda, 9, 143-59
Makars, 46, 170
Mandeville, Bernard de, 17-18
Marischal College, Aberdeen, 128, 129-30, 136
Marples, M. 207, 208
Marshall, G., Rose, D., Vogler, C. and Newby, H., 76

Marshall, T.H., 123
Martin, Henry, 17
Marx, Karl
  on alienation, 20
  on history, 16, 173
  on production, 93, 99
Marxism
  cultural analysis, 191-2
  and nationalism, 8, 31, 39-51, 73-4
  sociology, 6
Mary, Queen of Scots, 181
Maxwell, John, 17
media, 8, 66-7, 88
  and experience of the state, 78-9, 81-6
  and football violence, 10, 207, 208, 214, 215-18, 221-6
Mercantilist school, 17
merchant capital 95-6, 99
Meyrowitz, J., 81
middle class, forgotten, 123-40
Miles, R., 93
Millar, John, 8, 14-16, 21, 46
Miller, Karl, 11
Miller, W.L., 81
ministers, professionalism, 130-2, 138-9
M'Neill, Malcolm, 112-13, 116, 121n.
mobility, social, 25, 75, 83-4
modernity, problems of, 203, 204
monarchy
  De Wit portraits, 180-5
  early Scottish, 178-80
  symbolic, 178
Moorhouse, H.F., 10, 195, 207-26
Mouat, Thomas, 101
Muir, Edwin, 172
Munro, Hector, 217
Myers, M. 17
myths and nationality, 3-4, 35, 39, 167-72, 178-86

Nairn, Tom, 2, 31, 37-8, 39, 51, 61, 161-4, 166
Napier Commission, 104-5
nation, historical status, 31-5
nation-state, 6-7, 31-6, 93, 171
nationalism, 8, 31, 38, 68-9, 198
  cultural, 58-61, 65-7, 161-73
  cultural sub-nationalism, 162-4
  economic, 80
  and football violence, 215, 216
nationality, 1, 3, 5, 7, 8
  Marxist approach, 39-51
  non-Marxist approach, 38-9
  Scottish anomalies, 35-8
  as social construct, 41

# Index

Nead, L. 144
neonationalism, 161, 172
neurosis, and Scottish nationalism, 162, 164, 166, 170-1
Nicholson, Arthur, 101
Nisbet, R., 13

Orange Order, 48, 87

parties, political, dealignment, 83-4
patronage, 124, 127, 130-1, 134-6, 138-9
penal system, nineteenth-century, 143-5, 148, 149-52, 157
periphery, *see* core-periphery relations
Perkin, Harold, 9, 123-4, 127, 138
Peterkin, W.A., 119
Petty, William, 17
Philip, Winifred, 23
Pia, Simon, 189
police, and prostitution, 146-7, 149
Police Act (1866), 146-7, 148
politics, and social analysis, 3, 4-5, 8, 10-11
Poll Tax, 57, 63, 65, 68
Poor, Board of Supervision for the Relief of, 9, 110-20
Poor Law Act (1845), 110, 114, 115, 118
poor relief, 25, 110
poorhouse, 116
population
    eighteenth-century, 25, 100, 125
    nineteenth-century, 125-6
post-materialism, 172
power
    economic theory, 194
    relational concept, 194-5
presbyterianism, 46-7, 48, 50, 109, 114, 138
Priestley, Joseph, 17
privatism, 77-8, 83-6, 87-8
production, mode of, 92-3, 98, 100-3, 105-6
professionalism, 9, 123-4, 126-7
    consulting professions, 127, 132-7, 138-40
    scholarly professions, 127, 128-32, 138-9
professors, university, 128-30, 132, 138-9
proletarianization, of women, 151-2
property, private, in Ferguson, 20-1, 23
Proscription Act (1747), 165
prostitution
    nineteenth-century, 9, 143-58
    probation and surveillance, 152-5

rescue work, 144, 146-7, 149-52, 155, 157
resistance to reform, 156-7, 158
Protestantism, and Conservative Party, 86-7
public health, *see* health, public

Rafter, N., 151
Rawlinson, Major, 165
reform, and remaking of working-class culture, 146, 158
reformation, Scottish, 46
Regional Aid, 64
relations, social, capitalist, 104-6
religion, 59, 86-7
rent, Shetland Islands, 94-5, 104
Rifkind, Malcolm, 58, 163
Robertson, 15, 163
Rodger, E.H.G., 133, 137
Ross, John, 133
Rowley, Andrew, 140n.
royalism, 185-6

schizophrenia, of Scottish culture 166
science, beliefs in, 175-6
Scotland
    academic research, 1-7
    constitutional status, 1, 4, 7, 36, 47, 58-60, 89
    as different from England, 8-9
Scots, literature, 172
Scott, Walter, 162, 165, 198-9
Scottish National Party (SNP), 35, 51, 58, 60, 62-3, 68-9, 73, 83, 87, 161, 215, 218
Scottish Office, 60
self-government, 35, 37, 47, 60
Shetland Islands, and world economy, 9, 91, 106
Skelton, John, 111-12, 115-16, 121
Smith, A.D., 31, 34-5, 37, 38, 39, 44
Smith, Adam, 8, 14-16, 17, 21, 25, 27n., 46, 163
Smith, H.D., 92, 99
Smith, Richard, 9, 91-106
Smout, C., 1, 4, 25
Smythe, John, 111-12, 114-15
society
    civil, 16-19, 22, 33-4, 37, 38-9, 46-7, 58, 162
    commercial, 17, 18, 21
    definitions, 5-7
sociology
    figurational, 193-5, 201, 204
    origins, 13-14, 18-19, 22-3, 24, 26-7
    in Scotland, 1-7, 9, *see also* history; politics

Sombart, W., 16
sport, 189, 190-5, 204, *see also* football;
    Highland Gatherings
state changing experience of, 77-83,
    85-6, 88
    and welfare, 109-10, 112-13, 119-20
Stewart, Dugald, 13, 15
Stewart, James, 17
Stewart monarchy, and tradition, 10,
    180-6
structure, social, and electoral
    divergences, 76
succession, monarchic, 180-1, 184, 185
surveillance, community, 152-5
symbol, national, tartan as, 164, 166,
    198

Tait, William, 145
tannistry, 181
Tartanry, 161, 164-70, 172-3, 177
television, political impact, 81-3, 84-6,
    88
Telfer-Dunbar, J., 165
Test Act, 129
textile industry, Aberdeen, 125-6, 134
Thatcher, Margaret, 57, 64-5, 67, 87-8,
    219
Thatcherism, 57-8, 61-5, 87
    and cultural nationalism, 65-7
Therborn, G., 13
Thomas, W.I., 186
trade, and Shetland Islands, 92-6, 102-3,
    106
Trades Union Congress, Scottish, 51
tradition
    as social construct, 10, 175-6, 178,
    180-6, 377
    *see also* authority, traditional
Trevor-Roper, Hugh, 164-6
Truck Commission, 92, 97-9, 103, 104

unemployment, levels, 62, 63-4
Union with England 47-8, 58, 163
    possible break-up, 67-9
Unionism, 48-51, 87, 112
unity, national, 178

vagrancy, 114, 116, 120
Victoria, Queen, and Highland
    Gatherings, 200

violence, football, 10, 207-9, 211, 217-18
    definition, 212-14, 225
    and popular culture, 218-24

Wales, nationalism, 36-7
Walker, John, 105
Walker, William, 110-12, 115-19
Walkowitz, J., 144, 156
Wallerstein, I., 9, 92-3
Wardlaw, Ralph, 145
Weber, Max, 10, 32-3, 169, 175, 176-7,
    219
Webster, D., 196, 202
welfare government, 109-10, 113, 119-21
Westminster, dependence on, 58-61,
    66, 69
whaling industry, and Shetland Islands,
    98, 101-2, 103
Williams, Raymond, 84, 190
Wills, J. 92
Wilson, William, 165
Wittgenstein, L., 175, 177
Wolpe, H., 93
women
    in employment, 75-6, 151-2, 155,
    157
    and penal system, 143-4, 148,
    149-52, 157
    proletarianization, 151-2
Wood, N., 144
working class
    attitudes to, 109-10, 112-14, 115-20
    and Conservative Party, 86-7
    culture, 168
    depoliticization, 154-5
    female, 144-6, 149, 153, 155, 156,
    158
    and nationality, 42, 48-9
    and privatism, 83
world economy, and Shetland Islands,
    91-106
world-systems theory, 9, 92-3
Wright, Patrick, 173

Yearley, Stephen, 10, 175-86
Younger, George, 67

Zagladin, V. 40
Zetland Method, 94-7, 100-1, 103-4